Poverty Reform in Canada, 1958–1978

CRITICAL PERSPECTIVES ON PUBLIC AFFAIRS
Series Editors: Duncan Cameron and Daniel Drache

This series, sponsored by the Canadian Centre for Policy Alternatives and co-published by McGill-Queen's University Press, is intended to present important research on Canadian policy and public affairs. Books in the series are by leading economic and social critics in the Canadian academic community and will be useful for classroom texts and the informed reader as well as for the academic specialist.

The Canadian Centre for Policy Alternatives promotes research on economic and social issues facing Canada. Through its research reports, studies, conferences, and briefing sessions, the CCPA provides thoughtful alternatives to the proposals of business research institutions and many government agencies. Founded in 1980, the CCPA holds that economic and social research should contribute to building a better society. The centre is committed to publishing research that reflects the concerns of women as well as men; labour as well as business; churches, cooperatives, and voluntary agencies as well as governments; disadvantaged individuals as well as those more fortunate. Critical Perspectives on Public Affairs will reflect this tradition through the publication of scholarly monographs and collections.

GETTING ON TRACK: SOCIAL DEMOCRATIC STRATEGIES FOR ONTARIO
Daniel Drache, Editor

THE POLITICAL ECONOMY OF NORTH AMERICAN FREE TRADE
Ricardo Grinspun and Maxwell A. Cameron, Editors

POVERTY REFORM IN CANADA, 1958–1978
State and Class Influences on Policy Making
Rodney S. Haddow

Poverty Reform in Canada, 1958–1978

State and Class Influences on Policy Making

RODNEY S. HADDOW

McGill-Queen's University Press
Montreal & Kingston • London • Buffalo

Legal deposit fourth quarter 1993
Bibliothèque nationale du Québec

Printed in Canada on acid-free paper

This book has been published with the help of a grant
from the Social Science Federation of Canada, using
funds provided by the Social Sciences and Humanities
Research Council of Canada.

Canadian Cataloguing in Publication Data

Haddow, Rodney
 Poverty reform in Canada, 1958–1978: state and class
 influences in policy making
 Includes bibliographical references and index.
 ISBN 0-7735-0990-9
 1. Public welfare – Canada – History. 2. Poverty –
 Government policy – Canada – History. I. Title.
 HV105.H23 1993   361.6'8'0971   C93-090266-1

Typeset in Palatino 10/12
by Caractéra production graphique inc., Quebec City

Contents

Acknowledgments

Several persons deserve thanks for their generosity in assisting in the preparation of this book. The manuscript evolved from my doctoral dissertation at the University of Toronto. Professor David Wolfe supervised that project, and I owe him a debt of gratitude for his insight and his patience. Professors Ronald Manzer and Meyer Brownstone were very helpful and sympathetic members of the thesis committee. Much of the research base for the book consisted of documents from the National Archives of Canada. Archivists there worked hard, sometimes overtime, to make records available to me; the efforts of Sylvie MacKenzie were especially valuable. Many public officials and non-governmental actors involved in the events and developments examined in the book – 42 in all – devoted a considerable amount of their time to interviews with me; the interviews were particularly useful in writing chapters 5 to 8; these former participants receive my anonymous thanks. Philip Cercone of McGill-Queen's University Press provided generous advice on how to revise and shorten the manuscript; he and the press expedited passage of the manuscript through the many hurdles encountered on the road to publication. St. Francis Xavier University assisted in printing various stages of the manuscript.

Poverty Reform in Canada, 1958–1978

CHAPTER ONE

Canadian Poverty Policy and State Theory

Significant improvements were made in Canada's social security programs for the poor during the early 1960s. These changes culminated in the adoption in 1966 of the Canada Assistance Plan (CAP), which provided the best anti-poverty program achievable within the narrow confines of the traditional social assistance approach. But the increasingly manifest inadequacy of that approach led to widespread criticism later in the decade, and a more thorough reform of poverty policy – the Social Security Review – was launched in 1973. Although the Review failed to achieve any of its stated objectives, these two undertakings – the Canada Assistance Plan and the Social Security Review – were the most extensive federal attempts to reform Canadian poverty policy during the postwar era.

The present study sets out to explain and compare them, examining the forces that stimulated their emergence and subsequent development, and those which determined their quite different fates. The book has a second purpose: it addresses a central theoretical concern in the contemporary study of public policy – namely, the dichotomy between state- and society-centred perspectives on the modern state. For the most part, the debate on this issue has not proceeded beyond a simple confrontation between these two approaches, seen by their respective proponents as mutually exclusive: most participants attempt to prove the merits of one approach and to knock down its rival. Here, a case is made for an alternative strategy, based on the integration of state- and society-centred (in particular, class-based) theories in seeking to explain poverty policy.

WHAT IS POVERTY POLICY?

Poverty policy can be defined as a set of decisions taken by governments in the areas of income maintenance and social services, aimed primarily at improving the material circumstances of poor people. In developed capitalist societies, absolute definitions of poverty have almost universally been replaced by relative ones[1]: what a citizen "needs" and should properly receive from the community is not the minimum to sustain life but a standard that reflects the prevailing norm within that community. Poverty policy measures are designed to bring the least advantaged citizens closer to this level. They are therefore selective and, in that respect, differ from a variety of other social security measures (such as family allowances and Old Age Security pensions) that are universal in coverage or that are based on the social insurance principle. While these broader measures may play an important role in preventing or eliminating penury, their origins and structure suggest that this is not their primary purpose.

Poverty policy therefore does not encompass all social programs that affect the poor. Indeed, in those welfare states which have been the most successful at eradicating destitution, poverty policy (as defined here) has usually played a relatively minor role.[2] Where universal and broad social insurance measures are predominant and where they are complemented by economic policies designed to achieve full employment and promote the retraining of unemployed workers, both the incidence of poverty and concern about poverty as a policy issue are more modest. Programs targeted primarily at the poor are very minor elements in the Scandinavian welfare states, for example, and indeed in most non-Anglo-Saxon societies. In the United States and Canada, by contrast, where poverty programs are prominent features of the welfare state, the incidence of penury is high, and the broader social and economic measures capable of preventing it are less utilized than elsewhere.[3] The major implication of this, paradoxically, is that to the extent that policy debates in Canada focus on poverty issues, they are the reflection of a welfare state that has failed to address adequately the problem of destitution.

The Canada Assistance Plan and the Social Security Review were the two most comprehensive attempts ever made by the federal government to reduce poverty; as such, they represent an appropriate focus for a book on Canadian poverty policy. With the creation of CAP, the federal government made its first-ever commitment to share almost all of the costs of provincial welfare programs. Today, CAP remains the main instrument for federal intervention in the area of social assistance. The Review represented a more extensive effort at poverty reform by the federal government; had its objectives been achieved, many aspects of the Canadian welfare state would have been fundamentally altered.

STATE- AND SOCIETY-CENTRED THEORIES: TOWARDS A SYNTHESIS

In the late 1970s, a fiery debate began among public policy analysts between the proponents of a state-centred approach and those who favoured a society-centred explanation – that is, between theories that find the fundamental influences on public policy within the state itself and those which view the important influences on policy as coming from outside the state. Theda Skocpol, one of the foremost champions of the state-centred approach, has never entirely rejected society-centred explanations, but she has frequently attacked them, and her concrete applications of statism are often dogmatic.[4] Other proponents of statism have similarly assailed society-centred alternatives and treated them as errors to be refuted. The adversaries of statism have been quick to issue equally categorical rebuttals.

In Canada, the acrimony of the state/society debate was evident in the well-known exchange on unemployment insurance (UI) that took place between Leslie Pal and Carl Cuneo in the mid-1980s. Pal disputed Cuneo's class-based account of depression-era UI policy, arguing that a decisive role was played by bureaucratic ideology and federal/provincial relations – two phenomena "specific to the state's internal structure, and [not] easily reduced to class or other societal factors."[5] In his view, societal influences have had only a very modest impact on UI.[6] Cuneo dismissed Pal's analysis as "psychological and ideational reductionism." While admitting the need for an explanatory model that "combines the objective class struggle emphasized in my own model with the subjectivism of state actors stressed in Pal's," Cuneo conceded that "neither of us have come close to establishing this model."[7]

The present study tests the possibility of a synthetic model as an alternative to these sectarian confrontations. Robert Alford and Roger Friedland provide a useful starting point for such a synthesis. Following a commonly used typology, they contend that, for the most part, social scientists have failed to transcend the limitations of the three different theoretical perspectives from which the state has been studied – statism (which Alford and Friedland usually refer to as the "managerial perspective") and two society-centred alternatives, pluralism and the class perspective. Each of these approaches offers valuable insights, suggesting the need for "a synthetic framework out of which a new theory of the state can be constructed from these three perspectives, rescuing and integrating the major contributions of each."[8]

Alford and Friedland use the concepts of "levels of analysis" and corresponding "contexts of action" to characterize the contribution of each theory (or "paradigm") and to suggest a basis for their integration. "The three paradigms," Alford tells us, "focus upon distinct social and political forces that shape the state and legitimate its actions: individuals and groups for the pluralist paradigm, bureaucratic organizations for the elite [statist] paradigm, and social classes for the class paradigm ... Each paradigm gains its explanatory power by focusing upon a particular context of action – a situation context within which individuals and groups choose to mobilize to influence political decisions, for the pluralist paradigm; an organizational context within which bureaucracies deploy their resources, for the elite paradigm; and a societal context within which social classes shape institutions that reinforce their rule, for the class paradigm."[9] An adequate theory of the state, Alford and Friedland argue, must incorporate all three levels of analysis. They note, however, that the value of each model will vary in specific situations, depending on the context of action exercised in and by the state.[10]

In explaining developments in poverty policy during the CAP and Review periods, the present study focuses on two of Alford and Friedland's three levels of analysis – the societal and the organizational – and on their corresponding paradigms – the class perspective and statism. Pluralism is of considerably less relevance. As Alford and Friedland note, the context of action championed by pluralism is the exercise of "situational power," which "exists where open and informed competition between relatively equal participants – individuals and groups – gains support from issue-oriented constituencies and exercises influence over responsive political leaders."[11] We know, however, that the poor and other socially marginal people have few resources for organization or political activism and that they largely lack the self-confidence to act effectively in politics. Thus poverty policy is unlikely to involve the exercise of significant situational power by, or on behalf of, its potential beneficiaries.[12] The structural power of state elites and the systemic power embedded in prevailing class relations will therefore be the main focus of our attention. Nevertheless, research for the book included a thorough investigation of the impact of such individual level phenomena as non-class interest groups, especially among the poor.

A FRAGMENTED STATE

The statist tradition focuses on "organizational structures that have different resources for domination of each other and of the society.

The state is first and foremost the dominant *organization* of society."[13] An issue of fundamental importance, from the state-centred perspective, is the degree of centralization or fragmentation in the state. Some states are more centralized than others and are therefore less ridden by crippling conflicts among departments and agencies; such states have a much greater capacity to achieve desired objectives than do fragmented ones.

The statist tradition includes an extensive literature on the variable capacity of states. A distinction is commonly made between "strong," relatively centralized, states and "weak," more fragmented, ones.[14] A strong state is "differentiated from other organizations operating in the same territory; [it is] autonomous [and] centralized; and ... its divisions are formally coordinated with one another."[15] Weak states, by contrast, remain fragmented and poorly integrated. France is very much the archetypal strong state, having developed a highly centralized administration with considerable directive capacity; Britain and the United States are the most frequently cited examples of weak states.[16]

Weak states are not incapable of pursuing public policies of their own creation. But these do not involve long-term planning by ambitious and highly trained bureaucrats or the coordination of decision making across many policy sectors, as is the case in strong states.[17] The problem with policy making in weak states is that "bureaux pursue narrow, short-term goals that often draw them into conflict with other bureaus engaged in similar strategies. Their inclination to treat problems sequentially sets the stage for ... 'sectoral decomposition', the tendency to break large decisions into simpler, more manageable ones."[18]

In making the distinction between strong and weak states in their study of industrial policy, Michael Atkinson and William Coleman have little trouble placing Canada in the latter category. Canada, they write, has a fragmented bureaucracy: "What cannot be found is an organizational centre of gravity from which consistent political and bureaucratic instructions can be expected to flow."[19]

Stefan Dupré's interpretation of Canadian executive federalism provides an overview of the chronically fragmented structure of the Canadian state. But it also documents substantial organizational changes during the postwar era, reflecting an unsuccessful effort to centralize the federal government. Dupré's model is an excellent vehicle for applying the statist perspective to Canadian poverty policy.

For Dupré, the central feature of the Canadian state is executive federalism, defined by Donald Smiley as "relations between elected and appointed officials of the two orders of government."[20] How executive federalism works depends on the relation of the first of its two pillars to the second – of federalism to the cabinet-dominated form of government. And cabinet structures are subject to change: "Without altering one iota of the constitutional conventions that give them their central energizing force, cabinets can operate in vastly different ways,"[21] leading to parallel changes in the structure of federal/provincial relations. Dupré identifies two "historically distinguishable modes of cabinet operation" – the departmentalized and the institutionalized – which in turn give rise to two distinct models of executive federalism. One model is relevant to an understanding of the events leading to the adoption of the Canada Assistance Plan in the 1960s, while the other is applicable to the following decade, when the Social Security Review took place. Both models reflect the fundamentally fragmented nature of the Canadian state but have substantially different implications for the prospects of federal/provincial policy making.

From the 1920s to the 1960s, the federal government had a departmentalized cabinet. It had five key features, relating to the organizational *origins* of policy initiatives, the dominant *norms* in policy making, the *scope* of initiatives, the *range* of interests, and the *level of conflict* produced in the policy process. Each feature was reflected in corresponding attributes of federal/provincial relations:

1 First, initiatives emerged from parallel program-administering departments or offices at the two levels of government. New ideas would result, for example, from the interaction between federal and provincial foresters, or between federal transportation specialists and their provincial counterparts.

2 These initiatives reflected the norms shared by officials of corresponding federal and provincial program departments, who often had a similar professional background; in many cases, they had gone to school together and belonged to the same professional associations. Policy making involved modest, incremental departures from existing measures, with which these officials were familiar and, on the whole, comfortable.

3 The scope of policy initiatives, both within the federal government and in federal/provincial relations, was largely circumscribed by the pre-existing jurisdictional boundaries – or "turf" – of the originating departments. For example, a new health initiative would involve health matters, and nothing else.

4 Since these initiatives were within departmental turf, policy making in specific areas was dominated by a single set of

program- or department-based interests common to the two levels of government.

5 Finally, conflict over policy making within the federal cabinet and in federal/provincial relations was low. This was possible because policy making occurred within the confines of departmental turf and parallel federal and provincial departments, where consensus could emerge easily.

A negative consequence of this, of course, was that the state had a limited capacity to generate broad and systematic policy initiatives. It was that limitation which led to the reorganization of the federal government during the 1960s, especially after Pierre Elliot Trudeau became Prime Minister in 1968; similar changes occurred in some provinces. The departmentalized system gave way to an institution-alized one, designed to coordinate government activities across several policy areas. But institutionalization created problems of its own: "The institutionalized cabinet has as its theme the quest to make contemporary government decision making more manageable. It arises initially as the response to the perceived defects of the depart-mentalized cabinet in the face of the range, complexity and interde-pendence of the decisions that contemporary governments are called upon to make."[22] Under Trudeau's influence, there was considerable interest in "planning, policy formulation, and co-ordination"[23] – capacities traditionally associated with the strong-state model.

Institutionalized cabinets and federal/provincial relations have five features, corresponding to those of the earlier departmentalized form:

1 The origins of policy making are much more diffuse, involving central agencies (e.g., the Prime Minister's Office, the Privy Council Office, the Treasury Board Secretariat, and the depart-ment of Finance) to an unprecedented extent, alongside the pro-gram-administering departments.

2 The old program officials with their professional loyalties remain. But other norms now become relevant to policy making. Central agencies and their ministers are expected to bring a different orientation to policy making by stressing "the collective concerns of the cabinet." While the departmentalized cabinet "tended to subordinate the power, status and prestige of individual govern-ments to programmatic objectives, executive federalism [under an institutionalized cabinet] does exactly the opposite."[24] As a con-sequence, federal/provincial relations become less focused on pro-gram goals and take on a more strategic outlook, with each level of government seeing the other as an obstacle to its plans. The

new emphasis on planning, policy formulation, and coordination means that the institutionalized cabinet also departs significantly from the incremental thinking typical of a departmentalized cabinet. Central agencies bring with them a more systematic, large-scale orientation to policy making.

3 Under the influence of central agency officials, the scope of policy initiatives and federal/provincial discussions expands considerably, transcending the turf of single departments.

4 Cabinet decision making and federal/provincial relations involve a variety of disparate interests, including various program departments with contrasting professional loyalties and central agencies with government-wide and strategic concerns.

5 This diversity of interests substantially increases the potential for conflict among federal and provincial departments and agencies with distinct program and government-wide objectives. Federal/provincial relations in the age of institutional cabinets are fraught with pitfalls on the road to agreement.

The five defining features of each of the two cabinet systems and of the corresponding patterns of federal/provincial relations are summarized in the figure.

Cabinet Systems and Corresponding Federal/Provincial Relations

	Departmentalized	*Institutionalized*
Origins of policy	Program departments	Central agencies and program departments

Norms of participants	incremental program focus	central agency
		  systematic
		  strategic
		program department
		  incremental
		  program focus

Scope of initiatives	departmental	supradepartmental
Range of interests in policy making	homogeneous: similar program departments	heterogeneous: diverse program departments and central agencies
Level of conflict	low	high

In the name of comprehensive and planned policy making, the institutionalized cabinet curtailed the "sectoral decomposition" typical of the departmentalized cabinet. But in the end, changes in the structure of the federal state and in federal/provincial relations in the late 1960s and early 1970s did not alter the fundamentally weak, fragmented nature of the Canadian state. On the contrary, the reforms of cabinet undermined the one strength that the old system had – its ability to undertake modest, department-specific policy initiatives. As a result, the Canadian state remained incapable of generating comprehensive cross-sectoral initiatives.

Dupré's model inevitably simplifies the transition that occurred in the organization of the Canadian state during the late 1960s and early 1970s. While central agencies were less significant during the ascendancy of the departmentalized model, they were not irrelevant; the Finance department, in particular (as Dupré notes), has always exercised a significant influence. At the same time, the growing importance of the central agencies after 1968 did not obliterate the influence of program departments. And as noted above, the Canadian state remained fundamentally fragmented throughout the period. These continuities will become apparent in the course of this book, but the shift of power within the federal bureaucracy during those years was real and significant, and it had profound implications for policy making.

The Canada Assistance Plan emerged in an organizational setting that encouraged limited, incremental, department-specific reforms led by officials in program departments, thus facilitating the successful implementation of these modest policy initiatives. The context within which the Social Security Review took place allowed for much broader and more systematic initiatives, but it also inhibited their completion by involving in the policy process a welter of contrasting interests, both within the federal government and in federal/provincial relations. This book will assess the extent to which the two initiatives reflected these organizational parameters.

CLASS RELATIONS IN CANADA:
WORKING CLASS WEAKNESS
AND MARKET-ORIENTED
ACCUMULATION STRATEGY

While the domain of statism is the organizational level of analysis, that of the class perspective is the societal level; here, the focus is on "superorganizational relations stable enough to be described – polity, family, economy, religion, culture."[25] The analytical focus of the class perspective is different from, and more encompassing than, that of the statist perspective; this implies the possibility of their synthesis in a comprehensive perspective on the state.

All paradigms are divided among contending schools, but these fissures are deeper in the class perspective than in the others. Alford and Friedland distinguish two dominant traditions in the class perspective – one political and the other functional. The political tradition focuses on class struggle – on how the dominance of the capitalist class is always qualified, though to a much greater extent in some societies than in others, by conflict with working class interests. The functional tradition, by contrast, concentrates on the reproduction needs of capital – on how the state acts to secure the long-term stability of a capitalist society. Unfortunately, as Alford and Friedland note, "the paradox of the class perspective is that the two traditions are rarely brought together theoretically. Studies emphasizing capital accumulation do not normally deal with class struggle and vice versa."[26] The relevance of the political and functional variants of the class perspective will therefore be assessed separately in this book.

Political Variant

Class struggle is always present in capitalist democracies, but the balance among the classes varies substantially from one society to the next. The now-influential social democratic school of writers is a useful representative of the political class approach. For this group, the main determinant of the class balance of power is the ability of the working class to challenge the dominance of capitalist interests in the state. Working class power is "based in organizations which can coordinate ... individual wage-earners into collective action, that is primarily through unions and political parties."[27] In the state, working class power is reflected in the strength of social democratic and other parties of the left.[28] It has its primary expression in parliaments and the control of responsible executives.

The class balance of power is quite different in different capitalist democracies, because the strength of working class parties and their allies varies substantially among these societies. Compared with other developed capitalist democracies, the Canadian working class is relatively weak, and the political class balance of power is particularly favourable to capital. The Co-operative Commonwealth Federation (CCF) and its successor, the New Democratic Party (NDP), have had only modest success as national parties of the left, while organized labour has been weakened by regional and linguistic tensions.[29] The resulting "failure of the CCF/NDP to win electoral office at the federal level throughout the postwar period limited the influence that the working class could exert over the direction of state intervention in the economy."[30] As a consequence, policy making in the Canadian state during those years remained dominated by the Liberal Party, which enjoyed strong business support; this capitalist class preference has now been inherited by the governing Conservatives. Only on two occasions in the past half-century have political circumstances enabled the CCF/NDP to exert a modest influence on the state by inducing the governing Liberals to move to the left – during the immediate postwar years, and during the period of minority government led by Prime Minister Lester B. Pearson in the mid-1960s.[31]

Gösta Esping-Andersen, a leading member of the social democratic school, has developed a typology of capitalist welfare states that throws light on the implications of working class weakness for Canadian poverty policy. He contends that welfare states in capitalist democracies have not converged around similar programs and policies because the class basis of politics in capitalist democracies varies widely from one country to the next. The primary objective of working class movements has been to use the welfare state to reduce the market dependence of workers – their almost complete reliance on wages earned in the labour market to support themselves and their families. Where working class parliamentary power is significant, the welfare states that have emerged have substantially limited market dependence and reduced to a minimum the need for selective, social assistance-type programs – in our sense of the term, poverty policies. "Means-tested poor relief ... compels all but the most desperate to participate in the market," because it is usually designed to be less desirable than the lowest available wage; for that reason, it has "been a chief target of labour-movement attacks."[32] One of the most powerful correlations in Esping-Andersen's empirical study of eighteen capitalist democracies is the inverse link found between the extent of working class political mobilization and the predominance within a national welfare state of means-tested, poverty-oriented programs.

In Scandinavia, where social democratic welfare states developed under the long-term left-party control of governments, poverty-relief measures have been almost entirely eliminated. In a different way, market dependence is also limited in most of continental Europe, where the threat of working class power was strong in the past and where governments were long controlled by non-capitalist conservative forces that wished to stabilize their citizens' loyalty to the state. Social democratic and conservative welfare states replaced poverty measures with publicly funded income maintenance and social service programs that covered all or large parts of the national population instead of concentrating on the poor, and that offered generous benefits based on criteria independent of the market.[33] Because such programs are typically so broad in coverage, they have become the focus of equally widespread loyalty among citizens. In Esping-Andersen's terms, they embody considerable "solidarity"; any attempt to lower benefits is viewed as a threat by many voters and, as a consequence, is politically unattractive.

A third welfare state model, predominant mainly in Anglo-Saxon countries, is liberal. It is established by pro-business political parties in a climate of weak working class political mobilization. It differs substantially from the other two models in that it is dominated by a market logic. In the liberal welfare state, "means-tested assistance, modest universal transfers, or modest social insurance plans predominate." Assistance-type measures are far more prevalent in this model than in either of the other two. The fundamental principle underlying program design is that market relations, wherever possible, should prevail; the preferred form of welfare provision in the liberal state is through private channels.[34] Compulsory, public, social insurance and universal programs emerged only when this "ideal" was no longer politically acceptable, but they have in any case remained modest by conservative or social democratic standards. Much of the liberal welfare state remains narrowly targeted at the most socially disadvantaged population. As a whole, it embodies little solidarity and is more prone to attacks by hostile political interests.

Those who have applied this typology to Canada, including Esping-Andersen himself, have been unanimous in identifying this country with the liberal model. Nevertheless, as Esping-Andersen points out, welfare states that mainly belong to one model may include traces of others. Indeed, despite its mainly liberal character, there are sufficient traits of universality in Canada's welfare state to make its liberalism impure. This "impure-liberal" quality reflects the pattern of political class relations that has shaped the Canadian state. Poverty-relief measures – public assistance and associated services – represent about one-sixth of all social security expenditures in Canada. Among the nations surveyed by Esping-Andersen, only the United States spends a larger proportion on means-tested benefits; in most other countries, such measures have become unimportant.[35] In 1986, 1.9 million Canadians were assistance recipients at some time during the year, representing 7.5 per cent of the national population.[36] Assistance therefore persists as an important element in Canada's welfare state, and measures targeted at the poor remain a focus of policy debate.

Universal and social insurance measures, though modest, are not absent: Canada does have universal income security programs (such as Old Age Security), non-actuarial elements in its social insurance programs (especially unemployment insurance), and an important universal program for the provision of health insurance. But these measures are small by international standards, and other features of the Canadian welfare state identify it as clearly liberal. For example, the actuarial design considerations typical of market-oriented, liberal welfare states played an important role in structuring Canada's social insurance programs, including unemployment insurance and the Canada/Quebec Pension Plans. In addition, "in the area of labour market and employment policy, Canada consistently ranked behind the major European democracies."[37] The range of human needs that are satisfied by social policy is narrow; this is typical of the liberal model, which encourages market dependence.[38]

Reflecting this impure-liberal pattern, Esping-Andersen's quantitative scores of welfare state characteristics give Canada a very high rating on "degree of liberalism" – a rating rivalled only by those of the United States and Switzerland. Canada has no significant traces of conservatism. However, while universality, the essence of Esping-Andersen's measure of socialism, is the reigning principle only in Scandinavia, it is approximated to some extent in a few liberal regimes such as Canada and Switzerland. On his measure of degree of socialism, Canada's score is midway between the lowest (the United States) and the highest (the three Scandinavian countries).[39]

Of what relevance is Esping-Andersen's model for the study of Canadian poverty policy? In at least three ways, the policy legacies of Canada's quasi-liberal welfare state could encourage policy makers to make continued use of poverty-relief measures in developing social policy:

1 The heritage of a liberal welfare state might condition the ideological environment of policy makers, sustaining the belief that targeted, poverty-relief measures are an appropriate and legitimate means for providing social security.

2 Organizations within the state that administer poverty-relief measures and have a vested interest in their preservation and expansion are likely to be larger and to embody more bureaucratic power and expertise than is true in non-liberal settings, where social assistance is much less important.[40]

3   Canada's universal and social insurance programs are comparatively inadequate and would probably require substantial improvements in order to alleviate mass poverty. Policy makers
seeking pragmatic solutions to the problems of the needy might
therefore be encouraged to strengthen existing measures directed
at the poor as a more realistic alternative.

Esping-Andersen's model also has implications for determining
who will and who will not be interested in poverty reform. Universality is the agenda of working class politics, and its introduction into
policy debates will likely reflect the influence of parties of the left.
But where poverty-relief measures are concerned, these parties are
unlikely to be more reformist than non-left parties; on the contrary,
their market-curtailing ambitions will make them more hesitant than
non-left parties to support poverty reform. In any case, the limited
electoral appeal of poverty-relief measures is likely to make them of
only modest interest to politicians of all stripes; poverty reform is at
least as likely to be led by bureaucrats who are motivated by the
ideological, organizational, and pragmatic considerations listed
above. Union federations attempting to influence policy making will,
like their left-party allies, stress universality and the reduction of
market dependence; business federations would be expected to do
the opposite. In assessing the relevance of the political variant of the
class model to Canadian poverty policy, this study will look for
evidence of these patterns.

Functional Variant

The functional stream of the class model stresses the role played by
the state in reproducing capitalism. In David Wolfe's terms, "the
centrality of capital to the investment process, upon which both the
overall rate of economic growth and the steady improvement in the
standard of living depends, places it in a privileged position in the
policy process. This privileged position is reflected in the pattern
of interaction between capital and the state: relations tend to be
less visible politically (i.e., seldom open to public scrutiny), more
technical in nature ... and more consensual (in terms of mutual
acceptance of the necessity of an adequate rate of return for the
vitality of the accumulation process.)"[41] As one might expect, this
imperative is accommodated to large extent within the bureaucracy,
where this "less visible and more consensual" dynamic can unfold
relatively insulated from the unpredictable quirks of parliamentary
democracy.

From a functional class perspective, the reproductive needs of capitalism in any country reflect the structure of that country's capitalist class. In Canada, this class is dominated by its financial and commercial parts (or "fractions"). Industrial capital is, by comparison, quite weak and relatively isolated. These features reflect the history of Canada's economic development. Industrialization has been modest and has largely served a small domestic market rather than foreign markets. Growth in the past was largely based on "the export of those resources in which Canada was deemed to have a comparative advantage to metropolitan markets abroad, especially Britain and the U.S.,"[42] thus providing opportunities for capital accumulation for the financial and commercial interests. Reflecting the isolation of industrial capital from the dominant fractions of Canadian capital, "neither the commercial banks nor state institutions [historically] played a significant role in directing the flow of investment capital" to industry. This historical pattern departed from the Japanese and French models, for instance, where finance capital, working closely with the state, has performed an important role in directing industrial investment.

The strategy pursued by the state to reproduce capitalism is carried out by its dominant department.[43] There is agreement among many class and non-class commentators that Finance is the dominant department in the Canadian state, frequently possessing veto power over policy proposals emanating from elsewhere in the bureaucracy. There is also agreement that the Finance department's stature stems from its specifically economic role: it "remains the most important economic portfolio," and the Finance minister is the government's leading spokesman on economic policy.[44]

From a functional class perspective, Finance's institutional pre-eminence has enabled it to pursue the accumulation needs of the dominant financial and commercial fractions of the capitalist class. This can be observed in its approach to economic policy during the postwar era, as outlined in the 1945 White Paper on Employment and Incomes.[45] That approach was based on the assumption that "Canada's economic strength lay in its traditional role as an exporter of staple [i.e., non-manufactured] products."[46] Finance's orientation also reflected the traditionally limited role of the Canadian state in directing industrial development. Wolfe concludes that a bias was introduced into the selection of policy alternatives against "the adoption of policies affecting the allocation of credit, government procurement or indicative planning to influence the intersectoral allocation of investment capital."[47] These were the development tools used by the state in more interventionist capitalist economies.

Finance's perception that state intervention in the economy should be kept to a minimum and that the market is an autonomous, self-sufficient sphere, best able to perform when unfettered by the state, is typical of societies where industry has developed without extensive guidance from the state or from the financial sector. As Douglas Hartle points out, the usual philosophy in the Finance department is: "Let the market work until it can be shown that there is a better alternative."[48] Finance's pro-market orientation motivates it to protect the economy against departmental proposals for major infrastructure investments or fiscal transfer programs. Thus "Finance failed to find any criterion of general economic policy more sophisticated than a reflex anti-spending posture."[49] This has resulted in persistent conflict with other departments that have non-economic responsibilities which are seen as separate from, and antithetical to, sound economic policy.[50] This battle, and the market orientation that Finance brings to it, constitute a powerful force, representing a functional class influence on social policy. While other bureaux in the federal state acquired greater influence during the 1970s, they did not fundamentally challenge Finance's pre-eminent position nor did they pursue an alternative accumulation strategy.[51]

If a functional class model is relevant to explaining poverty policy making during the 1960s and 1970s, it should be reflected in Finance's pro-market approach to accumulation or perhaps in the similar position adopted by other economic policy-making bureaux that became more important in the mid-1970s. Finance would be expected to oppose significant new social expenditures in the poverty field and elsewhere. Where such initiatives nevertheless had to proceed for political reasons, Finance would attempt to restrict their fiscal impact and to minimize their negative consequences for market activity.

EXPLAINING POVERTY POLICY

This study attempts to demonstrate the utility of integrating different levels of analysis in the study of public policy. How can this be done? Alford suggests an "additive" methodology, which is based on the assumption that "an important element of contingency or 'slippage' exists between these levels, each of which is causally important and cannot be reduced to the others ... Each level ... sets limits upon the other levels, but does not completely determine structures within them."[52]

What is being tested in this book is not the comparative merits of statism and the class perspective but the viability of a synthetic approach to policy studies – one that integrates elements from each of two potentially complementary levels of analysis. Each variant of the class perspective elaborated above claims to explain important societal preconditions for policy making within the organizations of the state. Policy making is shaped by the policy legacies of Canada's largely liberal welfare state, which reflects the historic weakness of working class politics. And it is also influenced by the market-oriented accumulation strategy pursued by dominant economic bureaux within the state. Reconciled with statism in additive terms, the class perspective concedes that statism can explain which specific organizations will be involved in policy making, what the relations between them will be, and how they will engage in policy making. Here, the fundamental determinants of policy are historically evolving structures of executive decision making and federal/provincial relations. A singular merit of the period spanned by the two reforms examined in the chapters that follow is that it witnessed a significant transition in these internal arrangements of the Canadian state, which altered the organizational context of policy making but not the essentially fragmented nature of the state. The cases examined here therefore provide an excellent opportunity to document the impact of distinct forms of state organization on policy making. If the organizational model is of value, poverty policy in the two periods will have differed substantially in origin, organizational norms, scope, and range of participating bureaux – and most importantly, in the intensity of organizational conflict emerging in the reform process.

CHAPTER TWO

The Origins of Comprehensive Assistance Reform, 1958–63

Poverty relief remained an essential feature of Canada's welfare state after the Second World War – a legacy of the liberal welfare philosophy and weak working class mobilization that had prevailed before the war. Federal interventions in the area of social assistance continued during the 1950s; and, late in the decade, a debate about further federal activity began among federal and provincial bureaucrats who met under the auspices of the Public Welfare Division of the Canadian Welfare Council. As pressure for change mounted, concepts debated at the bureaucratic level eventually received the sanction of politicians, culminating in passage of the Canada Assistance Plan in 1966.

The dynamic group of welfare officials who led the reform movement reflected their societal environment, and their proposals were justified by arguments that confirmed their liberal background. The very existence of this group was testimony to the continued importance of the programs that its members administered. The political dynamics of the liberal welfare state were also evident in the role of the politicians in power. As Esping-Andersen observes, poverty-oriented social security measures embody little social solidarity and therefore have little political attraction. The primary focus of politicians was not on social assistance but on broader social security initiatives that were of interest to large numbers of voters. The New Democratic Party played an important role in stimulating this preference, confirming that social democratic influences on government tend to undermine, rather than encourage, assistance reform. Societal influences of a more functional type were also apparent in this early period, in the form of the market-oriented opposition to reform by the department of Finance.

A LIBERAL SETTING

Until 1940, Canada's welfare state was straightforwardly liberal and did not include any significant universal programs. The only noteworthy social insurance measure, available in most provinces, was workmen's compensation. The federal government played a minimal role: its sole ongoing commitment was the Old Age Pension Act (OAP), which required it to pay 50 per cent of provincial relief payments to poor elderly and blind persons. During the Great Depression, the only social security available to most Canadians consisted of provincially and municipally administered "relief" – what in later years would be called social assistance. The federal government shared these relief costs on a purely ad hoc basis, and it disclaimed any constitutional responsibility for them.[1] Even as late as the mid-1950s, provincial assistance standards remained stingy. In many provinces, benefits were available only to those who could prove that they were unemployable.

The proposals advanced by social policy experts during the 1940s reflected the continuing power of liberal ideas in Canadian society. Charlotte Whitton, long an influential commentator, argued that assistance should remain important in Canada's welfare state because it deterred work avoidance. Harry Cassidy, the author of a widely read proposal for postwar social policy, took a similar view.[2]

Both during and after the war, however, Canadian social policy acquired important universal elements. A national program of unemployment insurance was initiated by the federal government in 1940. Family allowance payments, available on a universal basis to Canadian families with children, began in 1944. And in 1951 the selective OAP system was replaced by the federally financed Old Age Security (OAS) régime, providing a modest universal pension to all elderly persons over the age of 70.

These measures represented a substantial expansion of the federal presence in social policy, but they did not entail a decisive break with liberalism. Nevertheless, the significant advances represented by UI, family allowances, and OAS, coupled with the continued (albeit now qualified, or "impure") liberalism of Canada's welfare state, reflected a new pattern of working class mobilization. Working class power had increased substantially during the war, but it remained modest by international standards. Support for the CCF surged during 1943 and 1944: the party won a provincial election in Saskatchewan, acceded to "official opposition" status in Ontario, and placed first in a national public opinion poll. This groundswell contributed to Prime Minister William Lyon Mackenzie King's endorsement of family allowances, to

generous though vague promises of social reform in his Liberal government's 1943 and 1944 "speeches from the throne," and to ambitious
reform ideas – including proposals that prefigured OAS – released by
the government in its 1945 Green Book.[3] A significant growth in labour
union membership during the war reinforced the spirit of innovation.[4]

But the Liberals' "dramatic shift to the left"[5] successfully undercut
the CCF, which in the 1945 election was relegated to minor party status,
where it remained until it transmuted itself into the New Democratic
Party in 1961. Having headed off the social democratic threat, the
Liberals lost their enthusiasm for reform. Within a year of their 1945
re-election, they were sounding a more cautious note, criticizing organized labour's suggestions for further change.[6] The Liberals sponsored
no major new innovations in social policy until the 1960s. During the
formative period of the postwar welfare state, then, pressure from
the political left did stimulate important departures from the liberal
model, but not the radical changes that would have been needed to
extract Canadian social policy from that liberal mould.

Initiatives in social assistance therefore found an important place
among the federal government's new commitments after 1945.
Income security expenditures at the three levels of government
reflected the continued prominence of assistance during the postwar
years. In 1950, about 80 per cent of provincial and municipal expenditures in this area (excluding employee pensions) were of the assistance type. Almost three-quarters of assistance expenditures went to
poor blind and elderly persons, with half of these costs being
absorbed by the federal government under OAP. But for all other
categories of assistance – general assistance, and assistance for the
disabled and for mothers – there was no federal help;[7] people in
those categories, especially the employable unemployed, received
very inadequate benefits or no benefits at all.

When the OAS legislation was passed in 1951, providing pensions
to all Canadians over 70, the provinces were relieved of a large part
of their assistance costs. Two pieces of assistance legislation were also
introduced at this time. The Old Age Assistance Act (OAA) extended
the age-related benefit to the 65–69 age group, while the Blind Persons
Assistance Act (BPA) simply continued blind allowances previously
covered under OAP. In 1954 the federal government extended its assistance role by passing the Disabled Persons Assistance Act (DPA), which
gave benefits to the "totally and permanently disabled." Together, these
three measures became known as the "categorical" programs. They
provided benefits to highly visible persons who, in liberal terms, were
"deserving" because they were not expected to work. The benefits
were based on a "means test," which exclusively involved a calculation

of what means (i.e., income, savings, and so on) were available to the claimant. The categories involved highly restrictive conditions about who could qualify for benefits and how high the latter could be. The provinces also had to meet a number of conditions to obtain federal funds. During the 1950s and 1960s, they constantly complained about the resulting rigidities.

The Unemployment Assistance Act (UAA) of 1956, which covered half the costs of provincial assistance for employable unemployed persons, was the most significant federal intervention in the assistance field during the 1950s. Aside from its potentially much larger caseload, UAA also differed from the categorical programs in that it used a "needs test" and had much looser standards for federal cost-sharing. The needs test meant that benefits not only reflected the claimant's available resources but also his/her particular needs. Because of the loose standards, it was the federal welfare authorities who complained about them after the passage of UAA. A major theme in federal reform efforts during the 1960s would be the drafting of new legislation with tighter national standards than existed in UAA, although not as stringent as those embodied in the categorical programs.

Even with the categorical programs and UAA in place, many provincial assistance costs were still not shared by the federal government. The most important exclusion was that of mothers' allowances. In 1960, some 50,000 families across Canada received help, totalling almost $45 million, from provincial mothers' allowance programs.[8] Another non-shared element resulted from the fact that the provinces could not share the costs of either their departmental administration or their casework. As rehabilitative social services gained in significance during the early 1960s, this exclusion became increasingly important. Also excluded from cost-sharing arrangements were assistance to employed persons and child welfare costs. There had been some discussion about including a differential cost-sharing formula into the UAA, which would have enabled the poorer provinces to receive more generous financial arrangements than the richer ones, but this proposal was not adopted. These exclusions, the administrative complications caused by the fragmentation of federal assistance commitments into four different programs, and the national standards issues alluded to above were the focus of the pressures that led to CAP.

THE PROFESSIONAL ARENA

Almost all of the assistance reforms discussed in the early 1960s had been anticipated in proposals of the Canadian Welfare Council's Public Welfare Division (PWD). The division was nominally a branch of a non-governmental organization, but during the late 1950s it provided a forum for a vital fraternity of federal and provincial welfare officials who developed common views on assistance issues there without appearing to meddle in matters that were properly the responsibility of their political masters. Given the continuing importance of poverty-relief measures in Canada's welfare state, thinking about how to improve social policy naturally meant thinking about social assistance. And the extent to which Canada's welfare state was still a social assistance distribution system meant that large bureaux of program administrators existed to engage in this thinking. They found a home at the PWD.

The Public Welfare Division of the Canadian Welfare Council

From its inception in 1920 until its replacement by the Canadian Council on Social Development in 1970, the Canadian Welfare Council (CWC) was the leading non-governmental source of social policy innovation in Canada. The council comprised a number of divisions (including the PWD) that over time developed their own staff resources and their own policies. The PWD sought to "provide a means whereby persons or groups employed or otherwise actively concerned in public welfare may study and discuss methods of achieving the highest possible standards in Canadian public welfare services at all levels of government."[9]

While most of the research and policy-making activities of the CWC took place within its divisions, the council's board of governors and its executive secretary performed important roles in the life of each division. Between them, they secured a prominent role for the council and its divisions during the 1950s and 1960s. The board, which was the CWC's senior decision-making body, included a cross-section of the country's business, academic, and governmental elites.[10] It endorsed all PWD policies as its own, thus giving them a higher public profile than they would otherwise have had.[11]

Officials from the three levels of government completely dominated the PWD. In 1961, for example, 62 of the 77 members of the division's key "National Committee" were welfare officials,[12] including a substantial representation from the higher levels of the federal and provincial welfare bureaucracies. Joe Willard, who became deputy minister of the department of National Health and Welfare (NHW) after 1960, had been a member of the PWD's National Committee for many years during the 1950s. Richard Splane, director of the UAA program and Willard's foremost subordinate in the assistance field, was also a member of the committee during the 1960s and, if anything, was on even closer terms with the PWD. He sometimes gave the division's staff access to confidential departmental files, and he became intimately involved in the preparation of one of its policy statements. Later, he became the most forceful exponent of the CWC's assistance policy within the federal bureaucracy.[13]

Provincial representation on the PWD's National Committee was also extensive. By 1960 eight provinces were represented on the National Committee by their deputy minister of welfare. Among them was F.R. Mackinnon, who had co-authored *Social Security for Canada*, the CWC's landmark 1958 policy statement (see below), and later became deputy welfare minister in Nova Scotia; Mackinnon was active in PWD meetings throughout the 1950s and 1960s. He and his three Prairie colleagues supported the CWC's post-1958 policy positions and tried to convince their governments to do likewise. Deputy ministers from the other three Atlantic provinces and British Columbia also belonged to the National Committee and were on cordial terms with the division's staff.[14] The two exceptions to this harmonious *tableau* were Quebec and Ontario. The division was unable to develop an adequate representation from Quebec on its staff or to establish close ties with its provincial government. As for Ontario, its welfare deputy minister, J.S. Band, refused to be involved with the PWD after 1959; he disagreed with its 1958 recommendations and did not get along with its staff.[15]

The PWD gave senior public assistance officials an opportunity to reach agreement on policy reforms and to camouflage their activity as the product of a disinterested and prestigious non-governmental organization. When the division issued public statements, the practice of having the CWC's board of governors endorse them not only attracted a certain prestige to its pronouncements but also prevented criticism of government officials for taking an active role in proposing policies. As the division's executive secretary pointed out at the time, this practice "recognizes that members of the Public Welfare Division, most of whom are appointed officials, would be placed in an awkward position by having to take full responsibility for recommendations which might in effect be considered policy matters, and as such more appropriately the responsibility of elected officials or laymen."[16]

The Reform Agenda

In 1958 the PWD conducted a thorough review of assistance policy and published the results in a statement entitled *Social Security for*

Canada, which anticipated most of the reforms eventually included in CAP. Other CAP ingredients were also prefigured by PWD proposals developed after the 1958 statement. Both the process that led to these statements and the proposals that they embodied reflected their societal setting – i.e., the vitality of the public assistance sector, the predominance of liberal norms – as well as their organizational context – shared backgrounds and collegial relations among participating officials, and incremental and department-specific recommendations for change.

The process.   The 1958 statement resulted from several months of intense discussion among federal and provincial welfare officials who belonged to the PWD. The previous year, C.A. Patrick, a recently departed PWD official, had proposed that the division launch a policy review that would endorse federal sharing of all welfare costs and "enable provinces and municipalities to improve their assistance programs and to eliminate categories where that seems desirable." Norman Cragg, Patrick's successor at the PWD, agreed that "there is a major task here for the Public Welfare Division."[17] Cragg also believed that if the PWD's National Committee concurred, it might be a good idea to prepare a policy recommendation to be forwarded to the federal government. Because of "the problem faced by the Division in making statements that affect government policy," such a statement would have to "come through the Board of Governors of the Canadian Welfare Council. However the ammunition would have to be made by our Division."[18] National Committee members responded positively to Patrick's idea, and Mackinnon, then welfare director in Nova Scotia, was seconded from his provincial government to work on the statement.[19] Cragg and Mackinnon jointly drafted *Social Security for Canada* after extensive consultations with PWD members from across the country. Cragg made a five-week tour of western Canada, where he held eighteen meetings with public welfare officials about the document, while Mackinnon and another senior Nova Scotia public welfare official held a meeting with officials in the Maritimes.[20] Federally, while drafting the statement, Cragg and Mackinnon "had been in close touch with officials at all levels in the Department of National Health and Welfare, notably the deputy minister, George Davidson, the director of the Research Division, Joseph Willard, and other members of that division," including Splane.[21]

The statement was adopted by the CWC at its 1958 annual meeting and endorsed by its board of governors in June. Cragg then held a series of meetings in all of the provinces from October 1958 to

January 1959, in order to lobby for the document's proposals among a very large number of public welfare officials who had not participated in its creation, as well as among other influential members of the public. Cragg found that "support for the recommendations was not only enthusiastic but also, to all intents and purposes, unanimous."[22] Having produced a statement that reflected the views of individual actors in the public welfare sector, the PWD then successfully disseminated it more widely among others with an interest in the field, especially other welfare officials.

The proposals. The major recommendation in the 1958 document was for "a federal Public Assistance Act which would ... enable the Dominion government to share the aggregate costs to a province, and to the municipalities in a province, of providing financial assistance to all persons who are in need." The provinces would have the option of maintaining the three categorical programs separate from the general assistance legislation or incorporating them into the general public assistance program "with the same provisions respecting the sharing of costs as in the Unemployment Assistance Act." The new act would also extend federal cost-sharing to several other areas, including, most importantly, provincial mothers' allowances. In addition, the federal government would adopt a differential cost-sharing formula aimed at increasing the percentage of costs shared as a province's caseload rose above the national average. The federal authorities were called upon to provide technical and research assistance to the provinces. The statement emphasized the importance of federal cost-sharing for the maintenance of adequate standards in provincial assistance programs, but it was more ambiguous about how such standards should be achieved.[23] The PWD became more concerned with standards after 1958 and would eventually advocate a more ambitious federal intervention.

Thus the 1958 statement included four key propositions that became important ingredients in the federal/provincial reform consensus that emerged among welfare officials by the early 1960s. The federal government should 1) fully integrate its assistance acts; 2) extend coverage to include provincial mothers' allowances; 3) implicitly continue the use of cost-sharing in the assistance field; and 4) provide a differential cost-sharing formula for the poorer provinces. All of these proposals pertained to problems experienced with existing assistance programs and were aimed at convincing the federal authorities that they should extend or maintain their program coverage to resolve them; thus the proposals were incremental. For similar reasons, none of these proposals transcended the traditional turf of provincial assistance programs: they were department-specific.

In the wake of the 1958 statement, the Public Welfare Division suggested additional reforms that displayed similar qualities. Welfare departments at both levels of government were becoming concerned about the dearth of properly trained staff and about their own limited ability to provide rehabilitative services to their clients. This led the PWD to suggest two changes – stronger, federally set standards for provincial assistance programs, and federal sharing of provincial costs for administration and social services. The need for better standards in provincial programs was stressed in several PWD statements between 1959 and 1961. To mollify the provinces, which would no doubt be angered by such interference with their welfare programs, the PWD recommended that the federal government extend cost-sharing to provincial welfare administration and social services.[24]

Beginning in 1960, many municipal and provincial politicians demanded that the federal government share the cost of "work-for-relief" measures under the Unemployment Assistance Act. Work-for-relief involved either compelling recipients deemed employable to "work off" their benefits or discontinuing the assistance they received. The UAA legislation, as originally passed, precluded federal sharing of work-for-relief costs because claimants had to be unemployed. After extensive discussion among welfare officials from all three levels of government, the PWD strongly opposed work-for-relief, arguing that it would undermine the morale of those compelled to take it and would have only limited rehabilitative value. But the division also looked for positive alternatives and advocated "greater emphasis ... on physical, social and economic rehabilitation services which may be needed by individuals and families on assistance," specifying that "economic rehabilitation services should include education, training or re-training programs (which may include work activity), vocational counselling, and job placement."[25]

Behind the PWD's specific policy recommendations during those years lay a clear acceptance of the liberal foundations of Canada's welfare state. The 1958 statement affirmed that "social security for all – both working people and those who are unable to work – depends ultimately on the productivity of the community. It follows that income security measures should be designed and administered in such a way as to promote individual initiative and national productivity." Similarly, while the statement made recommendations for improving the universal and social insurance components of Canada's welfare state – including OAS, UI, and health services – in each case the proposals represented modest departures from existing measures.[26] Justifiably, then, most observers saw the social assistance proposals as the heart of the document, and the division did not have a reputation as a significant reformer with respect to other parts of Canada's welfare state.[27] Finally, the document recognized that no foreseeable improvement in the non-selective elements of the Canadian welfare state could eradicate an important residual need for social assistance. It proposed that "the number of persons requiring public assistance ... be reduced as much as possible, both through the adoption of preventive measures and through the development or expansion of social insurance and/or statutory welfare payments." But "even with these provisions, there would remain a residue of needy persons for whom assistance should be available."[28]

THE EXECUTIVE ARENA

The Public Welfare Division had, by 1963, developed reform proposals that touched upon all but one of the themes later discussed in the federal/provincial negotiations leading to CAP.[29] Once this reform agenda emerged among public assistance officials, support for it grew within the federal and provincial governments until it was endorsed by the politicians and a formal policy review was launched in November 1963. Throughout this period, welfare officials at both levels of government took the initiative in promoting poverty reform, and most proposals reflected prior agreement achieved within the Public Welfare Division. Politicians, typically, did not have a strong interest in assistance reform.

Pressure from Provincial Officials, to April 1963

In the years preceding the federal Liberals' return to power in April 1963, several provinces requested various reforms in federal assistance legislation, in line with the PWD's proposals. While this did not represent a formal consensus, provincial bureaucratic support for the PWD agenda grew apace. This support was strongest in those provinces whose officials had especially close relations with the division; it was weakest in Ontario, whose deputy minister had little regard for the PWD. Two of the PWD's ideas attracted particular attention among provincial officials – a fully integrated federal assistance act, and federal sharing of the cost of provincial mothers' allowances. In the matter of work-for-relief, provincial politicians, motivated by characteristically market-oriented liberal ideas, opposed the objectives of most of their bureaucrats, who sought an expanded and more generous assistance plan.

The Prairie provinces were the first to support integration of the federal categorical programs with needs-tested general assistance. Citing the PWD's 1958 proposal, Saskatchewan's deputy minister of welfare frequently stated his desire to integrate the four existing federal programs.[30] In 1961 Alberta took an important step on the issue of integration by passing a Social Allowances Act, designed to incorporate clients of all four federal acts into one provincial program. The new legislation was created by Duncan Rogers, Alberta's deputy minister, who acknowledged his debt to Norman Cragg and the Public Welfare Division: they had convinced him, he said, of the merits of an integrated assistance act.[31] Manitoba officials informed their federal counterparts that they wanted the categories abolished.[32] The Atlantic welfare ministers requested integration of the categorical programs with UAA, largely through Mackinnon's efforts.[33] By contrast, Band, Ontario's deputy minister, opposed the integration of the four programs.[34]

The most widespread request for change was that in favour of federal sharing of provincial mothers' allowance costs. These allowances were the most expensive provincial assistance program not covered by federal legislation. Welfare officials in Saskatchewan, Manitoba, Quebec, and Nova Scotia led the way in raising this issue, and they were soon joined by colleagues in all other provinces, although Ontario was, again, initially reluctant, insisting that it be allowed to maintain a separate mothers' allowance program.[35]

Other issues attracted attention from various provinces. A differential cost-sharing formula for social assistance payments was advocated by the Atlantic provinces, again often led by their officials.[36] On the other hand, provincial officials showed little interest in another PWD proposal, which favoured stricter federal standards, at least for the very loose UAA legislation. As CAP emerged, national standards became the key point of contention between federal and provincial officials – the only example of a significant breakdown in shared norms and non-strategic relations.

As noted above, policy development of another sort became popular among municipal and some provincial politicians after 1960. With relatively heavy assistance caseloads resulting from the high unemployment rates of the late 1950s, several communities in Ontario and British Columbia introduced work-for-relief plans. This development reflected the impact of a liberal welfare state, with its ideological focus on deterring non-participation in the marketplace by making those absent from it "less eligible" than those who are attached to the market.

Canadian labour unions, especially the National Union of Public Employees, pressured the federal government not to share work-for-relief costs. Federal officials, themselves opposed to the practice, complied. The federal restriction was denounced at conventions of municipal politicians in Ontario and British Columbia; in both provinces, the welfare minister also supported the practice. The issue reached its climax when an August 1962 conference of provincial premiers requested that the federal government set up a committee to study work-for-relief. Some provincial politicians present expressed strong support for the idea and the liberal ideas underlying it,[37] but their views were not shared by their welfare officials. While not departing from an essentially liberal perspective, the officials adopted the PWD's position that rehabilitative work activity measures were compatible with a market environment and were more in keeping with the goal of restoring the recipient to usefulness (i.e., to the work force). They were therefore eminently preferable to the punitive approach favoured by the politicians.[38]

Pressure from Federal Officials, to April 1963

Assistance reform also gained momentum within the federal government. Here too, welfare bureaucrats led the way, with concerns inspired in good measure by the PWD. Federal welfare officials first attempted to have their reforms adopted as government policy in 1961, during the final years of Prime Minister John Diefenbaker's Conservative government, but their proposals were defeated in cabinet. The Finance department temporarily endorsed NHW's agenda because its officials believed that the alternative social security proposals then under consideration were even more undesirable, but this alliance was overridden by the politically motivated preference for social security reforms of a more universal kind – a concern stimulated in part by the New Democratic Party.

After 1960 the dominant federal welfare officials belonged to a generation that was close to the PWD, and they became zealous reformers. Willard, the new deputy minister of NHW, played a central role within this group, but Splane, who still oversaw the UAA administration, was equally important. Throughout the early 1960s Splane was the most persistent federal lobbyist for a comprehensive assistance act.

Beginning in September 1959 Splane wrote a series of memoranda to Willard, extolling the virtues of assistance reform. He advocated federal sharing of mothers' allowance costs and tentatively linked this to a broader package of ideas, including the integration of the existing categories into a comprehensive assistance act, the sharing of provincial administrative costs, and stronger national standards for the new act than those found in UAA. The package proposed by Splane both parallelled, and was explicitly indebted to, the CWC's 1958 recommendations.[39]

Splane's memoranda struck a responsive chord. In November 1960, Willard forwarded to Waldo Monteith, his minister, a draft cabinet submission proposing a "Reassessment of Federal Public Assistance Legislation" – a document that does not appear to have reached cabinet.[40] At the same time, Willard instructed Splane to develop specific proposals for a more integrated assistance act.

The result was another document from Splane, making proposals "in harmony with a number of the proposals of the Canadian Welfare Council." It repeated his views on program integration and on federal sharing of provincial costs for mothers' allowances and for administration and services. It also suggested that these extensions be contingent on the provinces' agreeing to submit "plans of administration" to the federal authorities, who would then assess whether the plans, including assistance rates, met national standards.[41]

Three months later, in June 1961, Monteith submitted to the cabinet a memorandum proposing the establishment of an interdepartmental committee to study new social policy ideas. One of the four initiatives recommended for study was "a new and more flexible Public Assistance Act." Others included a contributory public pension plan and the possibility of an increase in universal OAS payments.[42] The cabinet authorized the creation of an Interdepartmental Committee of Social Security (ICSS) to assess the options. Besides Health and Welfare, the departments of Finance and Labour were represented on the committee. The proceedings of the ICSS and the eventual fate of its report reflected a temporary, partial agreement between the quite different objectives of NHW and Finance in the assistance field, but their alliance was stymied by the contrasting, politically motivated agenda of the Conservative cabinet. Officials from the two departments dominated the meetings of the committee, held in July and August. Willard and Splane were the key NHW representatives, especially when assistance was discussed, and Robert Bryce, then secretary to the cabinet, also played an important role.

At the ICSS meetings, Willard made it clear that the introduction of "a general and more flexible Public Assistance Act" was a high priority for him.[43] He also supported federal sharing of provincial mothers' allowance costs.[44] Other parts of the emerging reform agenda – the use of national standards, the sharing of administrative costs, and the issue of differential cost-sharing – were raised by Willard and Splane, but less emphatically.[45]

Willard's preference for an integrated assistance plan that would cover mothers' allowances was accepted by Finance officials. But Finance's rationale for supporting integration was very different from NHW's. In a later period, when the array of policy alternatives had significantly changed, this difference would be crucial. In addition, Finance did not support any of the more tentative suggestions formulated by NHW.

Finance was primarily concerned with the maintenance of a prosperous private economy. On the one hand, this would be done by avoiding the adverse economic consequences that were thought likely to follow from the introduction of a public contributory pension proposal or a significant expansion of private contributory pensions. On the other hand, continued prosperity was to be achieved by preventing unnecessary government expenditures, which would have a negative effect on economic growth. This would be done by avoiding the expansion of costly universal pension programs. Bryce, who was soon to become the new deputy minister of Finance, took the same position.

At ICSS meetings and in departmental memos, C.M. Isbister, Finance's main spokesman, criticized the economic and financial consequences of major expansions in either public or private contributory pensions.[46] He argued that the forced expansion of pension schemes would raise production costs and prices and that the "large-scale accumulation of funds to meet the requirements of solvency would exert deflationary forces which would not be in the best interests of the economy under present and foreseeable conditions."[47] Bryce concurred; "important fiscal and economic implications" led him to conclude that "schemes for graduated benefits should be left to private initiative within the provinces."[48]

As between the two remaining alternatives set out in the cabinet memo – an increase in OAS and categorical assistance rates, and the development of a comprehensive assistance act – Finance officials and Bryce supported the latter for similar economic reasons. Ken Taylor, the Finance deputy minister, accepted Willard's insistence that "federal sharing of mothers' allowance costs [be] part of an improved over-all public assistance program"; as a later Finance memo made clear, however, this was motivated by a desire to avoid more expensive increases in OAS payments, with which the categorical measures were associated: "The additional costs in respect of mothers' allowances would have been more than offset by the savings of Old Age Security and Old Age Assistance combined."[49] NHW's reform suggestions were accepted because, of those which the ICSS had been instructed by cabinet to discuss, they were the least expensive and the least likely to affect the economy.

Finance and Bryce accepted these basic reforms, but in a memo to Willard, Taylor expressed doubts about the sections of NHW's draft report dealing with the training of welfare personnel and differential cost-sharing.[50] Bryce also emphasized that "the nature of this program could be left to the discretion of the provinces who would share equally its costs with the Federal government," implying rejection of federal standards and of a differential cost-sharing formula.[51]

The interdepartmental committee's final report embodied a compromise between the positions of NHW and Finance. In keeping with Finance's views, the report rejected the development of a public contributory pension plan and increases in OAS and categorical rates: "It would be difficult to justify any new major undertaking involving large expenditures and future commitments because of ... our existing and prospective fiscal position ... Financing of any new program or of any substantial increase in expenditures under existing programs will involve either additional taxation or borrowing which will exacerbate the difficult economic and financial problems of the federal government under existing economic conditions." Concern had been raised at ICSS meetings about the impact of greater public regulation of private pensions on the solvency of some employers, and the report advocated no immediate action on this option, proposing further study instead.[52]

The section dealing with public assistance, on the other hand, largely reflected the arguments of welfare officials. It referred to provincial requests for integration of the four assistance programs and to the problems created by the omission of mothers' allowances from federal cost-sharing. After rejecting the other three options, the report endorsed "a new federal Public Assistance Act [which] could replace the four existing acts covering old age assistance, disability and blind persons allowances and unemployment assistance." The new legislation would also provide for federal sharing in the cost of existing provincial mothers' allowance programs. While the rudiments of a comprehensive assistance act were supported, there was no endorsement of administrative cost-sharing, a differential cost-sharing formula, or national standards – all items that were resisted by Finance and Bryce.[53]

Monteith presented the ICSS report to cabinet in October 1961. He spoke in favour of the proposal for a comprehensive assistance act – and Donald Fleming, the new Finance minister, apparently did not oppose it – but the cabinet, led by Diefenbaker, rejected its recommendation and instead decided on an abortive attempt to initiate a contributory pension plan. Some cabinet members saw assistance reform as the least politically advantageous of the available options.

They believed that if the government expanded selective assistance benefits, it "would be vulnerable to attack." If OAS payments were not raised, "the government ... might lose much public support." As for contributory pensions, it was thought that "this would have great public appeal."[54] Diefenbaker added that "the Conservative Party for many years had been in favour of a contributory old age pension." A cabinet committee failed to reconcile the different viewpoints; the Prime Minister broke the deadlock by instructing Willard to "prepare a proposal for the consideration of cabinet on Old Age and Survivors Insurance plan along the lines followed in the United States."[55] Diefenbaker constantly affirmed the political popularity of contributory pensions and warned that "the New Democratic Party had been using social security as one of the main planks of their platform."[56] At least in the short term, assistance reform had been derailed by competing social security objectives of a universal and contributory type, which were deemed to be more politically advantageous, especially in the light of pressure from the social democratic left in favour of their adoption.

The proceedings of the ICSS and the subsequent fate of its recommendations in cabinet provide a first view of divergent agendas impinging upon assistance reform within the federal government. Federal welfare officials encouraged acceptance of the assistance reform agenda now under discussion in the department. Finance officials temporarily supported some elements of reform, but only because the alternatives under consideration constituted, in their view, a more serious challenge to their fundamental goal – protecting the economy against unnecessary and burdensome new social security expenditures. Neither of these goals prevailed in the face of cabinet's preference for considering an expansion of the universal and contributory elements of Canada's welfare state. These priorities were clearly motivated by their greater political appeal, and the NDP was seen as having had an important role in stimulating public interest in those measures.

During the remaining months of the Diefenbaker government, bureaucratic pressure for reform subsided somewhat because the political authorities clearly were not interested, but federal welfare officials continued to recommend modest changes. In 1962, Willard set up, under Splane's chairmanship, a Committee on Unemployment Assistance, which undertook a detailed discussion of the new provisions that a revised Unemployment Assistance Act might include.[57] Willard hoped that the committee could produce a memo on a new Public Assistance Act, but the government's lack of interest made such an outcome unlikely. Instead, the committee proposed more modest ideas that could be implemented by amendments to the UAA. There is no evidence that even this quite cautious document, whose main proposal was "the gradual removal of the mothers' allowance deduction over a period of years," was discussed outside of NHW before the April 1963 election.[58]

Willard and Splane were also active on work-for-relief in the period before the election. They had persuaded Monteith that pressure by the provinces in favour of work-for-relief should be resisted. These pressures persisted, however. In a confidential expression of his personal views to the Saskatchewan deputy minister for welfare, Willard argued that "in developing a case against work-for-relief in 1963, it is ... not enough to refer ... to the failures of work-for-relief programs in previous periods." On the basis of the U.S. experience, he asserted that "work-for-relief projects can be organized and made to achieve some useful objectives, though only with very careful planning and considerable extra expense" – and with little impact on unemployment levels. Splane expressed similar views.[59] Another element in the emerging reform agenda – support for positive alternatives to work-for-relief – was now crystallizing among federal welfare officials.

Political Sanctioning of Assistance Reform,
April to November 1963

Diefenbaker's minority Conservative government went down to defeat in the federal election of April 1963, supplanted by a rejuvenated Liberal Party led by Lester Pearson, who formed another minority administration. Pearson's victory created significant momentum for social policy reform in Canada. After their crushing defeat in the 1958 election, the Liberals had adopted ambitious new social security objectives. These included a commitment to pension reform, preferably along contributory lines, and firm proposals for a comprehensive medical insurance act. The impetus for these ideas had come from the individuals who had drawn up the party's 1958 election platform and from a party-sponsored "thinkers' conference," held in Kingston in 1960. Tom Kent, already a close confidant of Pearson – and soon to become his major policy adviser within the Prime Minister's Office – was a major inspiration for these developments. The Liberals' shift to the left took place in a context where Kent and others in the party were acutely aware of the need to prevent the NDP, newly founded from the ashes of the CCF, from displacing it as the electoral alternative to Diefenbaker's erratic government. After the Kingston meeting, for which Kent had prepared the background paper on social policy, Walter Gordon, a future member of Pearson's cabinet, approached Kent, saying "I must shake the hand that has strangled the New Party before it's born."[60]

While a number of reforms of the Canadian welfare state were included in Kent's 1960 proposals and in the Liberals' 1963 platform, assistance was not prominent among them.[61] The overriding priority was a contributory pension plan. The Liberals were interested in social security reforms of a more universal kind, encouraged by influences from the social democratic left. Given the market-curtailing preferences of social democracy, the left would not be expected to favour assistance reform; and it did not.

Thus the 1963 election result was not initially seen by federal welfare officials as likely to advance assistance reform. Two planks in the Liberals' campaign platform presented particular obstacles. The first was the party's assistance policy, which favoured the categorical programs. Its replacement by a reform agenda that stressed an integrated act was to preoccupy NHW officials from April to September 1963. The second obstacle was the Liberals' commitment, in response to the demands of Quebec Premier Jean Lesage, to terminate existing and future cost-sharing arrangements, rejecting them as unwarranted intrusions into provincial jurisdiction. This goal was championed by the department of Finance, which used it to challenge any extension of cost-sharing agreements and to propose the termination of some existing ones. Meeting this challenge became the focus of NHW's efforts from September to November.

Turning the Liberals around.   In the 1962 and 1963 election campaigns, Liberal and NDP assistance proposals were perfunctory, concentrating exclusively on the categorical programs. Both parties promised increases in maximum monthly benefit levels; the Liberals also wanted to extend OAA payments to "single women and widows at age 60."[62] Willard and reformist provincial officials thought higher categorical rates would make it more difficult to achieve an integrated, needs-tested program. Accordingly, they had to persuade the new minister of National Health and Welfare, Judy LaMarsh, to abandon these ideas. Observing in a memo to Splane that "the new Government is committed to increase the allowances by $10 a month under Old Age Assistance, Disability Allowances and Blind Persons Allowances," Willard surmised that this "could mean that it will be some time before our proposal for a new Public Assistance program will be supported and given effect."[63]

Willard tried to prevent such a delay. Within a week of LaMarsh's appointment on 22 April, he sent her two memoranda advocating

comprehensive rather than categorical reform. If the Liberals decided
to improve categorical benefits, Willard argued, the provinces would
have to devote more resources to financing their share of these
improvements, even though they would prefer to spend any additional money on general assistance. Willard referred to the Alberta
deputy minister's preference for comprehensive reform and suggested that this was typical of provincial views. He also implied that
the provinces would accept greater national standards than existed
in UAA.[64]

LaMarsh was not immediately swayed and in mid-May she asked
Willard for his opinion on the advisability of convening a meeting
with the provinces to discuss improvements in the categorical programs. He replied by restating his earlier position that "there is an
area of conflict between the approach proposed by the Government
for the continuation of the [categorical acts] and the approach which
a number of provinces would like to follow with regard to assistance
to needy persons. Some of the provinces wish to abandon the means
test approach set out in these categorical programs in favour of a
general assistance measure based on a needs test."[65]

Three days later, he again expressed these views and, for the first
time, revealed that federal welfare officials had themselves preferred
comprehensive reform for some time. Willard now also included
mothers' allowances cost-sharing in the list of proposals.[66] He
returned to the subject in an 11 June memo, which contained a
detailed discussion of recommendations for greater national standards in a new act, including the proposal for plans of administration
and for the inclusion of "provincially established rates of assistance
and conditions of eligibility" in agreements reached under the act.[67]

On 20 June, Pearson wrote to the provincial premiers about the
agenda for the following month's conference on the Canada Pension
Plan (CPP). He suggested that the conference would also have to
discuss "the whole question of old age assistance and disability
allowances," implying that if imminent changes were likely in the
assistance field, they would affect the categorical schemes. Splane
used a number of briefing documents prepared for LaMarsh's use at
the forthcoming conference to make another effort at altering the
government's approach. He cited "communications which have been
received from [the provinces] and ... the position many of their
officials took as participants in drafting the Canadian Welfare Council's statement on social security in 1958" in recommending that the
discussion revolve around an integrated assistance act instead of the
reform of the categorical measures.[68]

Pearson's report to cabinet after the July conference made no reference to assistance,[69] although assistance reform had been raised by the provinces. Premier John Robarts of Ontario was concerned about the impact of the Canada Pension Plan on the categorical programs; and Premier Duff Roblin of Manitoba raised a more diffuse concern "about mothers' allowances and provincial welfare standards in general." LaMarsh responded with a promise "to discuss these points with your officials at an appropriate time."[70] The appropriate time was to be another welfare ministers' conference in September, which had originally been intended to deal exclusively with a further discussion of CPP. Pressures from federal welfare officials for reform were increasingly reinforced by the efforts of their provincial counterparts.

The apparent willingness of the Quebec government, under the influence of its own welfare officials – and despite its official opposition to the continued use of cost-sharing – to consider an extension of the federal role in the assistance field, was of particular importance. A major signal of Quebec's new position was the release in July of the report of its study committee on public assistance (the Boucher Report). The committee discussed public assistance issues with welfare officials at the federal level and in all other provinces, as well as with the PWD's staff, before preparing its recommendations. These included an endorsement of the needs test; support for the development of "a new general assistance act on social assistance ... which should form an integrated whole adapted to present and future welfare requirements"; and an emphasis on the importance of rehabilitative social services.[71] The Boucher Report and the Quebec government's decision in August to seek its implementation brought that province firmly into the group of those which favoured comprehensive reform.[72] In late September, Roger Marier, Quebec's deputy minister for welfare, contacted Willard, proposing that their respective departments meet in October to discuss a number of social security issues, including the integration of assistance programs. After that meeting, federal welfare officials were confident that Quebec would support a comprehensive federal assistance act, notwithstanding its apparently contradictory desire to terminate cost-shared programs.

Meanwhile, the provinces that had already endorsed comprehensive reform continued to do so. Newfoundland, Nova Scotia, Saskatchewan, and Manitoba, both in correspondence and at the September conference, pressed the federal government to broaden its sharing of provincial assistance costs.[73] At the meeting, LaMarsh finally responded positively to mounting pressure from the provinces and from her own officials for a more comprehensive review of assistance, and the conference participants agreed to a communiqué affirming "that the whole field of social assistance should be jointly re-examined in the hope of developing one general assistance program based on need."[74] Thus federal welfare officials were provided with the support of their minister and with a justification for launching their first approach to cabinet on comprehensive assistance since the defeat they had endured in 1961. Henceforth, the major obstacle would be opposition from the federal treasury.

Beating Finance. The department of Finance attacked assistance reform – a position that reflected its traditional market-oriented rationale – but senior NHW officials launched a counter-offensive to protect their agenda. This conflict culminated in a decision by cabinet in November to resolve the dispute by testing provincial interest in reform at an upcoming first ministers' meeting. This, in turn, led to the authorization by that conference of preliminary federal/provincial bureaucratic discussions about significant changes in federal assistance legislation.

Finance accepted the idea of integrating the four existing assistance acts, but it opposed any reforms that implied an extra burden on the federal treasury, including federal sharing of mothers' allowance costs – a proposal it had accepted in 1961. Although a number of factors may account for this hardening of position, the most important would appear to be that while reform of contributory and universal pensions was seen as an alternative to a broader assistance act in 1961, the federal government was now moving in the direction of a contributory pension scheme; in addition, increases in OAS and in the categorical programs, promised in the election, now seemed inevitable. Fiscally conservative Finance officials therefore could now oppose expanded assistance coverage without risking even more expensive alternatives elsewhere.[75]

This anti-spending attitude was now augmented by Finance's broader effort to implement the Liberals' election promise to terminate cost-shared programs. Writing in 1963, Smiley observed that "the attitudes of senior financial policy officials ... toward conditional [cost-shared] grant arrangements are usually critical or even hostile." In the eyes of Finance officials, these arrangements created budgetary uncertainties that "relate largely to the 'open-end' programs like that in unemployment assistance where federal contributions are determined by provincial actions." Furthermore, "in their more violent moments financial officials are tempted to view shared-cost arrangements as deliberate conspiracies against the public purse by program departments eager to escape what are regarded as desirable measures of political and financial control."[76]

Such views were widespread in Finance documents of the period; they reinforced the department's negative approach to assistance reform.[77] Finance did not learn of NHW's ideas for comprehensive reform until late October. In a memo to his minister, Bryce, who had become deputy minister by then, laid out his proposed response. He suggested that Finance support an integration of the four existing federal acts but that the federal government introduce a provision in the new integrated act that "would mean that the provinces would carry the normal load of unemployable persons" – i.e., that a part of the provincial assistance caseload roughly equalling the number of unemployable persons on assistance would be excluded from federal cost-sharing. This would be done by introducing into the assistance act a "threshold" that would exempt a proportion of the provincial assistance caseload from federal cost-sharing. Such a threshold had existed in the original version of the Unemployment Assistance Act, but it had been removed in 1957. Bryce anticipated that its reintroduction would exclude a large part of provincial assistance from federal cost-sharing – a share equivalent to 1 per cent of each province's population. The provinces would receive compensation for the withdrawal of federal cost-sharing in the form of "tax room" – i.e., by receiving a certain portion of a tax now collected by the federal government, the value of which could be anticipated well in advance.[78] Thus the motive for Finance's proposal to curtail assistance cost-sharing was its desire to reduce the uncertainty and open-endedness of Ottawa's financial arrangements in the assistance field.

Bryce's plan became the Finance department's position. He revealed it to welfare officials in late October, indicating that his department supported a consolidated act but wanted the threshold introduced. His rationale for the exclusion reflected the concerns for cost control and restraint noted by Smiley. Bryce

was concerned ... that a move to consolidate the categorical programs into one general welfare program would leave control over the level of Federal expenditures resting on the degree of self-restraint which provincial governments might exercise. The experience of the Unemployment Assistance Program where this approach was adopted consciously had proven to be difficult. To leave to the provinces the responsibility for the standards to be applied in the program, the administrative efficiency and discretion of determining the granting of assistance under the program presented some dangers ... The only way of ensuring provincial responsibility appeared to rest on such measures as the reintroduction of the threshold concept which had been in force some years ago. A larger provincial share in the cost of the program would mean, presumably, more provincial concern with the level of expenditures.[79]

Finance also opposed two other aspects of NHW's reform package that might lead to higher costs. In the matter of standards, Bryce suggested that under the new program "the provinces would determine the scale of assistance and the conditions of eligibility ... The value of leaving control to the provinces would be lost in any attempt by the Federal Government to lay down in regulations what standards and means tests would be applied."[80] When Bryce learned of NHW's plan to include mothers' allowances in the new act at a cost of $25 million per year, he wrote to one of his subordinates: "I don't like the 25 million in Mothers' Allowances – How can we avoid?"[81]

Finance's attack on assistance reform provoked a counter-offensive from NHW. After seeing one of the Finance documents, Willard contacted a senior official in the Privy Council Office. He noted the provincial consensus in favour of comprehensive reform, adding that the CWC had recently renewed its request for the same thing. He then suggested that "it would seem highly inadvisable to design policies for presentation to the November Conference which fail to take into account these developments."[82] Splane complained that the Finance document "bears the marks of hasty preparation" and that some of its premises "look highly questionable." It also reinforced his "impression that there is a strong movement at the highest policy level below the cabinet to terminate a number of [grant-in-aid] programs without sufficient consideration of the consequences in individual cases."[83]

The competing policy agendas collided in cabinet on 21 November 1963, where it was decided that "the recommendations of the Minister of National Health and Welfare would need to be considered further in the light of the position which the provincial delegations took and of other developments at the Federal-Provincial Conference."[84] At the cabinet committee meeting held the next day, some ministers objected to NHW's suggestion of a possibly expanded new assistance act. Maurice Lamontagne, who was strongly in favour of terminating cost-sharing, said that NHW's ideas were incompatible with this goal. The committee decided that "reference to expanding the program should be kept in general terms [at the federal/provincial conference] and should be deferred until the position of the provincial governments on the general question of fiscal arrangements and shared-cost programs became more clearly apparent."[85] Whether NHW would be able to proceed with assistance reform would depend on the position of the provincial governments at the federal/provincial first ministers' conference of 26–29 November.

As a consequence, LaMarsh's opening statement at that conference was confined to advocating the categorical increases. She did, however, invite provincial views on other improvements and asked whether these should be discussed by a working party of officials. The eight smaller provinces all explicitly indicated their willingness to discuss assistance integration, and some mentioned coverage of mothers' allowances. Ontario was silent on the merits of an integrated act. Throughout the conference, Quebec also refrained from mentioning comprehensive assistance reform, repeatedly stressing its desire to terminate, with fiscal compensation, the existing conditional grants and to be exempt from future ones. Nevertheless, neither Ontario nor Quebec used the *in camera* discussions on assistance to oppose debate on a comprehensive act.[86] In Quebec's case, this confirmed the view held by federal welfare officials that the province was prepared to discuss reform, even though its overall objective was to terminate cost-sharing.

The final conference communiqué noted that "[a] federal-provincial working group is to review the operation of all joint welfare programs, in preparation for further discussion by Ministers." Federal welfare officials had finally obtained political consent to proceed with public assistance reform. The communiqué did not specify which of the list of issues of importance to them could be covered by the working group, but Pearson's statement that "the working party should consider all aspects of public welfare, including those which are not of federal concern at the moment" ensured that discussion could include themes beyond the four specific concerns that federal officials had raised with LaMarsh.[87]

From November 1963 to February 1964, federal welfare officials used this broad mandate to include in the official discussions *all* of the key reform issues that had been raised in PWD discussions. By eliciting a positive response from provincial politicians, they obtained political consent to undertake an assistance reform that would conform to their agenda and to that of most of their provincial counterparts rather than to that of Finance.

CONCLUSION

Assistance policy making in the early 1960s was shaped by its societal context. The reform agenda that emerged in the late 1950s and early 1960s reflected political class influences – the policy legacies of a largely liberal welfare state, which emerged under the predominance of bourgeois parties only intermittently challenged from the left. In a liberal welfare state, poverty-relief measures play a significant role, and the reform of assistance measures therefore remains a matter of importance. This was the broader societal setting within which reform was launched in the early 1960s. The Public Welfare Division of the Canadian Welfare Council, source of most reform ideas, embodied a vital fraternity of assistance officials in Canada, reflecting the continued importance of programs that they administered. The division's seminal 1958 policy statement also reflected ideological assumptions typical of a liberal welfare state, and it indicated that reform interest was motivated, in part, by the realization that the existing components of Canada's welfare state would not suffice to provide for the needy.

Bureaucrats at both levels of government were the source of welfare reform; politicians took little interest. Here again, Esping-Andersen's political class model is corroborated. The social security concerns of politicians centred on broader universal and contributory measures that embodied more social solidarity. Such interest was evident, to a degree, among Conservative ministers before the 1963 election, but it was much more typical of the Liberal government that succeeded them. In both cases, the political threat of the NDP, very much a champion of social democratic universality, was a significant motivating factor.

In functional class terms, assistance reform was affected by the prevailing accumulation strategy of the Canadian state; the department of Finance, as the dominant economic department, had primary responsibility for pursuing this strategy, the overriding feature of which was a concern to foster economic growth based on minimal state intervention in market relations. In the early 1960s Finance was hostile towards significant new social security expenditures; it only accepted poverty-relief reforms when they represented an alternative to broader and more costly initiatives. The priorities of Finance officials were consistently justified in terms of their market-oriented definition of the prerequisites of economic growth.

Assistance reform also reflected organizations; it was moulded by the prevailing departmentalized structure of cabinet and of federal/ provincial relations in Canada. Reform was instigated in parallel program departments at the federal and provincial levels; central agency officials and bureaucrats in departments outside the welfare field played no role in stimulating it. The predominance of welfare officials was manifest in the composition of the PWD in the decisive period from the late 1950s to the early 1960s, as well as in the background of those who participated in formulating its policy statements. This predominance was again evident within the federal and provincial governments in the early 1960s. The reform consensus emerged among officials who shared the same professional background and norms, and who maintained cordial relations and were able to interact in a non-strategic way. The PWD was, in effect, a venue in which federal and provincial officials could foster a common identity and shared objectives. While a consensus favouring reform did not develop immediately at the provincial level after 1958, by 1963 welfare officials in all provinces, with the partial exception of Ontario, were committed to a number of common reform goals. Only in the areas of national standards and, to some extent, differential cost-sharing did cooperative relations between federal and provincial welfare officials eventually falter. But these tensions were not yet apparent in late 1963.

The specific components of this reform agenda reflected two other aspects of policy making in a departmentalized setting: the initiatives envisaged were incremental, and they were confined to the traditional responsibilities of the originating departments. The PWD's reform agenda consisted of seven key elements – the continued and unrestricted use of cost-sharing in the assistance field; the integration of the four existing federal assistance acts on a needs-tested basis; the extension of federal cost-sharing to provincial mothers' allowances; the use of a differential formula for cost-sharing; federal sharing of provincial costs for administration and social services; federally supervised minimum standards for provincial programs; and the development of work activity programs. All represented modest, incremental alterations (or non-alterations) in existing federal measures to share the costs of provincial social assistance. And with the exception of the work activity concept – which had been adopted by welfare officials largely in response to regressive, ideologically motivated political pressures – these elements were confined to the traditional concerns of welfare departments. The work activity proposal touched upon the typical manpower-related concerns of federal and provincial labour departments.

The bureaucrats did not agree about all of these ideas: federal standards would always be opposed by most provinces; and other elements of the agenda were accepted by some provincial officials more quickly than others. Nevertheless, by the end of 1963 there was substantial agreement among federal and provincial welfare officials on most of the elements in the PWD-sponsored agenda. As the formal review process began in 1964, this consensus would deepen.

CHAPTER THREE

Assistance Reform Triumphant, 1964–66

The Public Welfare Division of the Canadian Welfare Council ceased to play a significant role in assistance reform when direct federal/provincial negotiations began in February 1964. Most of the officials who had taken part in the PWD's work in the late 1950s and early 1960s were now actively engaged in bargaining on behalf of their respective governments; they felt that they could no longer be seen to be participating in the division's lobbying activities, however discreetly.[1] Thus from 1964 to 1966 the focus of bureaucratic consensus-building shifted entirely to bilateral and multilateral negotiations between the federal and provincial governments. And indeed, the PWD had little to complain about as the Canada Assistance Plan emerged: CAP included almost all of the reforms that its members had supported and promoted.

POLITICAL AND INTERDEPARTMENTAL RESISTANCE

Assistance reform was formally launched at a February 1964 meeting of federal and provincial welfare officials. Planning for the meeting had begun in December when, on Willard's advice, an Interdepartmental Committee on Public Assistance (ICPA) was established to prepare an agenda for the February meeting. The committee, chaired by Willard, was largely dominated by NHW officials. At the ICPA meetings, they raised all of the policy concerns that had been discussed within the department since 1960 and usually suggested that these issues be included on the conference agenda as possible features of the new assistance act.

The four issues that had keenly preoccupied NHW officials the previous autumn remained top priorities. One of these – the future of cost-sharing – was temporarily out of their hands, as it was now the subject of parallel discussions among central agency officials. At the first ICPA meeting, Splane re-introduced an earlier departmental memo that focused on the three other issues – federal sharing of provincial mothers' allowance costs, program integration, and the use of administrative plans to secure national standards. In subsequent meetings of the committee, each of these ideas was the subject of detailed and positive submissions by Splane and Willard.[2] Only in the case of national standards did federal officials want to proceed regardless of potential opposition from the provinces. They wanted to include provision for plans of administration in their proposal to cabinet for a new assistance act, but they decided to hide this fact from their provincial counterparts and to be evasive in their discussion of standards at the February meeting.[3] This represented their single departure from an otherwise consensual, non-strategic relationship with provincial officials.

At the ICPA meetings, federal welfare officials also discussed the merits of other elements of the reform agenda that they had not promoted very actively since the 1963 election – namely, administrative cost-sharing, positive alternatives to work-for-relief, and a differential cost-sharing formula – but here their approach was more tentative. Willard had not yet made any attempts to win the Liberal cabinet's support for these reforms, and he knew that they would be opposed by other departments, in particular Finance and, in the case of work activity measures, Labour. Also, with the single, important exception of national standards, NHW officials were unwilling to force any reforms upon the provinces: there was reason to expect that each of the three reforms might be opposed by at least some provincial governments. Nevertheless, Willard won the ICPA's agreement to include two of them – administrative cost-sharing and work activity – on the agenda of the February meeting, along with the central preoccupations of program integration and mothers' allowance cost-sharing.[4]

When the federal/provincial meeting convened, its participants easily reached agreement on integration and mothers' allowances, enabling NHW to prepare a cabinet memo that claimed unqualified provincial support on these two points. On integration, Ontario dramatically reversed its traditional hostility.[5] The future of cost-sharing could not be discussed in detail, but Willard pointed out that agreement on any of the other issues would be meaningless if the provinces did not accept new cost-shared grants. It was already becoming clear that Quebec was no longer incontrovertibly committed to the end of cost-sharing. NHW officials presumably still believed, as they had the previous autumn, that their Quebec counterparts were interested in extending shared-cost programs in the assistance field, even though their political masters were ambivalent. This was confirmed by the conduct of Quebec's deputy minister, who remained agreeable throughout the meeting, affirming that "the contracting-out issue [which was the main focus of discussions on cost-sharing] is largely a political decision with which I do not think I am concerned."[6]

A broad consensus also emerged between federal and provincial officials on work-for-relief, although reservations were expressed by Ontario. But progress here was hampered by the presence of federal Labour officials anxious to defend their turf. Most provincial officials explicitly dismissed work-for-relief, though they readily acknowledged that there was much public and political pressure in favour of it. Willard and Splane concurred in this rejection, but they also alluded to the need for positive alternatives. There was much talk about the merits of establishing "work rehabilitation" programs within welfare departments. But Labour officials spoke defensively about their own programs, suggesting that new measures could be accommodated within them. As a result of these divergences, the discussion did not proceed beyond generalities.[7]

On administrative cost-sharing, there was less agreement among welfare officials. Alluding to Finance's long-held view, Willard warned that "there was some feeling on the part of the Federal Government that we might become involved in decisions with respect to the operation of provincial departments, and that this was not appropriate." Willard did disclose his personal interest in rehabilitation – and in administrative cost-sharing as a way to improve it – but there was resistance from provincial officials: federal sharing of administrative costs was generally thought, at that time, to imply greater influence of the federal government over provincial programs. Quebec therefore expressed reservations, while Ontario voiced outright opposition.[8]

Willard wanted to prepare a cabinet submission immediately after the February meeting, based on the limited consensus that had materialized there, but he was asked to postpone this because the politically much more salient Canada Pension Plan was absorbing all of NHW's (and much of cabinet's) time. The memo finally went to cabinet on 4 May. It recognized the limited mandate for change that had emerged from the February meeting but made provision for further efforts to extend agreement on reform except where entrenched provincial resistance made such an outcome unlikely. Where a consensus did exist (on federal sharing of mothers' allowances costs and on the integration of the four existing federal assistance acts), the memo recommended that the federal government make the suggested improvements – presupposing, of course, the continuance of cost-sharing. In exchange for the expanded coverage to mothers' allowances, the provinces would have to accept national standards, enforced by federal review of provincial plans of administration. The memo made no mention of the fact that this provision had not been discussed with the provinces. In areas where interjurisdictional disagreement had arisen at the meeting or where there was conflict within the federal administration (on work activity and a differential formula), the memorandum recommended that the issues be subject to further discussion within the ICPA. As NHW had dominated the committee's proceedings in setting the agenda of the February meeting, it could presumably hope that its views would prevail again if the body was resurrected. Finally, the memo recommended no change on the issue of administrative cost-sharing, where there was substantial resistance to reform from Ontario and, to a lesser extent, Quebec.[9]

Despite their modest scope, Willard's suggestions were rejected by cabinet. From February until the end of May, reform faced insurmountable obstacles from competing bureaucratic and political agendas within the federal government. Finance continued to oppose NHW initiatives that could result in a burden on the national treasury; with the support of political forces within cabinet that were motivated by different considerations, it won the day. NHW was still unable to win key political allies for its agenda at this time, and indeed there remained a strong commitment to categorical assistance programs in cabinet, reflecting the promises made by the Liberal Party during the 1963 election campaign.

In cabinet, LaMarsh spoke in favour of assistance reform. Noting that the proposals had their origins in the public welfare sector, she said that she supported them despite the objections of groups representing categorical recipients.[10] Nonetheless, she agreed with other ministers that none of the items recommended for further study by the ICPA should, in fact, be held for such consideration.

LaMarsh could easily have anticipated the Finance department's hostility to her memo. In an earlier meeting with Willard, Bryce had argued that because of an impending deficit there was no money left in the federal treasury for a new assistance measure.[11] The position adopted in cabinet by Walter Gordon, the Finance minister, paralleled that of his deputy minister. He did not oppose an integration of categorical and general assistance acts, but he resisted the two components of the proposed assistance act that would cost more money. On mothers' allowances, Gordon said that "on financial grounds any assumption by the federal government of an additional burden of $25 million annually should be resisted and this objection was reinforced by the fact that more than half of this amount would benefit the province of Quebec." He also emphatically opposed the use of national standards to secure adequate assistance levels in the provinces, reflecting a stance that Finance adopted consistently throughout the development of CAP.[12]

Allan MacEachen, the minister of Labour and chairman of the cabinet's Social Security and Labour Committee, led the way in defending the categorical programs. He described the integration proposal as "a retrograde step" – a position that reflected a common perception that the categorical programs were "pensions" and not "assistance," and that their recipients were a more deserving category of the needy. He complained that if the four programs were integrated, "recipients of categorical allowances would become welfare cases," which suggested that they were not that already.[13]

In the end, the cabinet adopted Gordon's position: the federal government would inform the provinces that there could be no new social assistance legislation in 1964. A new act integrating the four categorical programs would be possible in 1965, but there would be no new money from the federal treasury – in other words, no coverage for mothers' allowances.[14] Prime Minister Pearson contributed very little to the cabinet discussion.[15]

MacEachen's defence of categorical benefits did not prevail in cabinet, since there had already been an agreement in principle to the integration of the assistance programs. However, NHW had warned cabinet that the provinces would not accept program integration without new funding for mothers' allowances and that they would, therefore, certainly reject the package endorsed by cabinet. The combination of Finance's bureaucratic obstruction and MacEachen's political opposition killed the immediate prospects for comprehensive assistance reform.

POLITICAL CONSENT, JUNE 1964–APRIL 1965

The May 1964 cabinet decision blocked assistance reform for the remainder of that year, but in succeeding months federal welfare officials found the political support they needed to triumph in 1965. A federal/provincial welfare ministers' meeting in May provided political sanctioning for the bureaucratic reform consensus, which had broadened since February. Later in 1964, Tom Kent, who had not encouraged reform in the spring because he was preoccupied with the Canada Pension Plan, was (in the words of an interviewee) "converted by Joe Willard to the view that replacement of the categorical plans was a very important social reform." But it would have to wait until passage of the pension plan was completed. This provincial and federal political support was decisively brought to bear on the Prime Minister at the end of the year. Meanwhile, NHW secured its position on two key issues – the continued use of cost-sharing and work activity (albeit in a reduced form, in the case of the latter) – in its disputes with Finance and Labour. With strengthened political support and reduced interference from other departments, federal welfare officials were able to return to cabinet with another reform memo in the spring of 1965.

Gaining Political Support

Federal welfare officials, intimately familiar with their provincial colleagues, had correctly assumed that without any new offers of money at the May 1964 meeting, the provinces would be unwilling to proceed with a new assistance act. Along with their minister, NHW officials were clearly unhappy to have so little to offer.[16] As a consequence, the conference was "abortive," in the words of the Ontario welfare minister, because it provided no basis for agreement on new legislation. But the meeting was also important because it secured the support of provincial ministers for a partially expanded bureaucratic reform consensus.

In most respects, the provincial ministers took positions identical to those of their respective deputies at the February meeting. There was one important extension of agreement, resulting from a more positive attitude to the sharing of administrative costs by Ontario's deputy minister. Band had opposed administrative cost-sharing in February, fearing that it would "involve an intrusion into provincial autonomy," with the federal authorities exercising rigid control over how the provinces administered their public welfare programs. But following discussions with their federal counterparts after the February meeting, Band's officials had concluded that his apprehension was unfounded. As one interviewee noted, this change of perspective "happened very quickly," and thereafter Band "ceased his objections entirely." Ontario and Quebec now joined the other provinces in requesting that administration costs be included in the new act. The political support that the welfare ministers were able to contribute to assistance reform, and the extension of the latter in this one important direction, would enable federal officials to push their agenda again when the time was ripe.

In fact, Willard wanted another welfare ministers' conference to be held in the fall in order to achieve final agreement on a reform package. But LaMarsh said that it would be impossible to proceed with assistance issues until after the upcoming election.[17] Thus by December 1964 NHW officials and their sympathetic minister were still unable to obtain cabinet support for a comprehensive assistance act. It was at this point that Kent, who had become convinced of the merits of the measure while working with Willard on the Canada Pension Plan, used his considerable influence over Pearson to push for a new assistance act. This decisive development created the political preconditions for reform.

With the pension plan now very nearly a reality, Kent and others with influence over the Liberal government believed that the administration "needed a second wind." Pearson had been elected on a reformist platform in 1963, and it was important to take new initiatives aimed at restoring the government's faltering momentum. This would be done by developing a new agenda for reform, and Kent had ideas of his own about what should be on this agenda. While assistance reform was not initially one of these, he became convinced, under the influence of Health and Welfare public servants, that in addition to the issues of particular concern to himself, "there was also a need to get the assistance measures into the kind of shape that was created by the Canada Assistance Plan" – the name now selected for the proposed reform package. In December, Kent drew up a memorandum for Pearson in which "a new thrust for '65" was proposed. This document included a recommendation in favour of a comprehensive assistance act. When the memo was presented to Pearson in January 1965, "he was convinced very promptly." While Pearson "played no part in the details" of the assistance proposal, either at that time or later, he fully agreed with its general goals.[18]

Interdepartmental Wars

Finding political allies was not the only preoccupation of NHW officials in 1964. They were also concerned with two conflicts in the interdepartmental arena over issues that would have to be resolved before the new assistance act could take shape. The more important of these was the prospect that cost-sharing for social assistance might be terminated; here, the major rival remained Finance. The second issue was the desire to find a positive alternative to work-for-relief – a stand that was opposed by the department of Labour.

Conflict with Finance over cost-sharing. Scholarly accounts of the debate about "contracting-out" – the federal legislative provision, adopted in 1965, that allowed the provinces to withdraw from shared-cost programs while receiving compensation from the federal government in the form of taxing powers – often treat it exclusively as an issue between Ottawa and the Quebec government. Contracting-out is sometimes portrayed as a federal concession to Quebec's demands for greater autonomy – one that in later years would lead to an unanticipated weakening of federal authority.[19] Others view it as a meaningless response by the federal government, desperate in its attempts to defuse hostilities with Quebec but unwilling to make any real concessions.[20] From the perspective of assistance reform, however, contracting-out can be viewed in an interdepartmental context. No province – including Quebec, as it turned out – wanted to end cost-sharing if this were to jeopardize a new social assistance act. When this became clear, NHW was able to win an important battle against Finance, which believed there were excellent fiscal grounds for terminating cost-sharing and used that argument to attack any proposal to spend more money in that area.

Intergovernmental meetings of treasury officials on cost-sharing took place in early 1964, while welfare officials were discussing assistance reform. These meetings slowed the momentum towards the elimination of cost-sharing. The English-speaking provinces, some of which had seemed well disposed towards contracting-out in November, were now much more cautious.[21] It was clear that the same cleavage existed among provincial bureaucrats as had already become manifest at the federal level. In the eyes of provincial treasury officials, cost-sharing tended to distort provincial priorities and create inefficiencies; program officials, on the other hand, were pleased with its tendency to stimulate program expenditures.[22] In addition, Quebec's detailed proposal for contracting-out, which had been forwarded to the federal authorities, clearly did not envisage the full termination of cost-sharing as an immediate objective. Instead, it provided for an interim period, from January 1965 to January 1967, when Quebec would continue to participate in cost-shared programs.[23]

That interim period had not been anticipated by the department of Finance and was not well received there. The immediate termination of assistance was no longer seen as an appropriate goal, because even Finance supported the integration of the categorical programs as a preliminary step. But Bryce advised his minister that in other areas, such as hospital insurance, immediate termination would be a better idea than Quebec's proposed interim arrangement.[24] In effect, he was more aggressively interested than Quebec in ending cost-sharing.

Quebec's proposed interim arrangement was readily accepted by Pearson at a first ministers' conference. The contracting-out legislation, passed in 1965, ensured that cost-sharing arrangements could continue to develop between the federal government and all of its provincial counterparts.[25] Finance was thus no longer able to undermine reform by alluding to the political need to terminate cost-shared programs.

Conflict with Labour over work activity.   Municipal and provincial interest in work-for-relief declined precipitously during 1964.[26] With fewer demands for this punitive option, the prospects brightened for a rehabilitative alternative. There remained the question of whether it should be developed within NHW or the department of Labour, which jealously guarded its perceived mandate in the field.

The vociferousness of Labour's offensive in this area owed much to the vision of Ian Campbell, who was the coordinator of the department's rehabilitation programs. Campbell, who was not well regarded among his colleagues at NHW, was much more aggressive in his dealings with them than were other senior Labour officials, including the deputy minister, George Haythorne. Nevertheless, his superiors gave Campbell free rein to launch an offensive against NHW's attempts to expand its programs into the rehabilitation field.[27] In various speeches and memoranda throughout 1964, Campbell drew a distinction between what were, in his view, the proper roles of the two departments.[28] He distinguished between non-vocational rehabilitation, where NHW had a role, and specifically work-related counselling and training, which should be provided through an extension of the existing Vocational Rehabilitation for Disabled Persons Act, which was administered by Labour.[29]

NHW officials defended their proposals by insisting that they had the support of the provinces.[30] In October 1964, Willard presented LaMarsh with his first concrete proposals for a positive alternative to work-for-relief. Noting that Ross Thatcher, the Premier of Saskatchewan, was still pressing for change and no longer wanted work-for-relief, Willard suggested that the best response to his obscure request for "training and job creation" was to amend the Unemployment Assistance Act to provide for federal cost-sharing in projects that would emphasize "training in the work provided."[31] To prove that provincial welfare officials supported his views, Willard convened another meeting, devoted specifically to the work activity theme.[32] Predictably, given their own desire to find alternatives to work-for-relief, provincial officials supported their federal counterparts' position.[33]

This response gave NHW the support it needed to include community work programs in a draft cabinet memo on public assistance reform that was completed in early January 1965. The proposed program had four basic features: persons with the potential to re-enter the labour market would have access to two kinds of complementary projects – a rehabilitation component and a work-training and employment-skill-enhancement component that would enable participants to re-enter the job market; persons who "prove incapable of competing in the labour market but capable of performing some work of value in the community" would have access to sheltered workshops; finally, the provinces, in setting up community work programs, would deal exclusively with NHW at the federal level.[34]

Conflict now erupted between NHW and Labour. When Labour officials saw the draft, they called for a meeting with NHW officials to voice their objections.[35] By the time the memo went to cabinet on 9 February 1965, Labour had succeeded in substantially reducing the community work provisions.[36] The February memo lacked two provisions central to the January draft: for the potentially employable, it no longer made any mention of work-training and skill-enhancement programs; and it no longer provided for NHW to exercise exclusive control over the program. Any further development of this part of the legislation would have to be done jointly with Labour, and provincial project proposals would require the approval of both departments.[37]

These changes represented a substantial reduction in NHW's reform objectives in this, the one area where its aspirations stepped significantly beyond the traditional statutory responsibilities of a welfare department. They also resulted in a significant reduction in budgetary allocations: while the cost of the Community Work Program proposed in January had been estimated to reach at least one million dollars for the first year, the February "work activity projects" proposal was priced at only half that amount.[38]

A Return Visit to Cabinet

With Pearson now supporting reform and with major interdepartmental disputes resolved, NHW prepared a new cabinet memo. Some proposals of the February 1965 memo were identical to those made in May 1964: the new program would operate on a shared-cost basis and would extend federal cost-sharing to include provincial mothers' allowances; and the provinces could integrate their categorical programs. The recommendations pertaining to program standards were also virtually identical to those proposed in 1964, although they still had not been discussed with the provinces (nor with Finance) since the last memo.[39]

Nevertheless, interaction with the provinces since the May 1964 memo had given federal welfare officials an opportunity to venture more boldly into areas discussed very tentatively the previous year. Work activity was, of course, one of these, but the most important was administrative cost-sharing. More generally, the consensus achieved by the provincial ministers in May 1964, which contrasted with the purely bureaucratic consensus that had preceded it, enabled NHW to insist that its proposals were supported by the provinces – something that it could not have claimed convincingly the previous year.[40]

Long before it was discussed in cabinet, Willard knew that the memo would be attacked by Finance. Indeed, Bryce had already criticized the proposals in a memo. The inclusion of mothers' allowance costs in CAP would, Bryce argued, have to be considered with great care because "the incidence [of costs] is quite uneven and it will not be easy to make a general adjustment." On administrative cost-sharing, the deputy minister of Finance was "concerned about the implications for other programs" and recommended that "we start off without them"; it would be possible to cover such costs "after [the new legislation] has been worked over for some while." Finally, on national standards, Bryce argued that "we think this would be quite contrary to the whole spirit and purpose of this arrangement" and recommended that the provinces set their own standards. Referring to the entire package, Bryce wrote that "we would like to keep the effects out of the budget for next year" and advised that it not be implemented until 1966.[41] Willard quickly replied to Bryce's memo, informing him that not only LaMarsh but also "Mr. Kent felt that action in the field of public assistance should be announced in the Speech from the Throne."[42]

On 3 March, as the NHW memo was about to be raised in cabinet, Kent, Splane, and Bryce met to discuss the proposal it contained. Kent's influence was much in evidence. He declared that "the time when the provinces could be put off with generalities was over and that the Minister had to be in a position to indicate a specific and

constructive federal policy." Bryce now adopted a less negative attitude. In February, he had still voiced opposition to mothers' allowance cost-sharing, but under Kent's pressure he now stated that he
understood its desirability and that "there would be no opposition
from the Department of Finance to the broad lines of the proposal,
although there was continued concern about four of five features of
the Plan." In fact, his only real retreat was on mothers' allowances,
the sharing of which could be "handled though fiscal adjustments."
He specifically questioned administrative cost-sharing and was concerned about work activity.[43]

Where Finance was now fully amenable, cabinet concurred. Cabinet agreed to share provincial mothers' allowance costs, to integrate
the four existing programs, and to continue the use of cost-sharing
for assistance.[44] On three other important issues, NHW was not as
successful; here, it would have to accept a compromise or, effectively,
a postponement of the final decision.

First, on administrative cost-sharing NHW settled for a limited
victory. In February, Bryce had opposed any administrative cost-
sharing, at least in the immediate future. But in the face of Kent's
stand, Bryce accepted the sharing of welfare field-service costs but
not of head-office costs, as long as cost-sharing did not begin until
1967. J.E.G. Hardy of the Privy Council Office (PCO) agreed with
both of these proposed restrictions. To counter them, Willard suggested a compromise that would concentrate federal sharing mainly
on new administrative costs. Kent then proposed a similar formula,
which became the basis for cabinet's decision to provide for federal
sharing of all new administrative costs but not of existing ones.[45]
This compromise fell short of NHW's goal of full administrative cost-
sharing, but it met the department's main objective of using cost-
sharing to enhance the development of rehabilitative services in the
provinces, which would presumably be financed by new expenditures.

In the two other areas of conflict with Finance, the cabinet's decision reflected a curtailment of NHW's aspirations, but the meaning of
the result remained unclear – a matter to be resolved by further
jostling among the institutional interests involved. The work activity
debate was by no means settled by the concessions that NHW had
incorporated into its February memo. Labour continued to resist any
NHW involvement in the vocational field. Apparently not placated by
the earlier compromises, Labour attacked any NHW involvement in
work-related programs, supported in this by Finance. Bryce was
worried that "the areas of federal participation would be difficult to

limit" in the work activity field and that it might cause confusion in federal/provincial fiscal relations. Hardy and the Revenue minister both agreed with Finance.[46]

Willard defended his proposals at length. He was strongly supported by Kent, who contended that the program "was well-suited for solving the particular difficulty it was designed for." This support may have prevented a defeat of NHW's work activity proposal, but it did not secure victory. Instead, cabinet referred the proposal back to NHW and Labour officials for further consideration.[47] A truce had been called in a battle that would resume during the summer.

Health and Welfare and Finance officials, who had clashed over national standards in 1964, again were the main antagonists on this issue. The February 1965 cabinet memo made it clear that reviewing the provincial plans of administration would enable the federal government to enforce minimum standards: "A basic feature of the Canada Assistance Plan is its *requirement* that the provinces undertake to provide an adequate standard of assistance."[48] Bryce objected to "references in the Minister's memorandum to the federal government's fostering the achievement of adequate standards of general assistance. It was considered that the virtue of the assistance program lay in its adaptability, and it would be preferable to continue to rely on the provinces in the matter of standards."[49] Even Kent would not support NHW on this issue. Perhaps sensing defeat, Willard and Splane did not defend the more compulsory aspects of their proposal. No mention was made in cabinet of the program review as a means of requiring certain levels of assistance, and the two NHW officials argued, not entirely truthfully, that their only goal was to improve consultation with the provinces.[50]

The cabinet's decision on the standards question stressed the consultative nature of the federal/provincial relationship: "The legislation and regulations relating to the Canada Assistance Plan should provide only for very general standards ... It would be the responsibility of the provinces ... to establish the more specific conditions and requirements governing the provision of assistance ... The federal government would rely on intensified federal-provincial consultation to ensure that the particular standards and conditions being applied in the various provinces were consistent and adequate."[51] The decision seemed to preclude the use of a program review procedure to enforce national standards in the provinces. But it did not specify what general standards could be set by the federal government and how these were to be distinguished from more specific conditions to be set by the provinces.

In summary, Kent's support for a comprehensive assistance package enabled NHW to gain cabinet acceptance of enough reforms to sway the provinces, since mothers' allowances appeared to by the single *sine qua non* of agreement in May 1964. It did not, however, allow the department's views to prevail on all issues. Compromises were necessary wherever reform encountered opposition from other departments. Kent's support for mothers' allowance cost-sharing was enough to end Finance's resistance to it, and this extension joined program integration on a cost-shared basis as areas of outright NHW victory. On administrative cost-sharing, Finance's resistance meant that a compromise solution, supported by Kent, was needed. On work activity and national standards, cabinet did not fully resolve interdepartmental conflicts. These issues would carry over to the next round of battles about assistance reform.

The Canada Assistance Plan was announced in the Liberal government's throne speech of 5 April 1965. Some effort was made to give greater political prominence to an issue that had emerged from the obscurity of bureaucratic policy making. The name of the legislation (which had been decided upon at a meeting between LaMarsh, Splane, and Kent in January) was an attempt to associate CAP with the much more politically salient Canada Pension Plan. The throne speech referred to CAP as part of the government's "war on poverty" – a much-hyped effort to mimic a similar initiative launched in 1964 by U.S. President Lyndon B. Johnson. Unlike the other elements of the war on poverty, which Kent had conceived of on his own, CAP "was a given at this time" (in the words of an interviewee), and it reflected Willard's ability to secure Kent's support. Including it in the package was therefore an effort to raise its profile.

Cabinet acceptance of four key aspects of assistance reform meant that for the first time LaMarsh was able to make an acceptable offer to the provinces, thus ensuring that a welfare ministers' conference in April would be a success. The conference accepted the package that LaMarsh had steered through cabinet. Passage of a new assistance act was now assured.

Assistance reform never did acquire much political appeal, however. LaMarsh was later to express disappointment that CAP attracted relatively little public attention and that she received very little recognition for her role in supporting it. A senior political adviser to the minister later recalled that despite her participation in the creation of the plan, it involved little work for the political staff, especially when compared with pensions and health insurance. CAP was seen by LaMarsh's political staff as a bureaucratic initiative that she had been persuaded to support. The announcement of the reform in the throne speech, and the subsequent successful federal/provincial ministers' conference that endorsed it, received little media coverage.

A SECOND ROUND OF REFORMS, APRIL 1965– MAY 1966

The final phase of assistance reform sorted out the remaining unresolved conflicts about reform. These included two issues that had not been decided by cabinet – national standards and work activity. Two other issues also now arose – differential cost-sharing, which had not been discussed in the federal/provincial context since the formal negotiations had begun in February 1964; and the inclusion of child welfare services in CAP, an issue that made its first significant appearance in any reform discussions. Debate about all of these issues proceeded through a number of stages during the months that followed.

Bureaucratic Discussions, April–November 1965

National standards. In 1965 the provinces gradually became more aware of, and opposed to, federal intentions to include national standards in CAP. Premier Lesage emphatically stated Quebec's opposition at a first ministers' conference in July: national standards "would amount to recognition of the federal government's right to oversee assistance measures which we consider to be within our own competence."[52] At a welfare deputy ministers' meeting in October, Willard tried to soft-pedal his intentions on national standards, disclaiming any desire to "veto" provincial programs. The provinces – especially Ontario and Quebec – were unmoved. All of them opposed some elements of the federal proposal for plans of administration. After Quebec's deputy minister stated his concerns in particularly strong terms, Willard relented, remarking that "it may be that the formal approach which we have suggested here is too formal."[53] With the provinces as well as Finance now firmly registering opposition to a significant standards-maintaining mechanism, NHW officials abandoned any idea that they might oversee provincial welfare standards.

Work activity. Despite the modesty of NHW's February 1965 proposals on work activity, Labour officials remained uncooperative after the March cabinet stalemate. To resolve the matter, a Sub-Committee on Work Activity was set up in the Privy Council Office.[54] Although it had previously been forced to retreat on work activity, NHW now held its ground. Kent intervened on its side, stating that Labour was being "very, very silly" in opposing the work activity proposal, which was finally presented to the provincial deputy ministers in October.

Their response was generally positive, but there was a clear lack of enthusiasm for a measure that had been significantly watered down. Everybody recognized that what was left of the work activity concept would be only a limited response to the work-related problems faced by welfare recipients.[55]

Child welfare. Full inclusion of provincial child welfare costs in a new assistance act did not become a major subject of discussion until 1965. It was the only important dimension of CAP that had not been anticipated by discussions within the Public Welfare Division. Its inclusion was nevertheless very much driven by a consensus among federal and provincial welfare officials.

During the summer of 1965, Ontario, which had earlier resisted federal involvement in its child welfare program, unexpectedly became a leading advocate. Its welfare officials suggested to Premier Robarts and to central agency officials that the province request the inclusion of child welfare in CAP.[56] Robarts followed their advice and at the first ministers' meeting in July declared that "Ontario believes that *all* child welfare services should be included with the cost-sharing provisions of the Canada Assistance Plan."[57]

Ontario's reversal, and the failure of Quebec or other provinces to raise objections, enabled NHW officials to consider seriously for the first time the possibility of expanding CAP to include all child welfare programs. They embraced it enthusiastically.[58] In October 1965, when it became clear that there was no longer any provincial opposition to child welfare cost-sharing, Willard raised the issue with LaMarsh.[59]

Before the October meeting of deputy ministers, British Columbia's welfare officials aggressively pushed for coverage of child welfare in CAP. At the meeting, their colleagues from Saskatchewan, Quebec, and New Brunswick all expressed sympathy with the idea. This consensus continued to crystallize after the October meeting.[60]

Willard's own sympathies were clear; his comments at the October meeting suggested that NHW would use the first available opportunity to propose the inclusion of all child welfare costs in CAP.[61] On 8 November 1965 cabinet received an NHW memo on child welfare and differential cost-sharing. To exclude child welfare costs from CAP while mothers' allowances were being covered, it argued, would force NHW to make an "undoubtedly artificial" distinction between cases where the custody of children had been transferred from the parents and those where this had not happened: "Sharing in child welfare maintenance and service costs on the same basis that applies to other assistance would deal with this anomaly and avoid a point of friction in the administration of the Plan."[62]

Differential cost-sharing. Differential cost-sharing had not received much attention in reform discussions since February 1964, but in mid-1965 the Atlantic provinces brought the issue back to the fore. Newfoundland's deputy minister proposed a differential formula in May.[63] Willard was sympathetic and proposed to LaMarsh that a differential formula be adopted for administrative cost-sharing. He nevertheless cautioned against any specific commitment to the provinces "in view of the fact that it has not received cabinet consideration."[64] There was good reason for this caution, as Finance was sure to raise its traditional objections to a differential formula. Nor could NHW make a case based on a provincial consensus in favour of differential cost-sharing, because British Columbia explicitly rejected the idea and Ontario was expected to join the western province in its opposition.[65]

In its 8 November memo to cabinet, NHW alluded to "strong representations" from the Atlantic provinces requesting a differential formula. It gave the most emphatic federal endorsement yet to differential cost-sharing, contending that, without it, "it is evident that the Atlantic Provinces will be unable to develop public assistance programs that will provide adequate levels of assistance." NHW directly addressed Finance's anticipated arguments by observing that "the Department of Finance, over the years, has favoured making differential adjustments through the fiscal arrangements with the provinces rather than through individual shared-cost programs." But it countered that "in a program which is designed mainly to assist the unemployed there is a special case for relating federal payments to provincial differences in the incidence of need."[66]

Unlike the other issues touched upon during the discussions that led to the creation of CAP, however, this one pitted the poorer provinces, which received a sympathetic hearing at NHW, against the more affluent provinces and the Finance department. As a result, there was no federal/provincial bureaucratic consensus, and federal officials faced considerable difficulty in selling the idea to cabinet. The provincial solidarity needed to turn aside Finance's objections was lacking.

Thus, by November 1965 two of the four outstanding issues had been resolved. NHW had protected its limited victory on work activity;

on national standards, by contrast, its agenda had been defeated: only very modest standards would now be included in CAP. Two issues were still unresolved – the sharing of child welfare costs, and differential cost-sharing – and these were the subject of very favourable treatment by the department in its cabinet memo of 8 November.

The November–December Cabinet Debates

Cabinet discussed the memorandum on 10 November, and an animated debate ensued immediately between LaMarsh and Mitchell Sharp, the new minister of Finance. On differential cost-sharing, Sharp said that he was "strongly opposed to the introduction of adjustments for fiscal capacity in the sharing formula [because] it could prejudice the work of the Tax Structure Committee in developing a satisfactory general equalization formula." Pearson concurred, observing that "in speaking on this subject, he had not gone beyond reference to the 50–50 formula." Sharp also argued that "the inclusion of broader child welfare costs would intrude on an established area of provincial responsibility, and as such should be examined in a broader context."[67] This was a somewhat incongruent position, since several provinces now strongly supported its inclusion in CAP.

Cabinet referred the disputes to an interdepartmental committee of officials drawn from Finance, NHW, and the PCO, under the chairmanship of the secretary to the cabinet, R.G. Robertson. At the same time, Allan MacEachen replaced LaMarsh as minister of National Health and Welfare. MacEachen's assumption of the portfolio made no difference in NHW policy since he followed his predecessor in accepting the positions of his officials. The erstwhile opponent of comprehensive assistance reform was now an ardent champion.

Presumably reflecting Robertson's greater sympathy for his fellow central agency officials at Finance, the interdepartmental committee's report sided with the Finance department's position over NHW's on both issues.[68] Cabinet discussed the report on 29 December 1965 and 5 January 1966. MacEachen attacked the committee's report and, perhaps because of his Nova Scotia background, was particularly aggressive in defending his department's position on differential cost-sharing. But Pearson now indicated even more clearly his support for Sharp, saying that "he foresaw difficulties in the suggested introduction of an equalization formula" in CAP and that an improved general equalization arrangement was preferable.[69]

Cabinet also sided with Finance over NHW on both issues. Only if MacEachen experienced "serious difficulty" with the provinces at the upcoming ministers' conference could he return to cabinet to discuss again the possibility of differential cost-sharing.[70] On child welfare, cabinet resolved "that federal contributions ... be limited to the costs of caring for 'assistance-type children' and not children in actual ward care."[71]

The Final Round, January–June 1966

Health and Welfare made another attempt at expanding CAP coverage in the early months of 1966. This time, it used the more persuasive tools of provincial political support and a broader reform consensus rather than the more limited bureaucratic agreement achieved the previous December. The two outstanding issues of differential cost-sharing and child welfare received considerable attention at a meeting of welfare ministers in January 1966, in subsequent cabinet discussions in Ottawa, and in another round of bilateral federal/provincial consultations and cabinet meetings that ended in May.

Child welfare.   In January, Ontario led the way in protesting federal unwillingness to share child welfare costs. Almost all of the other provinces concurred. The Quebec minister endorsed the idea for the first time, calling the exclusion an "enormous gap." MacEachen agreed that he could "appreciate the strength" of their arguments and promised to seek "a better position or a more acceptable one."[72]

NHW returned to cabinet on 18 February, attempting, for the second time, to obtain acceptance of differential cost-sharing and the coverage of child welfare. The provincial welfare ministers, the memo said, "made a strong and unanimous case for full and immediate coverage for children and youth." The memo emphatically endorsed the provinces' request, arguing that the measure would help to preserve the family unit and would be "in harmony with the general principle underlying the Canada Assistance Plan."[73]

The memo went to cabinet at the end of March. NHW's case for the inclusion of child welfare was now much stronger, in that it was backed by a ministerial consensus. Finance was either silent or no longer capable of overcoming NHW's arguments in favour of reform. Cabinet quickly approved full coverage of child welfare.[74]

Differential cost-sharing.   Predictably, the Atlantic ministers used the January meeting to reiterate their desire for a differential cost-sharing formula. Ontario and British Columbia did not explicitly object, but Ontario did make a proposal – surely without any expectation of its being agreed to – to the effect that all provinces should benefit from

75 percent cost-sharing from the federal government. As with the child welfare issue, MacEachen made no effort to defend his government's position on differential cost-sharing. He promised to inquire about the possibility of meeting the provinces' needs.[75]

The February cabinet memo again requested inclusion of a differential formula.[76] Here, NHW was much less successful than it had been on child welfare. There was a heated debate between NHW and Finance, and in the end, MacEachen was completely vanquished by Sharp.[77]

Over the next two months, cabinet resolved a number of outstanding technical problems. This enabled Finance to take parting shots at CAP. For example, it made sure that no projects of a long-term nature could be financed under the work activity component of CAP. Finance also obtained assurances that it could intervene in the project evaluation process if it wanted to.[78]

The Canada Assistance Plan in its final form was unveiled in Parliament on 14 June 1966. The legislation provided for federal cost-sharing with respect to the costs of provincial mothers' allowances, for the integration of categorical programs with needs-tested general assistance benefits, and for the continued use of cost-sharing in the social assistance field. In addition, the costs of all new social services and program administration were to be shared by both levels of government; modest provisions were made for work activity projects; and provincial child-welfare programs were covered. The legislation included only minimal standards – a prohibition on residency requirements and a requirement for an appeal process. It made no special cost-sharing arrangements for the poorer provinces.

CONCLUSION

The Canada Assistance Plan was a product of bureaucratic policy making. Where federal and provincial welfare officials achieved a consensus about reform, their ideas were implemented. This bureaucratic consensus was required to overcome a persistent obstacle – the indifference that continued to characterize political responses to assistance reform. During 1964 and 1965, the needed political support slowly emerged, but only once – and if – it was preceded by a bureaucratic consensus. The political support had two sources; the first was provincial welfare ministers, while the second was Tom Kent, whose views were highly prized by Prime Minister Pearson. And once these political actors indicated their consent, the bureaucratic consensus was able to overcome another persistent barrier – the opposition of the federal department of Finance. Where bureaucratic consensus was fragmentary, however, political support was equally incomplete, and Finance triumphed.

On mothers' allowances, program integration, the continued use of conditional grants, and child welfare, a federal/provincial bureaucratic consensus emerged in favour of reform. In each case, this consensus was eventually sanctioned by provincial ministers and by Kent. Once this occurred, Finance's opposition – which was vociferous on all of these issues, with the exception of program integration – was overcome. Similar provincial support emerged on administrative cost-sharing; in this case, NHW had to agree to a compromise with Finance, but one that nevertheless enabled it to realize its major objective.

On two other issues, a bureaucratic consensus did not emerge; as a consequence, neither did firm political support. Here, Finance was victorious. The richer provinces opposed their poorer cousins on differential cost-sharing, and thus Finance was able to override NHW's support for reform in this area. Similarly, the provinces resisted NHW's pressure to impose national standards. Again, Finance was able to use provincial reservations, especially in Ontario and Quebec, to score a victory.

There was one exception to the pattern in which bureaucratic consensus led to reform. Work activity reforms – the one element of CAP that transcended the traditional parameters of a welfare department – engendered strenuous opposition from the department of Labour. Welfare officials were compelled to lower their aspirations in this area.

These developments continued to reflect the societal and organizational factors that had shaped assistance reform prior to 1964. First, developments within the state reflected forces best understood with a political class model: all items considered for inclusion in the act were advocated first and foremost by a vital fraternity of federal and provincial welfare officials, empowered by the continued predominance of the programs that they administered within Canada's liberal welfare state. The very existence of such a cohesive group, steeped in shared program commitments and reformist beliefs, is a typical manifestation of a liberal welfare state where working class mobilization is limited and where social assistance programs and their administrators play a prominent role.

The role of the governing Liberal Party was quite different from that of the bureaucrats, but it is equally amenable to explanation in political class terms. The political pressures experienced by the governing Liberals, who were motivated by a conscious desire to curtail a threat from the left, generally pulled them away from, not towards, assistance reform. The NDP's social democratic preferences helped sustain these pressures in the context of a minority government. The Liberal government's effort to capitalize politically on assistance reform by linking it to the Canada Pension Plan was unsuccessful, however. Political indifference towards assistance and public apathy about it are consistent with Esping-Andersen's observations about the political logic of social policy making: only broader social security measures, not narrowly poverty-oriented ones, embody much of the solidarity that makes them political priorities; and social democratic influences tend to discourage, not promote, poverty-relief reforms. That the NDP had this effect will become even clearer in the next chapter.

In functional class terms, every aspect of the reform agenda that represented a potential burden on the federal treasury continued to be opposed by the department of Finance, which cited, among other arguments, the parlous consequences that such expenditures would have on the government's fiscal situation and on the economy. Finance justified its position with the anti-interventionist and anti-spending arguments that are prominent features of market-oriented accumulation strategies. Presumably, Finance's defeat on most issues during this period owed much to the relative economic buoyancy of the 1960s, which restricted the persuasiveness of its dire warnings about the fiscal and economic consequences of increased expenditures and lessened the vehemence with which these arguments were advanced.

The Canada Assistance Plan also reflected the prevailing departmentalized organization of the Canadian state. Reform originated among program officials of parallel federal and provincial departments who generally shared goals and interacted in a non-strategic way, and their concrete objectives were incremental departures from existing arrangements. Only on the issues of differential cost-sharing and, most dramatically, national standards, was there a departure from non-strategic, program-oriented relations between federal and provincial participants. In addition, the reforms that were implemented fell within the traditional turf of welfare departments – with the exception of work activity, which extended beyond the traditional turf of assistance programs and gave rise to a debilitating struggle with the Labour department, as one would expect in a fragmented state structure. Inasmuch as these organizational features prevailed – that is, inasmuch as a federal/provincial bureaucratic consensus emerged on a number of issues and was confined to the traditional welfare turf – the reform initiative was successful.

CHAPTER FOUR

Parties, Interest Groups, and Poverty, 1958–68

Social assistance reform during the 1960s was led by bureaucrats in federal and provincial welfare departments, not by politicians – at least not in the executive settings examined in the last two chapters. But did political parties exercise any influence on reform in electoral and legislative contexts? Did the agendas pursued by other class actors – labour unions and business federations – contribute to poverty reform? Of what relevance were the activities of non-class interests? This chapter seeks to answer those questions.

POLITICAL PARTIES

The electoral platforms of Canada's three major parliamentary parties between 1957 and 1963 gave priority in assistance matters to improving the benefits offered by the categorical programs (OAA, BPA, DPA). The policy pronouncements of the three parties were almost identical,[1] and these platforms did not diverge from the typical interests of individual MPs. Throughout the period, references to social assistance in the House of Commons almost exclusively pointed out the inadequacy of the categorical benefits. Echoing the position adopted by MacEachen in cabinet, MPs frequently referred to the particularly "deserving" nature of recipients of these benefits, which were often contrasted with the "relief" received by other, presumably less worthy, assistance recipients. Many representations referred explicitly to requests for improved allowances by the groups concerned.[2] These requests reflected, in good part, the existence of a well organized lobby for the blind and of more diffuse demands for improvements for the other categories of recipients. But they also reflected, no doubt, the predominance of liberal norms in Canada's welfare state. Recipients of all three categorical programs were manifestly unemployable and thus were destitute through no fault of their own. Within a liberal framework, they could be exempted from the incentive-inducing eligibility considerations that applied to others.

Before the Liberal government announced CAP in its 1965 throne speech, only NHW's ministers, within Parliament, had shown any interest in the reform agenda – and that, only after they had been persuaded of the merits of reform by their officials. Waldo Monteith, the NHW minister in the conservative government from 1957 to 1963, was the first MP to mention specifically (in April 1962) the bureaucratic proposal for integration in the Commons.[3] After the Liberals came to power in April 1963, Monteith reverted to the Conservative Party's position of demanding improvements in categorical assistance benefits.[4] Similarly, before 1965 only Judy LaMarsh, among Liberal MPS, voiced support for the integration of the assistance programs. She gave her first indication of possible major changes in the federal/ provincial assistance programs in July 1963, in a speech introducing the government's initial proposals for a national pension plan.[5] As with Monteith, this only happened after strenuous lobbying by her officials (see chapter 3).[6]

Once federal/provincial discussions on assistance reform began in February 1964, demands for improvements in categorical benefits subsided, although the Opposition parties still made such requests on occasion.[7] No parliamentarian other than LaMarsh expressed much interest in comprehensive assistance reform until it was announced in the government's throne speech of April 1965. All parties then accepted the principles underlying the Canada Assistance Plan. But the most salient feature of the political handling of CAP during its journey through the Commons in 1966 was the extent to which it was treated as a proxy for a debate on universal pensions – an issue whose electoral potential made it far more important to politicians. The NDP was the most vocal in stressing this link.

Throughout its first term of office, the Liberal government was under pressure from the Opposition parties to raise monthly OAS payments from $75 to $100 and to lower the age of eligibility from 70 to 65. Something, it was argued, would have to be done for current pensioners and for those near retirement age, as this group would be unable to benefit from the CPP. Although the government agreed to lower the qualification age for OAS to 65, it did not raise the monthly benefit. As a result, it continued to face demands for increased OAS payments throughout the 1965 election campaign.[8]

During the election, the Liberals clearly wanted to link CAP to the pension issue and thus defuse pressure for higher OAS payments. The choice of name for the new assistance act was a conscious effort to associate it with the CPP. When Prime Minister Pearson discussed CAP in the Commons on 6 April 1965, he noted that the new needs-tested assistance program could be used to supplement the pensions of OAS recipients who did not qualify for CPP benefits: "In this way ... social insurance and social assistance measures are being coordinated."[9] The possible use of assistance funds to supplement OAS payments was emphasized in public speeches by LaMarsh. It was also the aspect of CAP that was of the greatest interest to Stanley Knowles, the NDP's critic on social security matters. In late May, he urged the government to pass CAP as quickly as possible "so that additional pension benefits for persons on old age security might soon be made available to them."[10]

Few issues made an impact on voters during the election campaign, but the Opposition did score points with its demand that OAS payments be raised to $100.[11] The Liberals attempted to counter this demand by implying that CAP could lead to even more adequate pension benefits for those who needed them. A party policy document observed that under CAP, "there is no limit to the amount of the assistance in which the federal government will share. Thus, if a province decides that older people need a total income of $125 a month, assistance will be paid at the necessary rate ($50 a month on top of the $75 old-age security) with the federal government sharing all of the cost."[12] This position was reiterated in Liberal speeches throughout the campaign to an apparently sceptical public; Pearson also devoted part of an important television appearance to this theme.[13]

The pension issue would not go away after the election, in which the Liberals were returned to power, again with a minority government. Fuel was added to the fire by the release in February 1966 of the report of the Special Senate Committee on Aging. The Croll Report – named after Senator David Croll, who chaired the committee – dismissed the use of assistance to supplement pensions for those who could not benefit from CPP. Instead of recommending a costly increase in OAS payments as an alternative, it proposed the introduction of an income-tested benefit. In effect, this would be a modest use of the concept of a guaranteed annual income, which was becoming popular in social policy circles. The new measure would supplement the universal OAS system.[14]

The Croll Report was not well received either by the Liberal cabinet or by federal officials. Pearson, MacEachen, Sharp, and other ministers all had reservations about the proposed income-tested benefit, but they acknowledged that there might be considerable political pressure to implement the idea.[15] Thus when MacEachen introduced the CAP resolution in Parliament on 14 June 1966, the Liberal strategy was to rely on it to deflect criticism of its pension policy.[16] Both the Conservatives and the NDP accepted CAP as an improvement in assistance arrangements, but this point was quickly brushed over. Instead, the Opposition concentrated on the plan's deficiencies as a response to demands in the pension area. They insisted that a needs test could be degrading for pensioners. Armed with the Croll Report, they argued that it would be unacceptable to supplement a pensioner's income with social assistance. While drawing heavily on the report's critique of the use of assistance, the Conservatives and the New Democrats were silent about the merits of an income-tested pension, preferring to continue pressing for improved universal pensions.[17]

The NDP would not relent. George McIlraith, the Liberal House leader, complained that while the other Opposition parties were willing to allow CAP to proceed so that the parliamentary session could be wound up, the NDP was preventing this with stalling tactics.[18] Indeed, Knowles was so much more interested in pensions than in assistance reform that during the second reading of the bill he moved that CAP be "not now read a second time" and that the House instead immediately consider a proposal to raise OAS payments to $100.[19] When the motion was ruled out of order, the New Democrats, now joined by the other Opposition parties, continued to stall House business. Finally, on 30 June, NDP leader T.C. Douglas rose to speak on the issue. He threatened the Liberal government: "I want to tell the government that unless they do something about the plight of old age pensions, the opposition parties in this Parliament will be justified in combining and putting this government out of office."[20] In effect, the NDP was willing to see the passage of CAP delayed indefinitely, either by having it withdrawn or by seeking to defeat the government that sponsored it, unless its own pension demands were met.

With the pension issue now jeopardizing its survival, the government acceded to these demands. While refusing to state explicitly what new benefits would be made available to the elderly, it informally told members of the press that an income-tested pension (what would later become the "Guaranteed Income Supplement") would be introduced before the end of the parliamentary session to help needy OAS recipients until the CPP reached maturity.[21] When MacEachen assured the House that something was about to be done to help the elderly, the Opposition relented, and CAP was quickly passed, with all parties voting in favour.[22]

ECONOMIC CLASS ORGANIZATIONS

Parliamentary parties are the primary vehicle for mobilizing working class power in the modern welfare state. Nevertheless, as Korpi and Esping-Andersen point out, working class power is also reflected in economic organizations. This section examines the role of organized labour – that of the Canadian Labour Congress, in particular. It also assesses the impact of business associations – notably the Canadian Chamber of Commerce, the Canadian Manufacturers' Association, and the Canadian Bankers' Association.

Organized Labour

Canadian organized labour – like its political ally, the social democratic CCF/NDP – has comparatively modest power resources at its disposal. In tandem with the CCF, Canadian unions became more powerful during the Second World War and in the immediate postwar period, and labour had a major impact on the social security reforms of the time. But this influence subsided considerably thereafter, as labour federations became more fragmented, failed to enlist workers aggressively in the white-collar sectors, and thus did not attain the levels of unionization typical of most Western European societies.[23] As a result, labour has had a limited capacity to convince government to translate its policy preferences into program commitments. This is reflected in the sharp discrepancy between the social democratic content of labour's social security policies and the persistently liberal form of Canada's welfare state.

During the CAP process, labour advocated a welfare state based on full employment and social security measures of a universal and contributory kind. Canada's welfare state, by contrast, remained predominantly liberal and continued to give priority to poverty-oriented measures. Labour's social democratic commitments, and the divergence between them and the prevailing liberal context, shaped its approach to assistance issues. First, social assistance, with its market-oriented character and its potential to erode solidarity, was not a preferred form of social security. But second, because of the prevailing liberal context, labour could not deny that assistance measures would, for the foreseeable future, have a role to play in the welfare state. For that reason, it generally favoured higher standards for assistance programs. Third, it was only when labour anticipated that assistance reform would be used to erode the security of organized workers that it devoted any substantial amount of energy to assistance issues. Only then were labour's concerns well known to state actors and were they possibly taken into account in policy making. Finally, this discrepancy between labour's social democratic agenda and the liberal context was also reflected in the ambivalent and muted approach of organized labour to the debate on poverty that began after 1965. For all of these reasons, labour's social security agenda had no significant impact on the design and development of the bureaucratic reform agenda reflected in CAP.

A social democratic agenda.   After it was formed in 1956, the Canadian Labour Congress (CLC) defined its social policy in broad terms and linked it to economic and employment policy. The congress stated that "social security should be based on a program of full employment deliberately planned and promoted by the Government."[24] Its proposals in the area of social security – unemployment insurance, health insurance, pensions, and housing – were typically social democratic in outlook, seeking broad protection for workers against market forces. On unemployment insurance, the CLC asked that coverage be extended to all workers and that benefits be made more generous.[25] On pensions, it proposed in the early 1960s a combination of expanded universal payments and the introduction of a public contributory pension scheme with broad coverage.[26] The CLC later endorsed the Canada Pension Plan in principle but called for higher benefit levels and greater elements of progressivity in the benefit structure.[27] It demanded the introduction of a universal health insurance program in the late 1950s. When the report of the Royal Commission on Health Services (the Hall Commission) was released in 1965, recommending such a program, the congress called it "one of the great social policy documents of the century."[28] All of these subjects received substantially more attention in the CLC's annual memos to the cabinet and in other statements than did assistance reform.

Curtailing the market in a liberal welfare state.   But full employment and generous universality were not achieved by Canada's welfare state in the postwar era; labour therefore accepted a continuing need for social assistance. On numerous occasions during the 1950s and early 1960s, the CLC supported the continuance of the categorical measures but usually suggested that they be transformed into universal payments.[29] As late as January 1965, the congress prepared a government brief requesting "a more liberal interpretation of disability under the [DPA] Regulations, for an opportunity to seek rehabilitation and gainful employment without threatened loss of income and so on."[30] Other assistance issues received minimal attention in

CLC policy proposals. General assistance was briefly treated in a letter to MacEachen in October 1963 in response to the Gill Report on unemployment insurance. It affirmed a "need for a social assistance program over and above social insurance programs for income maintenance purposes," but it also expressed concern "about the adequacy of social assistance and about the standards under which it is administered."[31] The letter did not mention, nor did it suggest any awareness of, the specific discussions now proceeding within the federal government on assistance reform.

The 1965 throne speech ended the CLC's attachment to the categorical programs. But what replaced this was a passive endorsement of the measures included in the Canada Assistance Plan. CAP was apparently first discussed within the CLC in late July 1966. Andy Andras, its director of legislation, asserted in a memo to Joe Morris, a CLC officer, that "we are bound to be in agreement with the proposal to establish the Canada Assistance Plan since it represents a progressive step in the development of our social assistance legislation." He added: "I would assume that the Congress would support the Canada Assistance Plan ... subject to its right to offer reasonable criticism." Andras went on to observe that "this is an area in which the Canadian Welfare Council is in a position to give very valuable advice and exert the right kind of pressures."[32] Several public responses to CAP during 1966 followed the path laid by Andras. CAP was generally endorsed, and the few reservations expressed – regarding the failure to include a differential cost-sharing formula in the legislation and to assure national standards – reflected the CWC's position.[33]

In sharp contrast to the CLC's attitude towards all other assistance matters, the congress and one of its affiliated unions took strong positions on work-for-relief when it first became a major political issue in 1960. Their attacks on this practice preceded those of the Public Welfare Division and were frequently referred to in federal discussions. A senior CLC officer of that period has plausibly claimed (in an interview with the author) that labour's position was a significant factor in forestalling federal sharing of work-for-relief costs.

The issue was first discussed by the National Union of Public Employees (NUPE), the union representing municipal employees, in March 1961, shortly after the federal authorities notified Ontario that work-for-relief costs were not sharable. R.P. Rintoul, NUPE's national director, complained to Monteith that work-for-relief "creates unemployment for regular municipal employees."[34]

Discussion of work-for-relief within the CLC began at the end of October 1961. Andras objected to this practice because it degraded assistance recipients and was impractical, and because there was a danger "particularly where municipalities are concerned, that the municipality may substitute the labour of relief recipients for that of employees that should ordinarily be on the payroll."[35] Andras's memo was received very positively by Rintoul and other CLC officers at a subsequent meeting of its National Committee on Employment.[36]

The CLC nevertheless made no public comment about work-for-relief until the provincial premiers issued their apparent endorsement of it in August 1962.[37] The CLC's executive council then released a statement on the subject as part of its annual memorandum to the federal cabinet.[38] Again, the document reflected a concern about loss of employment for municipal workers. Governments might be tempted to use the practice to get "work done on the cheap by replacing regular employees with relief workers ... The rate of pay should reflect standards established through collective bargaining or other recognized procedures. Failure to do so creates inequities and undermines existing wage scales."[39] Splane immediately wrote Willard a memo in which he expressed his approval of these remarks.[40] The Alberta and Ontario federations of labour, meanwhile, released statements endorsing the CLC's position.[41] NUPE, the union most directly concerned with work-for-relief, continued its own campaign.[42]

Interest in work-for-relief continued within the congress, even as clear-cut examples of the practice began to dwindle in early 1964. That year, British Columbia gave priority to welfare recipients in selecting those who qualified for jobs under the federally initiated winter works program. Although this was not really work-for-relief – in that there was no granting of assistance in exchange for compulsory work – it did run counter to the desire of labour organizations to reserve winter works jobs for their members. As Andras put it, "the Congress' position has been that people should be hired for winter works projects on the basis of the ordinary standards of the labour market: the right people should be hired for the right jobs." Measures to help those on relief to return to work should await future economic growth that might cause "demand for labour in general [to] go up."[43] The congress complained to federal Labour minister MacEachen about the practice of giving preferential treatment to assistance recipients and urged him to stop it.[44]

Suspicion that the provincial governments wished to introduce work-for-relief was so strong within the CLC that it viewed with great scepticism the non-sheltered component of the work activity measures that NHW wished to include in CAP. At a meeting with federal and provincial officials in April 1965, Andras argued that "a clear separation is necessary between relief and work and there should be a clear transfer from a state of dependency to a state of economic self-sufficiency." Government programs should "transfer persons from one state to another." Participants should receive a salary rather than a "work activity allowance," and "the rates of pay should be the established rate in respect of the job and should be divorced from consideration of relief or assistance."[45] Thus while Andras was not opposed to measures designed to improve the vocational potential of assistance recipients, his primary concern was that such a measure should not have a negative effect on wage rates. The CLC could not have been displeased when the scope of work activity was significantly reduced by attacks from the departments of Labour and Finance.

The pursuit of the social democratic goal of curtailing market dependence for workers is intrinsically problematical for labour organizations in a liberal welfare state, where significant numbers of people remain dependent on social assistance, effectively constituting a kind of "reserve army of the unemployed." Under these circumstances, for unions to protect workers against "the whip of the market" might imply that their needs are given priority over those of persons unprotected by a labour contract. Labour effectively adopted this priority when assistance measures threatened workers by undercutting their wages or jeopardizing their access to the limited supply of off-season work and training opportunities.

The rediscovery of poverty.   President Johnson's declaration of war on poverty evoked a faint echo in the Pearson government when it announced a similar program in its April 1965 throne speech. Organized labour's response to the poverty issue was muted. This again reflected the problematical position in which labour found itself by pursuing a social democratic agenda in a liberal context. Greater concern about poverty brought with it a variety of proposed solutions. In both the United States and Canada, such proposals largely concentrated on measures designed to address directly and selectively the needs of the disadvantaged. The new poverty reformers dismissed traditional assistance as ineffective, but the alternatives they advanced – such as a guaranteed annual income – were equally selective and, therefore, liberal. By contrast, the CLC adopted the social democratic view that universality and the extension of union rights were the best security against poverty. While expressing general sympathy for the needs of the poor, organized labour thus remained ambivalent.

The United Auto Workers took a singular interest in poverty, going so far as to declare its own war against it.[46] In March 1964 Mordon Lazarus, a UAW officer, recommended "a CLC-sponsored Public inquiry into poverty in Canada." A board of inquiry "would visit every province, and invite submissions from Federations, Labour Councils, Local Unions and from any other organizations which wish to make presentations."[47] A CLC committee endorsed the UAW's proposal in April and recommended to the executive council that "citizenship month" in 1965 be devoted to the inquiry's results. But this endorsement was reversed in May by a meeting of the CLC's directors: "The consensus of opinion was that we should avoid committing ourselves to an all-out project" on poverty. The congress could only undertake one major project at a time, and "it was the opinion of the ... Directors that priority should be given to the Royal Commission on Health." Instead, the congress would simply disseminate information about poverty issues to its member federations and affiliates, and the June issue of *Canadian Labour* would focus on those issues.[48]

A lengthy discussion on poverty took place at a meeting of the executive committee in July, showing clearly that this topic had only secondary importance in the eyes of leading officers within the congress. It also revealed that the CLC was willing to concede to the Canadian Welfare Council a leading role in poverty issues generally, as it had on social assistance. George Burt, who represented the UAW at the meeting, made a proposal that was even more ambitious than that made earlier by Lazarus: the UAW was now proposing "a program to eliminate poverty. This would mean the organization of all welfare organizations, the unemployed, church groups" and other groups with an interest in poverty. If the UAW's proposal were accepted, the CLC would assume a leadership role in organizing an ambitious political initiative to deal with poverty. Leading CLC officers responded coolly. Donald MacDonald suggested that "we should continue with our traditional methods of organization of the unorganized, collective bargaining and legislative action." Morris added that "the phrase 'war on poverty' was a misnomer in Canada. Poverty in the United States was much worse than in Canada, and this was not really descriptive of the situation we have." MacDonald further stated that "the Canadian Welfare Council was carrying out a study on poverty and we might be just duplicating this." Other speakers at the meeting concurred.[49]

The congress did not respond publicly to the government's war on poverty until its February 1966 memorandum to cabinet. The memo approved of the idea and observed that "it represents at the very least a public and official recognition of the fact that even in the best of times there are always to be found considerable numbers of Canadians who are poor according to any definition of the term."[50] Under Burt's influence, a more critical resolution was passed at the biennial convention two months later, alluding to the government's anti-poverty measures as "meagre efforts which will not suffice even to win the first skirmish, let alone the war against poverty." But even here the congress did not offer specific alternatives. The two proposed improvements relevant to federal social security policy, for example, were "a major revision, strengthening and expansion of our present inadequate social security and transfer payment program" and "income guarantees for those whose needs cannot be met within the regular social security framework."[51]

Except for work-for-relief, none of the CLC's stands on assistance or poverty issues appears to have received any attention within the government. In their May 1964 memorandum to cabinet, NHW officials referred to organized labour as a key opponent of work-for-relief in making their own case against it. This view was echoed by MacEachen at the January 1966 welfare ministers' conference. But in the NHW documents available labour was never mentioned in connection with any other assistance or poverty issue; nor were such issues discussed between the federal cabinet and labour leaders at their annual *in camera* meetings of 1965 and 1966.[52]

Business Federations

Business groups made no public proposals relating primarily to assistance policy during this period, and interviews with former NHW and Finance officials indicate that it is almost certain that they made no direct effort to influence federal efforts in this area. This reflected the broader class-based agenda of business in the social security sphere. Liberal welfare states maximize the market dependence of workers by subordinating social security to market imperatives and minimizing popular loyalty to extensive, universal social programs. These liberal principles reflect the interests of capital as much as social democracy embodies those of workers. Throughout the period of CAP's creation, the major business federations in Canada championed a thoroughly liberal image of the welfare state. This entailed emphatic opposition to new, universal social security benefits; reluctance about the use of social insurance measures; and the advocacy of greater actuarial soundness in the latter. Assistance was therefore preferred to universal measures because it reflected the market-oriented eligibility principle. On the other hand, business's preference for the market and its consequent hostility to all social expenditures by government gave it little motivation to recommend improvements in existing assistance measures.

Canadian Chamber of Commerce. The Chamber of Commerce recommended in 1961 that the unemployment insurance system be restored "to a sound financial basis." The program was no longer actuarially sound because it had been "expanded to embrace unemployment assistance by using contributions from non-seasonal employment to subsidize seasonal unemployment" and because it extended benefits to married women, some pensioners, and so on. The Chamber's *Statement of Policy* added: "A system of Unemployment Insurance ultimately necessitates, in addition, a system of rationally administered Unemployment Aid for the purpose of caring for need arising from unemployment not covered by Insurance Benefits."[53] Unemployment insurance and assistance legislation must be funded entirely separately.[54] The Chamber's most concerted attack on the social insurance approach was launched against contributory pensions. In 1964 it proposed further study before the federal government proceeded with the CPP. When this failed, it denounced the proposed legislation. Pressure to reconsider the plan continued until shortly before its passage.[55] On health insurance, the Chamber of Commerce advocated the provision of "adequate medical care through the medium of voluntary health care plans, with the government limited to helping those unable to help themselves."[56] Similarly, it argued that "future financial assistance by government be directed to those whose health care needs are beyond their resources."[57]

In a December 1960 submission to a parliamentary committee, the Chamber had set out a position on taxation and government spending that was to remain unchanged throughout the first half of the decade: "The burden of taxation is too onerous in Canada [and] personal and corporate income tax rates discourage initiative." Excessively high taxes were "the direct result of expanded government expenditures ... Governmental policy should be directed to the reduction of expenditures with a critical review of social and welfare payments to determine how these costs can be contained."[58]

Canadian Manufacturers' Association. The CMA developed a position that largely paralleled that of the Chamber of Commerce, preferring selective benefits to expensive universal and contributory measures, and resisting any increase in government expenditures because of the impact they might have on the economy. In 1961, the CMA warned against attaching "to unemployment insurance supplementary measures which ... cannot be based on sound social insurance measures ... Unemployment Assistance is now available to meet any hardship that might be caused through the operation of seasonal regulations [in the UI system]." Unlike the Chamber of Commerce, the CMA accepted the principle of a public contributory pension plan, but it insisted that the plan be built on what it considered sound economic principles.[59] In its brief to the Hall Commission, the CMA recommended "that no national health scheme applicable to Canadians generally should be considered." Instead, there should be special measures for the protection of "those with pre-existing medical conditions, those of advanced years and those who were indigent." The CMA also consistently argued that "corporation and personal income tax rates should be substantially reduced." When the federal government announced in 1966 that there would be tax increases to pay for higher social security expenditures, the CMA recommended that "the Government should [instead] reduce its own expenditures and institute economies so that additional revenue is not required."[60]

Canadian Bankers' Association. The CBA's submission to the Royal Commission on Taxation referred to the "heavy rate of corporation taxation [and the] steeply graduated personal income tax," which affected "costs of production in Canada, ... our competitive position in world markets, and ... the incentives to work and produce, which are the basic driving force of a free enterprise economy." Where possible, existing social security benefits "might be placed on a self-sustaining basis with the required contributions being made by those who would normally expect to be beneficiaries." This would make the programs less of a drain on the federal treasury and "would instil in each participant a sense of responsibility." Departing somewhat from the opposition to government financing of contributory measures that had been voiced by the other business groups, the CBA proposed that supplementary benefit costs under the UI system be met from general revenues so that "all taxpayers, and not simply those who contributed to the unemployment insurance fund," would pay for them.[61] Nevertheless, the CBA's position remained broadly liberal. For example, it did not want traditional social assistance displaced by social insurance. Under questioning at the hearings of the Royal Commission on Taxation, the CBA delegates said that "we certainly recognize that there are areas where welfare assistance is definitely needed. There is no suggestion we are going to eliminate welfare assistance in cases where it is needed."[62]

NON-CLASS INTERESTS

The organizations created to help the blind were by far the most vocal non-governmental pressure groups involved in assistance policy making. The most important of these was the Canadian National Institute for the Blind (CNIB), a service organization. A significant and largely parallel role was played by the Canadian Council of the Blind (CCB), a national federation of blind persons. Far from supporting the bureaucratic reform agenda, which advocated integrating existing federal assistance measures, the blind organizations consistently stressed the unique circumstances of their constituency and requested special benefits for the blind above and beyond those available to other needy persons. By 1965, groups representing the disabled were making similar demands.

The CNIB's role dated from the Depression period, when it lobbied the federal government for a blind pension "either in the way of an amendment to the Old Age Pensions (OAP) Act or through a special Blind Persons Act."[63] The federal government acceded to this request in 1937 when it extended OAP coverage to blind persons over the age of 40.[64] During the war, the CNIB fought to have these benefits increased and extended to all blind persons over the age of 21, and to have blind allowances covered under separate legislation that would make it possible to "deal adequately with the specific problems relating to the blind and the prevention of blindness."[65] Amendments to the OAP legislation in 1947 met the first two of these demands, and the third was accommodated by the passage of the BPA in 1951. In the late 1950s and early 1960s, the CNIB and the CCB requested a universal pension for blind persons, alongside an improved means-tested benefit.[66] As CAP was in the final stages of preparation in 1965 and early 1966, the two blind groups continued to request a universal blindness allowance in addition to whatever selective assistance benefits blind persons and their families might be eligible for.[67]

Groups representing the disabled became active in 1965. In January, the Canadian Rehabilitation Council for the Disabled publicly criticized the DPA legislation. As an alternative, it proposed a universal disability pension, similar to the proposal of the blind organizations.[68] The Ontario Federation for the Cerebral Palsied launched a similar campaign.[69]

Federal welfare officials and at least some of their provincial counterparts were well aware of the blind organizations' position and went to some length to oppose it. During the ICSS meetings in 1961, NHW officials criticized the request for a universal payment to the blind.[70] The deputy ministers of Alberta and Newfoundland both spoke privately to federal officials of pressures from categorical groups in their provinces, which were interfering with efforts to integrate categorical and general assistance measures.[71] Even after the federal cabinet's acceptance of comprehensive reform in March 1965, Willard was fearful of the reaction of the categorical interests. He warned provincial officials that in order to minimize the opposition of blind groups, the provinces should not cut benefits to categorical recipients if these groups were transferred to general assistance.[72] By then, however, political support for comprehensive reform was assured, and the pro-categorical interests were unable to halt the momentum.

CONCLUSION

The reforms described in chapters 2 and 3 were not championed by non-bureaucratic actors. In legislative and electoral settings, none of the political parties played a significant role in shaping social assistance reform. They were far less interested in assistance than in the broader components of the welfare state, which had greater electoral appeal. In this is confirmed Esping-Andersen's political-class model, which suggests that political parties are motivated by electoral pressures to consider social security measures that are broader in scope than those contemplated as part of assistance reform. The NDP, as a social democratic party, led the way in stimulating these broader interests; indeed, its universalist preferences nearly scuttled CAP as it proceeded through Parliament during the summer of 1966. Where the parties did develop an interest in assistance – in championing the categorical measures and, at the provincial level, sporadically supporting work-for-relief – this reflected the ideological legacy of liberalism.

The political and economic organizations associated with a working class agenda adopted a social democratic approach to Canada's welfare state, reflecting a working class commitment to policies aimed at eroding market dependence. Both the CCF/NDP and organized labour emphatically preferred universal and broad social insurance measures over selective ones. Assistance reform was always, with them, a secondary concern. The ambiguous and hesitant approach of both the political and economic wings of labour to assistance and poverty issues during this period reflected the dilemma posed by the pursuit of labour's social democratic agenda in a liberal context.

The economic organizations of capital also played a minimal role, and again this reflected the specific class interests advanced by these groups. The market-oriented principles of a liberal welfare state embody the interests of capital. Consequently, the three foremost business federations all championed a selective, targeted welfare state, and they opposed the introduction of universal or non-actuarial social insurance measures. Assistance was considered preferable, but business never advocated significant reforms in existing assistance measures.

Interests best characterized in pluralist terms also played no role in advancing assistance reform. There were no general organizations of poor people at the national level during the early to mid-1960s. Recipient organizations with an interest in assistance represented the beneficiaries of the categorical programs. These organizations advocated retention and improvement of the privileges available to them through the categorical programs, but bureaucratic reformers, well aware of the obstacle represented by categorical interests, were able to circumvent their influence.

CHAPTER FIVE

Genesis of a New
Poverty Reform, 1968–73

The implementation of the Canada Assistance Plan did not eliminate the impetus to reform Canadian poverty policy. In fact, CAP was legislated at a time of growing awareness in North America that poverty remained widespread. This rediscovery of poverty led many to reject social assistance and to search for a new strategy based on the notion of a guaranteed annual income (GAI). In Canada, the most far-reaching attempt at devising such a strategy was the Social Security Review.

Canada's liberal policy legacies had created an appropriate environment for a GAI. Its reception within the state was facilitated by the institutionalization of its decision-making structures. This reception occurred, first, in newly created, government-sponsored research bureaux, located outside government bureaucracies. Thereafter, a preliminary, limited application of the GAI was attempted within the federal administration, followed by a more ambitious effort in Quebec. That initiative, coupled with a more ambitious reorientation in reform thinking in Ottawa, led the Trudeau government to launch the Review in April 1973.

THE LIBERAL PARAMETERS OF
THE SOCIAL SECURITY REVIEW

The 1960s and early 1970s witnessed the second great period of postwar innovation in the Canadian welfare state: the Canada Pension Plan came into effect in 1966; the income-tested guaranteed income supplement (GIS) for pensioners was added in 1967; the Medical Care Act, creating a universal health insurance program, was implemented in 1968; and in 1971 substantial improvements were made in the Unemployment Insurance Act. These developments reflected a move to the left by the governing Liberal Party after 1960, in a conscious effort to contain the NDP. Persistent pressure from the left provided an incentive for minority Liberal governments of the mid-1960s to meet their electoral commitments to social reform. The reforms added significantly to the universal and contributory elements in Canada's welfare state, but they did not cause it to depart fundamentally from the liberal model. In 1972, for example, approximately 7 percent of Canadians received benefits from provincial and municipal programs financed under the Canada Assistance Plan. Assistance payments represented 17 percent of income security payments by all levels of government and accounted for more than half of the expenditures of provincial and municipal jurisdictions.[1] Thus poverty-oriented measures remained far more prominent in Canada's liberal welfare state than in social democratic or conservative welfare states.[2]

A rediscovery of poverty took place during the 1960s in liberal welfare states – the United Kingdom, the United States, and Canada.[3] The public debate on poverty was far more muted, if it took place at all, in the conservative and social democratic welfare states of Europe. Catherine Jones notes that "numerous books can and have been written on concepts of poverty – mostly by British and US writers, rather than by Swedes or Germans until recently [1985] at least ... The UK and US [tend] to be much more 'poverty-obsessed' than continental Europe." She observes that this preoccupation is related to the "relief" orientation of the British and U.S. welfare states.[4] Similarly, Roger Lawson and Robert Walker argue that, unlike in Britain, "in most European countries ... the relief of poverty has rarely been more than a subsidiary element in a social policy that is more concerned to regulate the relationship between capital and labour, foster solidarity, and to maintain the acquired living standards of those no longer in employment."[5] Concern about poverty has remained less salient in conservative and social democratic welfare states, reflecting the much smaller role of selectivity in those societies.

In Canada, the poverty debate inspired a search for solutions that went beyond traditional social assistance. The guaranteed annual income, first championed by American economists, was a liberal solution to a problem defined in liberal terms. Its singular avowed merit was (and remains today) to provide selective social security for the least advantaged, while maximizing the recipient's market dependence – in other words, to enhance work incentives and labour-market flexibility among low-wage workers.[6]

In its most popular version, a GAI delivers income maintenance payments to citizens by means of a negative income tax. A minimum payment (guarantee level) is received by all citizens who earn no income, the size of the payment being reduced only gradually as income rises from zero. Only a certain percentage of the payment is "taxed back" (or offset) as earned income rises. In effect, those whose income is deemed to be inadequate are subject to a negative tax. At the break-even point (or ceiling), earned income is high enough to offset completely the guaranteed income payment; those who earn income above this level receive no benefits and are expected to contribute to the positive tax system. As Patrick Moynihan points out, the GAI "introduced incentives for the poor to increase their incomes. Just as the positive guaranteed income tax steadily took more from the taxpayer as his income mounted, but never *all* the additional increment, so the negative income tax would give less as earnings increased, but never to the point of cancelling *all* advantages of increased earnings."[7] The importance of work incentives to the GAI reflects its liberal inspiration: it is designed to persuade individuals to earn a living in the marketplace by making alternative sources of livelihood distinctly less desirable.

The GAI's foremost popularizer, Milton Friedman, emphasized this goal to the exclusion of all others in his *Capitalism and Freedom*. Unlike virtually all existing social security measures, he argued, a negative income tax "does not eliminate [the incentives of those helped to help themselves] entirely ... An extra dollar earned always means more money available for expenditure." To be effective, the GAI's offset must be low enough to create work incentives, while the guarantee level must not be high enough to enable the recipient to support himself or herself. Since the GAI would replace almost all existing social security measures, Friedman implied that subsistence would not be possible for those unwilling to work.[8]

Other American economists (Robert Lampman, for example) also believed in the importance of incentives, but they saw the guaranteed income as a means of providing an adequate living standard. The guarantee level should, they argued, be high enough to assure survival. In effect, they attempted to combine adequate social security for the poor with the GAI's market-enhancing potential.[9] The proponents of this more generous version of the GAI were often willing to preserve alternative forms of social security, including modest universal and social insurance measures, alongside a new GAI.[10] It was in this tamer form, still liberal but of the "impure-liberal" variety, that the GAI became relevant to the Social Security Review.

THE NEW REFORM AGENDA

A new poverty reform agenda emerged in state-sponsored institutions in Canada during the late 1960s and early 1970s; it was centred on the GAI but included other proposals. Developments occurred both within the federal government and in the province of Quebec. In each case, reform proposals not only reflected the liberal setting described above but also the increasing institutionalization of the federal and Quebec governments. They therefore evidenced both societal and organizational influences.

Organizational Change in the Federal Government

In the late 1960s, significant changes took place in the organization of the executive bodies of the federal government and many of its provincial counterparts. Central agencies became more important as sources of policy initiatives; planning officials with systematic and strategic objectives partially displaced program-administering officials; and there was a greater focus on initiatives with a supradepartmental scope. While these changes did not fully materialize until Trudeau assumed power in 1968, they had been foreshadowed by developments earlier in the decade.

Trudeau was not alone in being mesmerized by the allure of rationalism. As Richard French put it, "the arrival of the pervasive state in the postwar period was the greatest single factor behind recognition of the need for improved planning of the activities of Western governments." This recognition coincided with "an explosion of activity in the social sciences. The analysis of public problems became a series of esoteric specialties, requiring lengthy formal training." The social sciences had, it was thought, acquired the knowledge needed to plan.[11]

As a result, before 1968 the federal government had already begun to sponsor research outside the "line" bureaucracy – that is, outside departments such as National Health and Welfare or Transportation, which were staffed by officials who administered programs directly – on important policy concerns. Research was often conducted by experts capable of rationalist and supradepartmental thinking because of their training in the social sciences and because they had no departmental loyalties or constraints.[12]

In social policy, the heightened stature of social science eroded the power of public welfare officials. The research tools of the newly ascendant social scientists displaced the hands-on wisdom of program administrators. Governments now sought solutions to social problems that represented fundamental, rather than incremental, departures from existing measures, and they preferred reforms that were much broader in scope than those of the past. In this environment, the GAI concept represented the kind of solution that was being sought. It was championed by economists and clearly reflected the preoccupations of marginal-utility economics. The displacement of program expertise occurred even within the once potent Canadian Welfare Council (see chapter 7), and the new demands rendered obsolete the professional network that had made the council's Public Welfare Division so effective during much of the 1960s.

The federal government's new social science capacities were applied to poverty research during this period. It sponsored several major enquiries into this subject, dominated by non-bureaucratic experts.

New institutions and poverty research.   The first contribution was the report by Senator Croll's Special Senate Committee on Aging, released in February 1966. The committee's research was conducted by outside experts from a variety of academic disciplines, who provided much of the analysis and wrote the final draft of the report. The committee concluded that existing welfare measures did not meet the needs of the elderly and recommended "the institution of an income guarantee program for all persons aged 65 and over."[13] This proposal was hailed by some as the first step towards a comprehensive GAI and influenced the creation of the guaranteed income supplement.[14]

Despite the Croll Report and the institution of the GIS, the problem of poverty among the non-elderly did not gain much public attention until the Economic Council of Canada published its Annual Review for 1968. The council, largely staffed with economists, reflected the new social scientific expertise: it was "a kind of research bureau which includes an advisory function."[15] Its 1968 review declared that "poverty in Canada is real," adding: "Its numbers are not in the thousands, but the millions." The council recommended "that serious poverty should be eliminated in Canada, and that this should be designated as a major national goal." Among proposed solutions, it mentioned "a careful evaluation of the advantages and disadvantages of new proposals such as the negative income tax and other forms of minimum income guarantee."[16]

The Economic Council's 1968 Annual Review had a significant public impact both in its own right and by precipitating another and more massive poverty inquiry, that of the Special Senate Committee on Poverty. As one commentator noted, "The Council's conclusions and recommendations on the subject, coming as they did from a prestigious body of experts for whom Prime Minister Trudeau's new government could not help having both an affinity and admiration, appeared to have a profound impact."[17] The federal government immediately acted to implement the council's recommendation that a

Senate inquiry "whose work could also be aided by a small but competent research staff,"[18] be established to study poverty further. David Croll was again appointed chairman of this committee.

As with the other statements on poverty reform published during this period, the preparation of Croll's second report involved a substantial hired staff, including economists and others with expertise outside the social welfare field. Four staff members, believing that Croll was not sufficiently radical in his analysis of the sources of poverty, resigned from the committee and produced their own *Real Poverty Report* shortly after the official report was released in November 1971.[19]

While the two documents differed substantially in explaining the social roots of poverty, they proposed quite similar designs as a solution. Each advocated a comprehensive approach that would eclipse needs-tested social assistance. A GAI was to be the centrepiece in both cases, but a variety of economic policies, including the vigorous pursuit of full employment, were also seen as necessary adjuncts. Finally, both reports advocated that social services be separated from income maintenance programs and that the latter be made more widely available. The main program-related difference between the two reports pertained to benefit levels under the GAI, the levels proposed in *The Real Poverty Report* being substantially more generous than those recommended in the second Croll Report.[20]

While Croll's poverty report was still in the making, the Royal Commission on the Status of Women in Canada released its final report. It was largely written by Monique Bégin, the commission's executive secretary, and proposed that a "guaranteed annual income be provided by the federal government to the heads of all one-parent families with dependent children" and that "a federal annual taxable cash allowance in the order of $500 be provided for each child under 16."[21] Bégin's interest in cash allowances for children was to have a bearing on events at the end of the Social Security Review, when she became minister of Health and Welfare in 1978.

Legacies of liberalism.   All of the major studies celebrated the market-oriented qualities of a GAI. The Economic Council's annual reviews, for example, stressed the need to increase work inducements for the poor. In 1965, the council noted that "welfare assistance is provided in a manner and amount that all too frequently undermines, rather than reinforces, the abilities and aspirations of recipients to participate productively in the economic system."[22] Work incentives were cited in the Croll Report on poverty to justify the adoption of a negative income tax. The authors of *The Real Poverty Report* observed that existing "welfare systems ... discourage any impulse a recipient might have to go out and make a living."[23]

These reports and studies also reflected liberal pragmatism – a belief that given existing and foreseeable levels of commitment to social security in Canada, the best way to meet need was to direct expenditures at the most disadvantaged. The Economic Council recommended that "those measures that will meet [the] challenge effectively and economically" be identified. Accordingly, "one of the greatest uncertainties is the extent to which the existing structure of policies in fact constitutes an attack on poverty – the extent, that is, to which its benefits flow to those most in need."[24] In the eyes of the Croll Committee, a new GAI "should be accomplished at minimum costs to the government and the tax-payer." To achieve this, "federal income maintenance legislation, as it exits at present, would be repealed. The G.A.I. would effectively replace Family and Youth Allowances, Old Age Security, the Guaranteed Income Supplement, and most of the other transfer payments programs now operated by the Federal Government."[25] The Real Poverty Report, by contrast, noted that there are various "programs that prevent workers from falling into poverty in the first place. Some of these programs are structural policies, which ensure demand for labour and so prevent large-scale unemployment and training programs ... Others are programs of social insurance." But these measures were viewed as being clearly inadequate to prevent poverty; so a GAI would be needed to "draw a line below which nobody ... will be allowed to fall." It would, in effect, constitute "the bottom layer of a number of other programs."[26]

The Quebec Government and the New Agenda

The most comprehensive proposal for poverty reform before 1973 was the report of Quebec's Commission of Inquiry on Social Affairs (the Castonguay-Nepveu Report), released in January 1971. The commission was chaired by Claude Castonguay, a Montreal accountant; Claude Forget, who had a similar background in economics, was a prominent member. Rather than recruit its staff from the traditional welfare sector, the commission employed many researchers steeped in economics, accounting, or statistics.

The Castonguay-Nepveu Report recommended a radical remodelling of Quebec's social programs, with a GAI as the cornerstone of the new system and the alleviation of poverty as its fundamental objective. Reflecting the broad scope of its enquiry, many of the commission's proposals went well beyond the traditional welfare field. They included a substantial improvement in minimum wage rates, the use of subsidies for workers in marginal sectors of the economy, and improvements in manpower training measures. The report's income security proposals had three elements, two of which – social insurance measures and universal family allowances – already existed. The third, "which constitutes the nucleus of the integrated system advocated by the Commission," was a general social allowances plan (GSAP) – the central element of the package. This program would, in effect, be a two-tier GAI. Social insurance programs and family allowances would be harmonized with the benefits that would be available under GSAP and, more generally, would become suitable weapons in the fight against poverty.[27]

When the commission completed its work in 1971, many of its social science-trained experts, including Forget, moved into a reorganized ministry of Social Affairs and worked there to have the commission's recommendations implemented. Castonguay, meanwhile, had been elected as a Liberal member of the Quebec National Assembly in 1970 and was appointed minister of Social Affairs by Premier Robert Bourassa. There he pursued the same goals that he and his former colleagues had advocated in the commission's report. Thus before the relevant sections were even released, the commission's report had effectively acquired the status of a prominent minister's recommendation to cabinet, based on advice from experts who had the training of planners.

Reflecting its ideologically liberal colouring, the Castonguay-Nepveu Report stressed the importance of incentives: "We underline here the lack of incentive in social assistance measures based on which ... each dollar earned by the recipient was subtracted from his assistance allowance. This measure ... discourages any motivation on the part of low-income persons to hold jobs and to earn income." Similarly, "income security programs must promote reintegration within the labour market." Since the existing universal and social insurance programs could not alleviate poverty, the report recommended that "generally speaking, universal programs be more selective so as to reduce privation among families or unattached individuals."[28]

EVOLVING STATE STRUCTURES
AND POVERTY INITIATIVES,
1968–SUMMER 1972

Although public discussion of poverty reform reached a peak between 1969 and 1971, it did not produce any major initiative during that period.[29] Alleviating poverty was a stated goal of Trudeau's first government, but it never received a significant financial commitment. On several occasions from 1969 onward, the Prime Minister categorically ruled out a GAI, saying that it was an untested concept and might be too expensive. John Munro, the minister of National Health and Welfare from 1968 to 1972, publicly repeated Trudeau's warnings against the fiscal dangers of a full GAI.[30] Until mid-1972, the federal government was committed to only very modest poverty reforms. A more comprehensive initiative did emerge in 1972, at a time when public interest appeared to be waning, but in the context of deteriorating federal-provincial relations and growing support for reform among planning officials.

NHW and Poverty Reform

The quest for more systematic policy making in Ottawa after 1968, reflecting the institutionalization of policy making, had an impact on program departments such as Health and Welfare. There was a significant move away from incrementalism, motivated by cabinet's desire for a more systematic approach. The foremost example of this influence in 1968 was a request that Joe Willard undertake a comprehensive review of the department's income security policies and make recommendations for improving them. A similarly wide-ranging study was requested the following year and prepared by department officials. These studies laid out the department's reform agenda until 1972.

Nevertheless, in important ways NHW remained a line department with characteristically incremental and department-specific concerns. This precluded the emergence of a truly comprehensive agenda in the department, where reform was still being viewed in piecemeal fashion, requiring the adaptation of existing programs; changes were to be confined to measures administered within NHW. Moreover, NHW initiatives were now less likely to succeed because policy-making structures were more institutionalized and gave greater prominence to the central agencies. NHW no longer had the influence required to have its agenda accepted in cabinet.

The department's new approach was outlined in a briefing note prepared for Munro in 1968. It advised that "the social security structure ... should be improved by emphasizing selective rather than universal measures." Family allowances "should be modernized so as to provide greater income support for those children who really need it." The elderly should continue to have access to OAS payments, but greater reliance should be put on GIS benefits to meet their needs.[31] Rather than moving immediately towards a comprehensive GAI, then, there should be a gradual development of income testing by adjusting, or adding to, specific existing measures on a piecemeal basis. Furthermore, reform was to be undertaken entirely within the programs administered by the department. NHW officials felt confined by this restriction – which had, in part, been imposed upon the department by cabinet – because it meant that they could not develop reform ideas relevant to programs under provincial jurisdiction (such as social services).[32] But NHW never, apparently, sought to develop reforms that transcended departmental boundaries at the federal level.

Willard's approach was typical of the NHW philosophy. As one actor at the time put it in an interview with the author, "Joe did not believe in the comprehensive view; he did things incrementally and he did them brilliantly"; he believed in "doing good by stealth." In 1968 and 1969, Willard advised Munro that the next important step should be the implementation of income-tested measures for families and for the disabled. The former could be developed either as an "add-on" to the universal family allowance or as a substitute for it; in either case, it would require the expenditure of new funds if the resulting measure was to be at all adequate.[33]

Willard convinced Munro to accept his piecemeal approach, and the reform priorities that the minister presented to cabinet in April 1970 reflected Willard's ideas. Munro proposed to the cabinet an increase in the GIS, a new income-tested measure for families (called the "family income security plan" or FISP), and a similar program for the disabled. The package presented by Munro received little support from the other ministers and was rejected. The cautionary public statements made by Trudeau and other Liberals in 1969 and 1970 suggest that poverty reform had a low priority within the government, despite the Liberal Party's use of the "just society" theme during the 1968 election. In addition, the proposals were attacked by Finance and Treasury Board as being too costly.[34]

Cabinet decided that NHW could move towards a selective measure with respect to family benefits only and that no new money would be available to finance it: the change would have to be financed from the savings yielded by the elimination of the universal family allowance.[35] A White Paper entitled *Income Security for Canadians*, embodying the results of the April cabinet decision, was released by Munro in November. It referred to a full GAI as a long-term possibility but added that budget restrictions and technical uncertainties ruled it out for the time being.[36] Instead, there would be a reallocation of existing funds in the direction of selectivity, and FISP was the only new measure immediately available.

FISP was a very modest response to poverty. This is explained, in part, by cabinet's unwillingness to accept any significant poverty reform initiatives coming from NHW. But the initial objectives of the department were modest in any case: NHW officials had made no effort to develop a comprehensive approach that would transcend existing departmental (or even program) boundaries.

The Organizational Sources of Comprehensive Poverty Reform

A much more comprehensive poverty reform agenda emerged within the federal and some provincial governments in 1970 and 1971, driven by organizational influences and laying the groundwork for the Social Security Review. First championed by the government of Quebec, this agenda soon became a major focus of federal/provincial tensions. It also acquired an important base within Treasury Board – a central agency of the federal government that actively engaged in the systematic and supradepartmental policy making typical of institutionalized government structures.

Conflict between Ottawa and Quebec. The fact that the authors of the Castonguay-Nepveu Report – including, above all, Castonguay himself – were now in the Quebec government ensured quick and thorough acceptance of the commission's recommendations, which became official policy in January 1971. From then on, "there was a considerable gulf between the pragmatic approach of the largely anglophone ministry in Ottawa and the planning-based-on-principle approach of the ministry in Quebec." This made the report's recommendation that Quebec obtain primacy in the social security field especially compelling for the provincial government: progress towards comprehensive poverty reform appeared unlikely if it required the cooperation of a federal government that seemed to have little interest in alleviating poverty.[37] But provincial primacy was resisted by the federal authorities, and the two governments became locked in a conflict not only about the scope of poverty reform but also about jurisdictional responsibilities. This deterioration in bilateral relations was compounded by the fact that the dispute arose during negotiations to reform the Canadian constitution. The disagreement about social policy contributed significantly to the breakdown of the famous Victoria Charter constitutional discussions in June 1971 – so much so that resolving social policy disputes with Quebec became a major objective of the federal government in 1971 and 1972. The Social Security Review would be the last and most far-reaching result of that endeavour.

Ottawa and Quebec discussed social security and constitutional issues on a number of occasions during the first six months of 1971. Castonguay was the main political participant for Quebec. On the federal side, central agency officials gradually displaced Munro and NHW as the main actors.[38]

At the earliest meetings, Castonguay set forth the Quebec government's social policy goals, extolling the merits of a comprehensive approach to poverty and attempting to convince the federal government and the other provinces to adopt it; he requested federal cost-sharing of Quebec's two-tier GAI proposal.[39] Trudeau refused, citing his established position that the expense would be prohibitive. Bryce, still the Finance deputy minister, also opposed Quebec's suggestion privately because he believed it would entail an open-ended financial commitment.[40]

As the constitutional discussions proceeded, the Quebec government became increasingly frustrated with the federal position on social policy. In February, it insisted on "legislative primacy" in the income security field, to be "enshrined" by a constitutional amendment, so that it could implement its social agenda with fewer constraints from Ottawa. If this proposal had been accepted, the federal government could have participated administratively and financially in income security programs, but the province would have acquired the power to determine their overall design. Quebec announced that it would only agree to constitutional reform if it obtained legislative primacy and thereby obtained the means to achieve its ambitious poverty reform objectives.[41] The federal negotiators, however, made only a modest effort to accommodate that position. They offered the provinces constitutional primacy in many areas of income security; but if Quebec withdrew from a federal program, it would not receive the fiscal compensation that it sought from Ottawa. The federal government also offered to allow income-testing under CAP as an interim step towards a GAI, but the proposal was subject to a restrictive financial limitation.[42] On 23 June, Bourassa announced that Quebec could not accept the Victoria Charter, citing differences between the two governments on social policy as the reason; the resolution of these differences remained a major goal for both governments during the remainder of 1971 and the first half of 1972.[43]

In September 1971 Bourassa wrote to Trudeau, suggesting that the two governments resolve their social policy differences on a piecemeal basis, outside the constitutional context, and that top priority be given to family allowances. Quebec continued to insist on legislative priority, but it would not demand a constitutional amendment guaranteeing this. Once this issue was resolved, other social security disputes could be dealt with. Thereafter, Quebec might consider the resumption of constitutional discussions.[44] Meanwhile, Castonguay indicated that Quebec was drafting new family allowance legislation that would "represent the first step towards the global and integrated income security policy that the Quebec government announced last January, and that it has since attempted to have adopted by Ottawa."[45]

Trudeau agreed to embark on a piecemeal resolution of jurisdictional problems. Negotiations on a more satisfactory version of FISP resumed for several months but broke off in May 1972. The federal budget of that month announced significant increases in OAS and GIS payments, without any prior consultation with the provinces. Outraged, Castonguay argued that these increases would create major anomalies in Quebec's social security system. The federal decision made it clear "that it is illusory to wait for sufficient agreement [with Ottawa] to assure a unified design for programs relevant to the guaranteed income"; one was forced to conclude that the piecemeal approach "has also reached a dead end." It was necessary to return "to the constitutional level and to seek modifications of it that not only affect the division of powers regarding social policy, but that also alter the division of fiscal resources and that limit the spending power of the government of Canada." Bourassa adopted Castonguay's position; at a Quebec Liberal Party conference at the end of May, he announced that the province would seek "a fundamental solution to the problem of the federal spending power instead of trying to obtain piecemeal concessions from Ottawa."[46]

Tensions grew even further when, because of a procedural problem, the revised FISP legislation died on the parliamentary order paper on 7 July. Castonguay held Munro responsible for this failure and complained that Quebec could no longer go ahead with planned revisions in family allowance and social assistance programs because complementary federal legislation would not be in place. Relations between Castonguay and Munro now degenerated to a state of open hostility.[47]

Thus social policy became a persistent and important source of tension between the federal and Quebec governments in the early 1970s. The adoption of comprehensive poverty reform by Quebec created tensions with Ottawa that became linked to the constitutional negotiations of 1971. Subsequent efforts to uncouple the two issues by piecemeal changes in social security policy completely broke down

in mid-1972. Now, the confrontation would spread to include several
other provinces.

The influence of the central agencies.   The second organizational influence encouraging comprehensive poverty reform came from the
newly strengthened central agencies of the federal government. This
development had its genesis in the constitutional debates and
resulted in part from Ottawa's need to generate an alternative to
Quebec's proposals. But it also reflected the quite independent
interest of federal planning officials and was elaborated by them
outside the constitutional context.

In 1971, the federal government was not willing to replace its
modest social security goals with Quebec's more ambitious reforms
nor was it prepared to abandon to Quebec the constitutional authority
it requested to pursue reform on its own. The federal constitutional
position had been set out in two documents, released in 1969, that
also indicated very preliminary interest in a poverty reform agenda
that was more ambitious than NHW's and more compatible with Quebec's objectives.

Al Johnson, who had gained experience in the Saskatchewan civil
service and later (from 1964) in the federal department of Finance,
joined the Privy Council Office staff in 1969. There, he played a
major role in developing the two federal documents, of which the
most important – entitled *Income Security and Social Services* –
defended a continuing role for the federal government in social policy.
Income security policy, which was divided between income support
and income insurance (or contributory and non-contributory) components, should, according to the paper, be an area of shared jurisdiction between the federal and provincial governments. Examples
of relevant income support programs included the demogrants and
a negative income tax. The main justification for federal involvement
in this area was that "it is highly unlikely that an equitable distribution of income across Canada will be achieved – that disparities
in the incomes of individuals and families will be alleviated – unless
Parliament has the power to support the incomes of the poor."[48]
Johnson was arguing, in effect, that the federal government had the
potential to alleviate poverty on a national scale and that guaranteed
income measures might be used to achieve that goal.

The document did not, however, envisage any major federal role
in social services. NHW's Richard Splane, who had worked under
Johnson in the PCO in 1969, took the department's traditional view
that it should be allowed to perform an active role in this as in other

areas of social policy. Johnson countered that social services were primarily a provincial concern. While the federal government had legitimate interests in the area of services, the paper observed, "we do not believe it should be expressed by giving Parliament power to legislate or regulate in these fields"; reliance should instead be made on cost-sharing arrangements with few federal standards attached.[49] The disagreement with Splane on services foreshadowed the differences that would arise between the positions of Johnson and of NHW officials at the start of the Social Security Review.

Johnson left the PCO in 1970 to become deputy secretary to the Treasury Board, which was then aggressively pursuing the kind of rationalist policy analysis that had become popular in Ottawa since 1968.[50] As Johnson described it at the time, the Treasury Board developed proposals for cabinet on how to allocate resources based on "the priorities of the government and its policy decisions, the effectiveness of the programs in achieving the government's objectives, and the efficiency with which the programs are administered." This approach necessitated a focus that transcended existing programs and, if necessary, existing departmental boundaries. Treasury Board must be "unencumbered by departmental loyalties to particular clienteles."[51] Its expert staff performed policy assessments, based on this philosophy, by means of a series of evaluations of programs in line departments.[52]

Johnson "obviously had a pent up interest" in the area of income security and poverty, as one interviewee put it. Soon after arriving at Treasury Board, he launched an assessment of existing NHW programs in the systematic terms suggested by the board's planning philosophy. He concluded that the programs, especially CAP, were not alleviating poverty. Meanwhile, Johnson assembled a group of economists (including Russell Robinson) who provided him with expert analysis of income security programs.

Johnson also considered that Health and Welfare's FISP proposal was undesirable; not only was it inadequate as an attack on poverty but it was politically unwise, because by substituting income-tested benefits for the universal family allowance, it would deprive many middle-class housewives of an important source of income. As FISP was being prepared for cabinet, Johnson wrote a detailed proposal on federal income security policy that amounted to an ambitious alternative to NHW's ideas. The universal family allowance should be maintained, he argued, but poverty could be attacked more methodically than was possible under the Canada Assistance Plan. Johnson's document was prepared independently of the Castonguay-Nepveu Report (which was released shortly after he completed his paper), but his conclusions were similar to the Quebec commission's. His central proposal favoured a guaranteed annual income that would replace CAP. He also stepped beyond the traditional welfare field by arguing that government must do more to improve employment opportunities for those outside the normal work force. The paper was silent about social services.[53]

The paper was sent to Trudeau and also found its way into the hands of Health and Welfare officials, who felt that it displayed a lack of appreciation for the merits of CAP and other NHW programs. Trudeau did not respond to the memorandum, but Johnson's model – and the attempt at systematic and supradepartmental policy analysis by a central agency that it represented – remained as an alternative to NHW's proposal. It was to receive more attention when the latter collapsed in the summer of 1972.

PRELUDE TO POVERTY REFORM, AUGUST 1972–APRIL 1973

The Liberals were returned to power with a minority government in October 1972; the government's survival now depended on the goodwill of the NDP. Shortly after the election, the federal government launched a comprehensive reform of poverty policy, but this decision was not made public until the January 1973 throne speech. On 18 April the federal government released *The Working Paper on Social Security for Canada* (popularly known as the Orange Paper), which laid the detailed groundwork for the federal/provincial review that was to be conducted over the next five years.

The Impact of Politics: Expanding Universality

The government decided on poverty reform by late November 1972, but it was not evident until the following April that it had been subject to political pressures to increase OAS and family allowance payments in the intervening period. By the spring of 1973, in fact, it was obvious that these changes would take priority over poverty reform. Eventually, they would seriously undermine it. In the case of the OAS benefits, the increase was traceable directly to the influence of the NDP; other political factors, as well as interjurisdictional considerations, played an important role in the case of family allowances.

Old Age Security was perhaps the most politically sensitive of the federal government's social security measures.[54] One of the last acts of the first Trudeau government, in May 1972, had been a small increase in the pension; at the same time, the government had reversed a decision made the previous year which had ended inflation-related adjustments in OAS payments. Both changes, which were widely praised in the media, had been demanded by the NDP,[55] but when they were introduced in the House of Commons, they were condemned by Stanley Knowles as a cynical pre-election manoeuvre and as being inadequate.

Pensions were the main social policy concern of the New Democrats after the election. In public statements and in private meetings with MacEachen, the Liberal House leader, between November and January, NDP leader David Lewis and Knowles made an "immediate and substantial" increase in OAS levels their main social security demand in exchange for their party's support of the government.[56] The Liberals realized that responding to the third party's demands was a *sine qua non* of their survival in power, and the throne speech of 4 January 1973 promised that "legislation will be introduced to improve the economic situation of old age pensioners," but no agreement had yet been reached with the NDP about how large the increase would be.[57] Lewis was pressing to have the monthly benefit raised to $150, but he reluctantly settled for $100.[58] Marc Lalonde, the new minister of National Health and Welfare, used a Commons speech on 11 January to announce the increase. Knowles, speaking for his party, declared that "that's the one sentence in the whole speech that meant anything," ignoring the fact that the speech was largely devoted to an elaboration of the government's plans for a major attack on poverty.[59]

The factors that had a bearing on the decision to increase family allowances were more varied, but political influences predominated. NHW's post-1970 reform agenda, which presupposed the elimination of the allowances, was abandoned during the election campaign. By the summer of 1972, FISP had "proved politically to be quite negative" for the Liberal Party, as one interviewee put it. From its beginning in 1970, the plan had raised a storm of protest among people, many not far above the poverty line, who were concerned about losing their "baby bonus." Even before its demise in Parliament, FISP had been condemned by the Conservatives and, more vehemently, the NDP, as an attack on universality. It was widely assumed in 1972 that a number of Liberal backbenchers opposed it on similar grounds and were quite happy to see the legislation die.[60] Liberal MPs returned to Ottawa from their ridings with reports of growing anger among their constituents about the proposed abandonment of the universal allowance.[61] During the fall campaign, Munro vaguely promised changes in FISP after the election,[62] and the January 1973 throne speech confirmed that the government was abandoning FISP and that family allowances would remain universal.[63]

Still, there was no indication that a major budgetary commitment would be made to family allowances. Another series of mostly political influences that made themselves felt the following spring changed this. When it introduced the Orange Paper on 18 April, the government announced that the family allowance would be tripled to $20 per month. This decision had been finalized only shortly before the paper was submitted to cabinet earlier that month.

Again, the NDP had a significant impact on the decision. When the party was consulted about the Orange Paper in late spring, Knowles made it clear that its support was conditional upon family allowances remaining universal, and he encouraged the Liberals to emphasize universal programs during the Social Security Review. As one major policy maker of that period put it in a later interview, "FISP was really the foot in the door for selectivity, and quite clearly this would have been seen as a challenge to the NDP, and we felt that just proceeding with FISP [could] be a cause of our defeat." The NDP's tough stand on family allowances contrasted sharply with its rather vague response to the poverty-related elements of the reform.[64]

The NDP's influence was reinforced by the views of a number of ministers in the Liberal government. When the proposals for a Social Security Review first went to cabinet, they contained no provision for a major new commitment to family allowances, focusing instead on poverty measures. Some cabinet ministers were strongly opposed to this approach, however. As one interviewee noted, this was "in good part for ideological reasons, fundamentally politics. Selectivity created problems among a certain part of the electorate, and middle and high income groups were very vocal and antagonistic to selectivity." As a consequence, the reform proponents refashioned their policy package, including a substantial increase in the universal family allowance as well as measures that were directly poverty-related. When the revised draft was sent back to cabinet, "the family allowance increase went through surprisingly easily." The poverty elements of the paper fared less well.

The third influence was a demand from Castonguay, first voiced in early February, that family allowances be increased to compensate Quebec for the federal government's unilateral decision to raise OAS pensions for the second year in a row. Caught between NDP pressure for an immediate increase in OAS payments and Castonguay's insistence that this would again aggravate distortions in the income security system, the government promised that more money would be available for other programs if Quebec agreed to participate in the Review.[65]

By April, then, it had been established that the poverty-related elements of the Review would be preceded by significant and expensive increases in the two demogrant programs, largely as a result of political influences, in good part emanating from the NDP. The increases were to have a profoundly negative impact on the poverty elements of the Review, its primary *raison d'être*.

Federal Commitment to a Comprehensive Poverty Reform

The federal commitment to an ambitious poverty reform reflected the interjurisdictional and bureaucratic influences described earlier. Political influences played a more limited role.

Interjurisdictional relations.   The social policy impasse with Quebec continued during the summer and autumn of 1972. Indeed, the conflict broadened considerably as other provinces now expressed sympathy for Quebec's point of view. Quebec still wanted control of the entire social security field, and Castonguay promised that he would take advantage of the election campaign to criticize federal social policies.[66]

Meanwhile, Quebec attempted a new strategy in its challenge to the federal government. For the first time since the Victoria conference, where it had been isolated in its opposition to Ottawa, Quebec reached out to the other provinces, using the premiers' conference in early August to seek support from them for a more decentralized view of the country. Bourassa achieved a measure of success: the premiers supported a weakening of federal authority in several areas while demanding more money from Ottawa.[67] As a prominent federal actor at the time put it, the provinces "were constantly knocking on our doors for more money and still asking us to stay away more and more from intervening."

Sympathy for Quebec's position among the English-speaking provinces took another step forward at a meeting of provincial welfare ministers held in Victoria in November. The conference was dominated by Castonguay, who called for a more concerted attack on poverty and for provincial control of the social security field, as well as for more money to be made available by Ottawa as a means to achieving this. The four western provinces, especially Alberta and British Columbia, supported Quebec's position on jurisdiction. Ontario was noncommittal but was seen by federal observers at the meeting as moving towards support for Quebec. Only the Atlantic provinces, especially New Brunswick, expressed serious reservations, fearing that a diminished federal role might reduce income redistribution between provinces.[68]

The conference's final communiqué was only slightly modified from an earlier draft prepared by Quebec officials. It declared that "all provinces see the elimination of poverty as the common and ultimate objective of their income security policies." Accomplishing this goal would require a more integrated social security system. Income security measures "whatever their source of financing, must be determined in the first instance through provincial initiative ... The Ministers agreed that the provinces should have the option, without financial loss, to administer the family allowance program within a provincial social security system." To achieve these objectives, a federal/provincial conference should be held early in 1973.[69] By proposing a social security system better streamlined to attack poverty and by picking the provinces as the logical jurisdiction to organize the system, the Victoria communiqué, agreed to by all provinces, substantially endorsed Quebec's social security agenda.

Federal observers at the conference reported to their superiors in Ottawa that "the agreement among provincial Ministers was more apparent than real," especially since, in their view, only Castonguay knew what he was talking about: "Some ministers did not seem to grasp the real significance of the final statement." Nevertheless, the conference made a major impression on these federal officials. One of them observed confidentially at the time that "from Quebec's point of view the conference was particularly successful ... Clearly there is growing provincial agreement that the lack of integration of income security measures is one of the main if not the main problem facing Welfare Ministers, even though most provinces are not yet prepared to accept the Quebec call for provincial legislative primacy in social security matters. It would seem that increasingly the dialogue between the federal government and the provinces in regard to income security will be conducted using the ideas and concepts introduced by Mr. Castonguay."[70]

The federal cabinet agreed. By the end of November, it had decided to launch the Social Security Review to find ways to implement a guaranteed annual income. Marc Lalonde's appointment as minister of National Health and Welfare was announced as the provincial welfare ministers were winding up their meeting, and an enthusiastic Castonguay immediately sent him a congratulatory telegram; progress, he thought, would now be possible. Al Johnson was asked to become Lalonde's deputy minister to guide the Review.

The main motivation for launching poverty reform was the growing federal/provincial crisis in social policy. The federal reformers accepted the substance of Quebec's poverty agenda while denying its premise of provincial supremacy in the area of social security. The agreement of the provinces to a continuing federal role in that area would be secured by promising them enough flexibility to enable them to meet their own program objectives. In one of his first public statements as minister (in December), Lalonde hinted at this strategy: "I share the ideas of Claude Castonguay and the ideas of other provincial ministers about an integrated social policy ... I think there is agreement on the fundamental objectives of such a policy." Lalonde did not, however, endorse the provinces' desire to control social security, promising instead that "if the provinces are ready to continue talks, so am I. If they want to wait, I can wait too. You can't be more flexible than that."[71]

The notes included in Lalonde's briefing book for the February 1973 welfare ministers' conference elaborated on this strategy. They discussed federal objectives for the next conference, scheduled for April. A main goal of the April meeting would be "to set the stage for a joint review of Canada's social security system, and ultimately for an appropriate balance in federal and provincial involvement in the administration of the system." What an "appropriate balance" entailed was also made clear in the document: "[Provincial] welfare ministers should be brought to recognize that only a common approach among themselves, *coupled with federal leadership*, will make possible the rationalization of the social security system." The provinces would be reminded that "the federal government is more likely to be able to allocate incremental revenues to social security than are provincial governments."[72]

Castonguay's position, grounded in the principle of provincial primacy in the rationalization of social security, was the obvious obstacle. A key component of the "federal-provincial objective" would be "to reveal to the provinces enough of the federal approach to provincial flexibility (provincial variation of federal payments, within broad limits) as to engage their support, and to throw into question the need for Mr. Castonguay's extreme approach (federal withdrawal from the whole social security field)." The major potential pitfall of the April meeting, furthermore, would be "Mr. Castonguay's efforts to achieve in part or in whole his objective of transferring to the provinces the federal elements of the social security system (per Victoria Constitutional Conference)." Three main strategies were suggested to counteract this: first, "the provinces [should] be urged to discuss the system that would be best for the Canadian people before they discussed which government should do what"; second, "the design of federal proposals should be such as to give Castonguay a victory – giving him credit for his pioneering via the Castonguay-Nepveu Report"; and third, "the Victoria alliance of Welfare Ministers should be broken by making it clear there are equally flexible but better federal-provincial arrangements than those proposed by Mr. Castonguay."[73]

The selection of Lalonde and Johnson to conduct the Review is also noteworthy. Neither had any background in the traditional welfare sector, and their accession to positions of responsibility in NHW further eroded the fraternity that had once existed there. But both had extensive experience in dealing with interjurisdictional problems. Lalonde, elected for the Liberals in 1972, had been primarily responsible for constitutional bargaining with Quebec while at the Prime Minister's Office; Johnson, for his part, had had extensive experience in provincial administration in Saskatchewan, in federal/provincial relations during his stint at the department of Finance in the 1960s, and in developing the federal government's position on social policy during the constitutional debates. The appointment of these two men was in itself enough to signal to the provinces that social security reform had become a high priority of the federal government.

Central agencies and supradepartmental policy making.   In August 1972, a number of PCO officials met with Johnson to explore the possibility of developing an alternative to FISP, since the latter measure would clearly not be passed in its present form. This led to a renewed interest, within the central agencies, in Johnson's poverty reform suggestions, which had been in limbo since 1970. A number of papers, largely inspired by Johnson's ideas, were prepared and, shortly before the election was called on 1 September, turned over to Lalonde, then still at the PMO.[74] These central agency documents were therefore available to cabinet when it made its decision to launch reform.

Johnson was highly regarded by Trudeau, who had entrusted him with important tasks in the past; several former officials interviewed by the author noted that Johnson obviously played a major role in launching reform and setting its agenda. Before being offered the deputy ministership, he had been asked to make two separate presentations to groups of ministers and central agency officials on his 1970 poverty reform proposals. Johnson explained his model, which was still centred on a GAI and complementary employment services. That model became the starting point for the Review.

In February 1973, Johnson was asked to prepare the document that would set forth the federal government's objectives for the Review – the Orange Paper. Writing the Orange Paper was "a personal thing" for Johnson, but he did require assistance from officials whom he could trust and who would be able to engage in broad-based and systematic policy making. Johnson thought that these skills were in short supply among the existing NHW staff, and he was therefore authorized to overhaul the department. He reorganized NHW's policy-making capacities around the planning officials who had worked for him at Treasury Board and around others who also had a training in economics and statistics.[75] Few had any experience or expertise in the welfare sector.

The newcomers were employed in a new branch – Policy Research and Long-Range Planning (Welfare) – with Russell Robinson as its assistant deputy minister (ADM). Most of the existing research capacity on the welfare side of the department was incorporated into a separate branch – Policy and Program Development and Coordination (Welfare) – with John Osborne, a long-time NHW employee, as its ADM. Robinson's group was expected to provide the focal point for the Review by coordinating the activities associated with it and conducting its central part, income security reform. While Osborne eventually gained Johnson's confidence, his branch was not judged capable of guiding the Review. From this point, then, the key policy-making body at NHW consisted of a group of people with the training and career experience appropriate for planning officials engaging in supradepartmental and systematic decision making. That they were inclined to use these skills was made clear in a paper written by Robinson some eighteen months after the beginning of the Review: "The idea was to rethink the basic concepts, examine the evolving nature of social security issues, and work from basic principles – i.e., 'from the top down' – in pursuit of viable reform proposals. Constraints resulting from potential costs, administrative exigencies, existing program patterns, and finally, difficulties with respect to financial arrangements or jurisdictional issues, were to emerge as the issues (and choices) became more and more specific. They were not to encumber the first stages of the review. The evolution was to be from the 'desirable' to the 'practical', with as little departure from the former as possible."[76] This style had already suffused the January 1973 throne speech, which called for a review of "Canada's total social security system."[77] Similarly, the briefing papers prepared later that month referred to the need "to open up the discussions which will lead to the reconsideration and reorganization of Canada's social security system."[78]

The secondary influence of politics. Party politics played a role in the launching of poverty reform in 1972–73, but in a far more indirect and general way than did the organizational factors. Immediately after the October 1972 election, the NDP used its influence over the Liberal minority government to demand improvements in demogrant programs; the evidence available suggests that the NDP was silent on the question of social security reforms aimed directly at the poor. While Vernon Harder has established that the NDP discussed the Social Security Review with Lalonde, he found that family allowances were the only program about which they were specific and that their influence was used to preserve and enhance that universal measure.[79] In addition, the New Democrats had not addressed the value of a GAI during the election campaign or in the months leading up to it; indeed, they had said much more about this during the 1968 campaign. Later on, after the Orange Paper was released in April, Lalonde asserted emphatically, in a television interview, that "there had been no previous consultation with the NDP at this time in this respect."[80]

Despite the NDP's apparent lack of interest, during the months following the election senior ministers and central agency officials assumed that the Liberals' minority-government status required a greater commitment in the social security field in general. As one of these participants later acknowledged, "we felt that, certainly, one way of assuring the support of the NDP ... was to give a high priority to social security, which would allow us to gain some time politically, because while we were working on it the NDP would give us their support, if we didn't make too many mistakes otherwise." The NDP's influence on poverty-related reforms was therefore secondary and indirect: it only served to encourage a poverty reform package that had already been developed in considerable detail within the Quebec and federal governments and that was now a compelling objective in inter- and intragovernmental contexts. The substantial increases in demogrant payments demanded by the NDP ended up severely circumscribing progress on poverty reform. On balance, then, the impact of the NDP and of other political factors on poverty reform was negative.

THE ORANGE PAPER

During the spring of 1973, three additional factors shaped the Review before its launching in April. First, the substantial costs resulting from cabinet's decision to expand the two demogrant programs meant that there could be no immediate funding commitments in the area of poverty relief. Second, the Finance department's opposition to the

Review was far more vociferous than its resistance to CAP had been in the 1960s, even though the economic crisis would not be felt fully until 1975. This opposition was already apparent as the Orange Paper made its way to cabinet. Third, several heterogeneous interests impinged upon the reform at this time. One made a positive contribution to the scope of the reform; but that factor, and several others, also contributed substantially to its fragmentation.

Some of these influences emerged as the Orange Paper was working its way through the bureaucracy and through cabinet, and they had a direct bearing on the specific proposals laid out in the paper. Others were reflected in the paper itself. And yet additional factors appeared only after the document was released.

On the Road to Cabinet

The impact of the demogrants.   The substantial and costly increases in demogrant payments became an immediate constraint on poverty reform. Tripling the value of family allowances would cost the federal government $800 million annually. The short-term cost of the increase in OAS pensions was smaller but when combined with the pre-election increase, it was also expected to tally up to about $800 million annually by 1975.[81] Lalonde and Johnson had not originally envisaged these demogrant increases, but the largely political influences described above made them all but inevitable.

Poverty reform was Johnson and Lalonde's objective, and they wanted to proceed as quickly as possible. In the first version sent to cabinet in April, the Orange Paper therefore set out a specific program for poverty reform; as noted by one participant, "it included all the answers." When the paper was discussed in cabinet, however, "all hell broke loose … It was manifestly unacceptable and we were in a state of considerable tension." Resistance by the department of Finance contributed to this state of affairs, but the major opposition came from a number of ministers who argued that they had already allocated huge sums to social security and were not prepared to give it more money from existing revenues or to raise taxes in order to acquire the extra funds required. As one former NHW official noted, "we were finally authorized to talk about the principle and consult with the provinces but not authorized to put forward a specific program." The department would have to wait until money became available through general increases in tax revenues to pay for poverty reform.

Instead of a specific program, the final version of the Orange Paper offered only "propositions" and "strategies" to be discussed with the provinces.[82] It noted that poverty reform would be implemented over a three- to five-year period. The justification for the timetable was that it would assure financing "within existing levels of taxation." Lalonde gave his provincial counterparts a frank explanation of the timetable at the *in camera* meeting of federal and provincial welfare ministers in April. He stressed the need to work within existing expenditure limits and told his colleagues, some of whom were impatient for immediate action, that "I don't think it would be very realistic, considering the direct addition of federal expenditures by this particular program alone [family allowances], to expect for next year a very substantial increment in terms of contributions by the federal government to provincial shared programs in the field of social security." He then noted that constant pressure to increase OAS pensions also left little money for other priorities that are "politically less sought after."[83]

Many Review participants, both among traditional welfare officials and in the non-governmental sector, were dismayed when they heard that the time horizon for reform was being pushed so far into the future: in three or more years, circumstances might no longer be propitious for reform. For the time being, however, it was only clear that the demogrant increases had postponed poverty reform.

The role of Finance.   Vehement opposition to the Review also came from Finance, especially from its deputy minister, Simon Reisman. As in the 1960s, Finance's view was based on the assumption that poverty reform would be bad for economic performance, which would best be served by minimizing state intervention; it reflected the department's historical market-oriented accumulation strategy.

An intense animosity quickly developed between Johnson and Reisman. At one cabinet discussion of the Orange Paper, the two men "were extremely vigorous with one another," in the words of a former NHW official, and almost came to blows. The Finance minister, John Turner, and Lalonde played secondary roles in the debate, although each firmly supported his deputy's position. The intensity of the confrontation made future conflict over the Review a virtual certainty.

Beyond expressing general opposition, Reisman created one specific obstruction to the Review. The income tax system was one possible option for delivering income security to the working poor, but Reisman used his control over tax policy to prevent NHW's gaining access to this possibility. For the time being, at least, the most suitable mechanism for federal delivery of income supplementation was not available.

Finance also had two specific objections to the Orange Paper. The first was fiscal: Finance wanted to restrain spending. In 1973, unemployment was rising, and Finance was concerned about rising inflation; increased spending could worsen the situation. These concerns were heightened by the Liberals' minority-government situation. Finance officials believed that the NDP's influence was "causing instability" because it tended to diminish cabinet's fiscal consciousness. Second, and perhaps more important, was a specific aversion to the idea of a guaranteed annual income. Finance viewed the GAI as a threat to work incentives. According to Reisman, the employment measures proposed in the Orange Paper amounted to "guaranteed employment"; he believed that a "guaranteed income" would also discourage people from exercising any initiative. A GAI could only undermine the incentives fostered by the private market working on its own.

State fragmentation: a positive contribution.   Unlike traditional welfare officials, NHW deputy minister Johnson did not envisage a major role for the federal government in social services. Thus the rough draft of the Orange Paper circulated in early 1973 did not mention them. Despite the bitterness felt by long-time NHW officials at the infusion of central agency officials into controlling positions in the department, Brian Iverson, ADM for the Social Services Program Branch, and two of his assistants decided to "jump on the bandwagon" by proposing to Johnson that the Review be extended to include social services. They were supported in this by others among the department's established staff. Although Johnson appears to have been reluctant to include services in the Review, they persuaded him to do so.

This difference of views went beyond the selection of specific programs that should be included in a poverty reform: it also reflected different philosophies of reform. The Orange Paper made it clear that Johnson wanted to place the Social Security Review in the context of economic growth and employment, thus reflecting its highly articulate liberalism. While not rejecting this objective, welfare officials did not give economic objectives as much attention. In the words of a Review participant, "the social workers believed in people; that meant they had a perception of the importance of social services that was terribly important, but they were also rather soft on the questions of incentives and quantification, etc. ... They were a little bit 'dewy eyed'." In later interviews, some of the key welfare officials involved said that they managed to convince Johnson to include services only "because he saw [them] in terms of a relationship to employment ...

The only justification for services was to get people back to work."
For their own part, however, welfare officials believed that services
had a relevance well outside this context, and they used their influence to move social service reform away from purely employment-related objectives.

Fragmented state structures could, on the whole, be expected to
inhibit policy making, but in this case they contributed to its broadening. Examples of the more typically negative consequences of state
fragmentation appeared soon after the Orange Paper's release.

The Orange Paper: Analysing the Text

The Orange Paper did two things. First, it set forth the rationale and
the desired *modus operandi* for the Review; these tasks were largely
accomplished in the paper's first sixteen and last four pages, respectively. And second, the paper presented the specific policy changes
that the federal government hoped to discuss with the provinces.

Rationale and methods: the influence of organizations.   In arguing the
case for poverty reform, the Orange Paper followed closely the inter-jurisdictional strategy recommended in the February briefing papers.
It also reiterated the arguments that Johnson had made for federal
involvement in the income security field in his 1969 constitutional
documents; it therefore reflected the two organizational influences
that underlay the government's commitment to poverty reform. The
Orange Paper insisted that the federal government must play an
important role in the Review, relating this to the poverty-alleviation
argument raised in Johnson's earlier document: "The Parliament of
Canada must continue to play a role in the income security system
… it has a responsibility to combat poverty by way of a fair distribution of income among people across Canada." As the January
documents had proposed, though, the paper also promised greater
flexibility: "We are anxious to avoid that degree of precision in what
we suggest which might leave the impression of 'cut and dried' or
'take it or leave it' proposals."[84] The Orange Paper therefore clearly
followed the strategy laid out in earlier documents: the federal government would secure a major role for itself in social security, but it
would also display greater flexibility in order to prevent the provinces
from adopting the alternative jurisdictional stand taken by Castonguay.

The paper also clearly embraced a rationalist approach to reform:
"We have sought, in developing our proposals, to comprehend the
whole sweep of social security policy and to develop a comprehensive,

logical and hopefully imaginative approach to this field. We have sought, too, to exercise our ingenuity in finding new, and if necessary radical, federal-provincial or constitutional arrangements, in order to achieve the kind of integrated social security system which will best serve the needs of the Canadian people."[85]

Like Johnson's constitutional papers and his Treasury Board memorandum, the Orange Paper saw the alleviation of poverty as the main goal of the remodelling of the system. This more integrated attack on poverty would require a high degree of coordination between existing policies and the new measures. A remodelled social security system must integrate the income support plans, including existing measures such as job creation and training, family allowances, minimum wages, and social assistance, as well as any new program that might emerge from the Review. It must deal with "the problem of the interrelationships between [these income support programs] and Canada's social insurance plans," including unemployment insurance and the Canada Pension Plan.[86]

Liberal policy legacies.   Among the various proposals for social policy reform made during the postwar period, the Orange Paper stands out as an eloquent testimonial to the normative premises of Canada's welfare state. Incentives were the key preoccupation. The reformed social security system must "operate in harmony with, not in opposition to, the motive forces of the economy." With existing assistance arrangements, "there is too little ... incentive to get off social assistance ... The social assistance may be higher than what one could earn at or near the minimum wage ... And ... if one does take a part-time or temporary job ... one loses, in most provinces, nearly $1 of social aid for every $1 of income from employment." The paper's specific proposals were designed to eradicate this problem by advocating "incentives to work and a greater emphasis on the need to get people who are on social aid back to work." For the working poor, "it would therefore be desirable to establish a *general income supplementation plan* ... to provide them with an incentive to keep on working rather than giving up and living on social aid. The supplementation ... should provide a continuing incentive to increase earnings from work."[87]

The Orange Paper also developed a model of the "ideal" social security system that laid primary emphasis on the private labour market as the main source of livelihood for Canadians. Ideally, employment would be the primary source of income: "For people who are of working age, and are able to work, there would be employment at least at a living wage. To ensure that a living wage is paid, the state would legislate a minimum wage. If the minimum wage were sufficient to support small family units only, income supplements would be available to meet the costs of child-raising in larger families." The next element of the system would be social insurance programs, financed from savings, "to meet the contingencies of life." Beyond this, "if someone somehow failed to receive an adequate 'income through employment' ... or 'income from savings', additional income support measures would be available ... The supplementary income support measures would be associated with social and employment services needed to assist in returning to employment those who were able to do so – services such as training, placement, rehabilitation and counselling."[88] Thus the program proposals set forth in the second half of the Paper were conceived as an integrated approach to meeting need within a context where employment in the private economy was the primary and preferred source of livelihood; social security reform was intended to enhance the attachment of recipients to the labour market, not erode it.

The Orange Paper also gave evidence of pragmatic liberalism: Canada's limited commitments to full employment and to universal and contributory measures necessitated the extension of poverty-oriented programs. The clearest example of this is found in the description of "Deficiencies in Canada's Social Security System." The first deficiency "arises from the simplistic assumption that Canada can, at any and every point in time, expect to achieve full employment."[89] While some conservative welfare states have achieved this goal and while it is a hallmark of social democratic welfare states,[90] the Orange Paper accepted the premise that Canada would remain a high-unemployment society indefinitely. Second, "incomes of people who *are* employed oftentimes are not adequate to meet the family's needs." This is partly due to modest minimum wage levels, and inadequate universal income security measures. The other deficiencies mentioned included the "inadequate levels" of benefits under the country's social insurance measures.[91] Also, even if the paper's generous family-allowance proposals were implemented, "there would still be families whose income ... would fall below an acceptable minimum." Poverty-oriented measures, such as income-tested supplementation, would be required for these employable persons.[92]

The proposals.   The second half of the Orange Paper translated principles into specific proposals; because cabinet would not endorse specific program commitments, these took the form of fourteen tentative "propositions" grouped into several "strategies," three of which were of direct concern to the poverty sector. In keeping with the liberal preference for the private market, the first strategy dealt with employment. The economy's inability to create enough jobs was a particular problem for certain groups of people – older workers, residents of depressed areas, and those lacking appropriate skills. The employment strategy envisioned "helping them equip themselves for employment, and providing them with employment opportunities which apparently are lacking." Therefore, "governments should consider the establishment of a community employment program, its purpose would be to provide socially useful employment to people who have been unemployed for an extended period of time."[93]

The core of the Orange Paper was its proposal for an income supplementation strategy, which included guaranteed income measures; indeed, income supplementation remained the primary focus of the Review, especially from 1973 to 1975. Like the Castonguay-Nepveu Report, the Orange Paper proposed two distinct income-tested programs – income support for those who were unemployable, and income supplementation for the employed and those expected to work.[94] Support and supplementation differed in two important respects: 1) support would have a guarantee level high enough to provide its recipients with a livelihood; supplementation would not, since it was seen as a supplement to earned income; and 2) supplementation, on the other hand, would be subject to a much lower offset or tax-back rate – in other words, recipients would retain a larger percentage of benefits as earned income rose above the guarantee level. This was because work incentives, which were intended to be a pervasive feature of the revised system, would be offered to employable claimants in a monetary form; in the case of the unemployable, for whom monetary incentives made little sense, they would be provided through employment measures and services.

The Orange Paper's preference for a two-tier support/supplementation program provides further evidence of its liberalism. Esping-Andersen observes that liberalism's objective of maximizing market dependence implies a dualism that carefully segregates those who are not in the labour force from those who are.[95] The two-tiered design is very much an embodiment of this liberal dualism. Charles Rachlis notes that this design in the Orange Paper "sharpens the distinction [between work and welfare] by effectively establishing two classes of people within the social security system: those who work and those who do not." This reflects a concern for "the 'motive forces' of capitalist market operation, and the determination that the government would not interfere with them."[96]

The third key proposal was for "a social and employment services strategy." The services covered by this strategy were expected to assist in restoring employment skills or the capacity to earn an adequate income: "The broad spectrum of social and employment services required to make the employment and income supplementation strategies fully effective and efficient should be extended and improved – training, counselling, placement, rehabilitation, special work situations, homemaker and child care services."[97]

The Orange Paper set forth a timetable for implementing the three strategies. The overall design of reform should be settled in two years; implementation would require three to five years and would be undertaken "within existing levels of taxation." The one explicit exception was that priority should be given to the immediate passage of the family allowance increases and to certain changes in the Canada Pension Plan; the recently passed Old Age Security increases were another, tacit, precondition of the reform.[98]

State Heterogeneity and the Fragmentation of Reform

The heterogeneity of interests within the federal government initially had a positive influence on the Review in the area of social services. However, it also had three negative consequences for the Review at this early stage. This negative effect was not reflected in the Orange Paper but appeared shortly after its release, and it led to a substantial fragmentation of what was supposed to be a systematic and supradepartmental review.

First, the restructuring of NHW created considerable tension within the department between the old and the new guard. The former group included those who had considerable experience in the welfare field, while the latter comprised the academically trained economists and statisticians in the new research branch. One newcomer to the department recalled in an interview that "we used to scratch and fight like cats and dogs ... I found it very uncomfortable, quite unsettling and annoying and threatening." He was only able to proceed with his work because Johnson made it clear that he would not tolerate such disruptions and "dissipation of energy." Another referred to the old guard as an obstacle to reform. The latter, in turn, considered themselves to be under attack by the newcomers – Johnson, in particular. Another former official felt that he was treated by Johnson as "the whipping boy for the old school." Yet another was considered "suspicious and hostile" because of his diminished role in the department after 1973. In general, this group was "concerned" about the remodelling of the department.

This tension led to wastage of time and energy on settling intradepartmental conflicts between groups with quite different dispositions. The newcomers saw a central role for a GAI in a reformed system, while the older group wanted more emphasis on social services. They also felt that the newcomers were conducting an overly rationalist reform and that incremental changes in CAP would have been a more sensible way to proceed. The new guard, by contrast, felt that the established group resisted change because they had a vested interest in existing programs and because they lacked vision.

A more tangible result of this divergence was that, for all intents and purposes, the income-security and social service components of the Review were conducted in completely separate branches of the department, with only the deputy minister bridging the gap between them. Income security was handled by the new guard in Robinson's branch, while the service reform, once it began in earnest, was largely conducted from the Social Services Program Branch under the guidance of social welfare professionals.

The second fragmentation was even more complete. In the reformers's opinion, it would be pointless to antagonize the Manpower and Immigration department by having the employment strategy implemented by NHW. Consequently, it was assumed from the outset that Manpower, which was responsible for existing employment programs, would control the strategy. While the deputy minister of NHW was at least able to bridge the gap between the other two strategies within his department, he could not do the same for the employment strategy. Some NHW officials, especially in the old guard, were of the opinion that Manpower officials had traditionally ignored the needs of welfare recipients and that they were unlikely to develop much interest in the employment strategy. As a result, NHW hoped to influence the strategy, but Manpower never lost its monopoly. Like the old guard at NHW, Manpower bureaucrats saw the new guard as "ivory tower" economists with "idealistic" and "intensely rational" notions about how jobs could be created. With their practical experience in the field, Manpower officials naturally believed that they escaped this curse. Idealism was thought to be reflected in the employment propositions of the Orange Paper itself, which were "quite unrealistic" and which could never be implemented without requiring that all existing programs of relevance in the Manpower department be dismantled. During the Review, Manpower officials also clashed with the old guard in NHW, rekindling a long-standing antagonism between the two groups.

A third type of fragmentation led to the effective exclusion of unemployment insurance from the Review. UI had become a political minefield; the federal reformers hoped to change this by developing an income support program that would cover those who would be excluded from a UI program based on sound, actuarial, insurance principles.[99] This again reflected their very liberal conception of social security. Johnson had always been suspicious of the 1971 reform of the Unemployment Insurance Commission (UIC) and considered his GAI a better way of filling the needs it was designed to meet.[100] Senior bureaucratic and political actors from some provinces (especially Quebec) concurred. But for Johnson it was clear from the beginning that "it would not be possible to include in the review a re-examination of Unemployment Insurance. The new UI plan had only just been enacted, and it was still the subject of great controversy and change."[101] Bryce Mackasey, the Labour minister, resisted tampering with his program, supported in this by other ministers; and UIC officials were suspicious of the Review throughout.[102] Mackasey's position in the cabinet was no doubt considerably strengthened by the fact that the NDP approved of the UI extensions and would have been unhappy to see them jeopardized. For Johnson, "what was wrong with the *Unemployment Insurance Act* of 1970 was precisely that it was charged with some of the income support/supplementation tasks that are properly a part of a guaranteed annual income, but not properly a part of a contributory, wage-related social insurance plan."[103] While some limited coordination with UIC was attempted during the Review, nothing of consequence emerged from this effort. The exclusion of unemployment insurance was a disappointment to both federal and provincial actors, and it limited the potential comprehensiveness of the Review. It was a clear example of the barriers to supradepartmental policy making created by the very institutionalized cabinet system that made possible initiatives of such breadth.

CONCLUSION

The Orange Paper was tabled in the House of Commons on 23 April 1973. It received considerable media coverage, although the immediate and dramatic increase in family allowances attracted far more attention than did the poverty-related elements of the paper. Castonguay understandably "took a certain amount of pride" in observing how close the income security elements of the paper were to his own proposals of 1971; his enthusiastic response made it quite likely that the provinces would accept the document as a basis for a federal/provincial reform.[104] This was confirmed at the welfare ministers' meeting of 25–27 April.

The Orange Paper was a comprehensive response to the new poverty reform agenda that emerged in Canada in the late 1960s and early 1970s. These concerns reflected both societal and organizational imperatives. Regarding the former, the agenda was shaped by political class influences. Despite the significant program innovations that came into being during that period, Canada's welfare state remained predominantly liberal, retaining a prominent place for targeted social security measures. This persistent liberalism made Canada an appropriate environment for a characteristically liberal rediscovery of poverty and for the associated development of a reform agenda centred on the GAI concept. Accordingly, a number of federally sponsored studies, as well as a thorough policy review by the Quebec government, advanced a reform agenda largely based on the GAI. Their proposals reflected specific liberal policy legacies – an attachment to the ideological heritage of liberalism, with its focus on incentives; and a pragmatic calculation of the need for selective social security reforms in Canada's liberal context. The Orange Paper itself provides the most eloquent testimony of its ideological debt. Also, there was little political interest in poverty reform during the first Trudeau government; the development of such a commitment during his second government owed something to the atmosphere created by the minority situation, but it was largely stimulated by intergovernmental and bureaucratic influences. The NDP, a party broadly advancing working class interests, had a very nearly exclusive preference for reforms in universal social security measures. This reflects the limited solidarity attached to poverty-relief measures and the preference of social democratic parties for universality. Functional class influences were not yet decisive in the Review, but they had already made an appearance. The department of Finance substantially weakened federal commitments in the Orange Paper and circumscribed their possible direction; this was done in pursuit of the market-oriented, *laissez-faire* accumulation strategy that typified Finance's philosophy.

The Review was also powerfully shaped by the newly emergent institutionalized organization of the federal and Quebec governments. Organizations defined the channels along which the liberal legacy moulded reform. The earliest poverty studies reflected the increased interest of governments in broad and systematic policy analysis, provided by newly prestigious expertise in the social sciences. Indeed, the GAI concept itself reflected this influence: it was an economist's idea, the product of the application of economists' skills. The emergence of a reform agenda within the federal government after 1970 followed the substantial remodelling of federal institutions undertaken by Prime Minister Trudeau. The seminal Orange Paper was produced by planning officials in central agencies. In part, it represented a strategic response by the federal authorities to increased interjurisdictional tensions in the wake of the failed Victoria

Charter. It was also a systematic and supradepartmental initiative by its central agency sponsors. The proposed reforms self-consciously departed from an integrated, ideal concept of what a social security system should look like, and they went well beyond the departmental responsibilities of Health and Welfare. Reflecting the tendency of institutionalized structures to fragment the very supradepartmental initiatives that they foster, bureaucratic heterogeneity led to an important extension of the reform agenda in the matter of social services, but it also ensured that this part of the reform – and many others – would be pursued in quite different bureaux, under the control of different organizational actors, and in pursuit of divergent objectives.

CHAPTER SIX

From Promise to Crisis, 1973–75

Meetings in February and April 1973 revealed deep tensions about the Social Security Review among federal and provincial welfare ministers. First, the breadth and high profile of the reforms included in the Orange Paper meant that responses from the English-speaking provinces often reflected government-wide priorities, including the ideological preferences of the party in power. Partisan diversity created tension in federal/provincial discussions and impeded agreement. Second, the officials who took part in these events had different professional backgrounds; they had not experienced the bonding that an institution like the Canadian Welfare Council had fostered and that had facilitated policy agreement during the 1960s. The federal officials who guided the Review came from central agencies and brought with them a rationalist philosophy; Quebec officials tended to have a similar approach and background. In most of the smaller eight provinces, by contrast, public welfare officials still held sway. They often retained the incremental-reform ethic that had created the Canada Assistance Plan and saw the gradual reform of CAP as the most realistic way to achieve change. Many of the old guard at Health and Welfare were in sympathy with this approach. The federal new guard and officials from the smaller provinces were often at odds with one another during the Review over the choice and implementation of priorities. These bureaucratic tensions compounded the political ones that arose when the goals developed by provincial politicians diverged from those of their federal counterparts.

AGREEMENT AND FRAGMENTATION

An Incomplete Federal/Provincial Consensus

At the February and April meetings, the provincial welfare ministers accepted the Orange Paper as a basis for discussion, but there were already ominous signs of divergence. Not surprisingly, given the origins of the Review, Quebec's goals were closest to those of the federal government. Quebec agreed with the Orange Paper's two-tier proposal for income support and supplementation, and shared Johnson's indifference to social service reform.[1]

Ontario was less enthusiastic about the Review, reflecting a weaker commitment to social reform on the part of its long-entrenched Progressive Conservative government. The latter wanted to proceed with income security reform cautiously and to target any new support program at "deserving" categories of recipients, especially the handicapped. Provincial treasury officials played an important role in developing Ontario's poverty reform agenda. Reflecting this influence, the provincial government proposed that new income security benefits be delivered through the tax system. Ontario believed there was no urgency in reforming social services.

Alberta's Conservative government was even more reluctant about reform. It was sceptical about the merits of a full support/supplementation program because of its potential cost and impact on work incentives. Like Ontario, Alberta proposed that a new support program be targeted, at least initially, at the handicapped.[2]

While the Alberta and Ontario governments were more cautious about reform than their federal and Quebec counterparts, those of British Columbia, Saskatchewan, and Manitoba – all of them under the banner of the NDP and with welfare programs that were still under the control of traditional welfare officials – were impatient to move further and faster. They supported a generous (and expensive) one-tier income supplementation program – that is, a program that did not have two separate components for employable and unemployable recipients. They also believed that the Review should include a major expansion of social services. They wanted social insurance programs to be integrated with any new income security program developed as a result of the Review. The NDP governments were impatient to begin reforms immediately and to implement them gradually – not to wait several years, as envisaged by the Orange Paper. Their strong commitment to the one-tier approach and to the integration of disparate social security measures suggests that their position broadly reflected a social democratic commitment to universality.[3]

Party ideology played a less obvious role in the poorer Atlantic provinces. Welfare officials remained in charge of the provincial departments responsible for social assistance and, for the most part, shared the general desire for reform, but they were also concerned about its cost. Still, Nova Scotia and Prince Edward Island were enthusiastic about both the income-security and social service elements of the Orange Paper – while giving priority to the latter – but they expected that the federal government would absorb most of the additional costs of any new program. New Brunswick was more reluctant about reform.[4]

Lalonde and Johnson responded to the views of the provinces by saying that the federal position was not carved in stone and could be revised once the Review had proceeded further. In fact, however, until 1975 federal policy makers never seriously considered anything other than a two-tier model, and they clearly preferred a system that would avoid targeting benefits at specific categories of recipients. On the reform timetable, the federal authorities were adamant: no interim incremental changes would be possible in the first two years (1973–75), as funds were unavailable for that purpose. Johnson was also concerned that if such changes were implemented before the question of program design was settled, this could threaten the comprehensive nature of the Review.[5] Ever loyal to their own grand design, the federal participants would not compromise.

A Fragmented Machinery

Meeting in May 1973, federal and provincial welfare deputy ministers set up the administrative machinery for the Review. At about the same time, the internal arrangements needed to conduct the Review within the federal government were established. Both developments revealed how much the professional diversity of the participants in the Review contributed to the fragmentation of reform.

At the May meeting, Johnson laid out the federal proposals for the Review's structure. Deputy ministers of welfare at both levels would form a "continuing committee on social security" to coordinate inter-jurisdictional bureaucratic activity for the Review. The committee would report directly to the ministers of welfare. And reporting to the committee would be bureaucratic working parties – one for each strategy outlined in the Orange Paper. These subcommittees would conduct much of the technical discussion between governments. The provinces generally accepted Johnson's proposal.[6]

While the working parties were expected to coordinate their efforts, it was already clear that their main point of contact would be through the deputy ministers. From the outset, therefore, the design of the Review implied significant fragmentation of policy formulation. Unlike CAP, the Review transcended professional and departmental boundaries; different strategies required different kinds of expertise and, particularly at the federal level, were to be executed through different departments.

Everyone agreed that income security would be dealt with in one working party – to be called the "working party on income maintenance" – because this matter was quite distinct from others in the Review. There was disagreement about whether employment and social services should be covered by the same working party, but it was eventually decided to keep them separate. A number of provinces stressed that they would be using different professionals in these two fields – a point that was made even more forcefully by Jack Manion, who represented the Manpower department at the meeting. For his part, Johnson noted that "we [in Health and Welfare] did not want to get into the employment business ... therefore these people [at Manpower] must assume this responsibility and anything we have to contribute we'll contribute to Jack and his people." He also observed that the relation between social and employment services "has been an issue of some difficulty within the federal government ... and we've got hell from [Manpower] for years ... for failing to coordinate." Manion added that "as far as the social services ... are concerned, I am not sure they are part of the examination we want to do in [the employment working party]." Consequently, there would be separate working parties for income maintenance, employment, and social services.[7]

Similar fragmenting tendencies were present in the structures erected to coordinate the Review at the federal level. In chapter 5 it was noted that the Review was fragmented from the outset within the federal government because each of its three main components was conducted in a different part of the bureaucracy – income security, in the new policy branch of NHW; social services, in its Social Services Program Branch (SSPB); and employment, in the Manpower department. A steering committee, which met approximately twice a week, was created within NHW to coordinate federal efforts and thus overcome this fragmentation, but it had limited success.[8]

The first constraint on the steering committee was that it was unable to overcome the divergence that existed within NHW between the new and the old guard; as a result, there was considerable friction among committee members. A second limitation was the fact that the committee played no role in the employment strategy, which was controlled by Manpower and Immigration. NHW created an internal office to maintain contact with Manpower about the employment strategy, but Manpower largely ignored it. Manpower set up its own internal committee, under Ivo Krupka, to guide its part of the Review. Unlike their counterparts in NHW, Manpower's officials mostly had a professional background in labour market policy.

FROM PHONEY WAR TO
DEBACLE

The Orange Paper proposed a two-year "developmental" phase for
the Social Security Review. As Lalonde admitted in private conver-
sations with provincial officials, the political priority attached to the
broader changes in social security meant that no money would be
available for poverty-related reforms until 1975. Serious discussion of
income maintenance reform did not begin until late in 1974, and
social service reform had to wait until 1975. Thus during its first year
the Social Security Review had a "phoney" quality, concentrating as
it did on an uncoordinated set of policy changes not directly related
to poverty.

When poverty discussions did get under way, they became mired
in intractable conflicts. From the outset, there was little effort to
coordinate the three strategies or to reconcile them with existing
social insurance programs. Each strategy became the subject of substantial friction between competing federal and provincial objectives
and, at times, among rival interests within the federal bureaucracy.
There was also intense partisan debate about the liberal character of
the federal proposals, and Finance maintained its market-based
opposition to reform.

Income Support and Supplementation

There were three distinct phases in the segment of the Review
dealing with income support and supplementation. From May 1973
to November 1974, the Review proceeded in a federal/provincial context, where it focused only very gradually on poverty issues; from
November 1974 until the following February, the focus shifted to the
federal cabinet; and for the next three months after that, it returned
to the interjurisdictional arena.

A slow beginning, May 1973–November 1974.   Three conflicts arose in
the earliest income-maintenance discussions. First, the politically
driven focus on family-allowance changes and the Canada Pension
Plan did not go unchallenged. The NDP governments, led by that of
British Columbia, protested the two-year hiatus imposed on income
security reform by the Orange Paper. When, in October 1973,
Johnson sent his provincial counterparts the agenda for upcoming
federal/provincial meetings about the Review, the main items were
the Canada Pension Plan and family allowances. British Columbia,
supported by Manitoba and Saskatchewan, demanded major changes

in the agenda: it wanted CAP reform to be the top priority, and it insisted that CAP be amended to permit the income testing of benefits and the universalization of social services. British Columbia also demanded that the poorer provinces benefit from the kind of differential cost-sharing formula that had been omitted from CAP.[9] Quebec, Nova Scotia, Prince Edward Island, and Newfoundland also reacted positively, especially on the differential cost-sharing issue. Alberta, by contrast, was opposed to additional funds being given to the poor provinces; New Brunswick wanted no changes in the system until agreement was reached on a completely new support/ supplementation program. Despite the forces aligned against him, Lalonde refused to budge. As previously, the demands for incremental reform were unacceptable to the Review's federal initiators, who were committed to a systematic design for reform. Lalonde told the provinces that the money already allocated to OAS and family-allowance increases made immediate improvements in poverty policies impossible.[10]

A second conflict arose over the link between the support/supplementation program and existing social insurance measures. The most aggressive position was again taken by the provinces with NDP governments, which favoured what Johnson subsequently called a "simplistic" solution for social security reform: a single, "omnibus" program that would encompass existing programs, such as unemployment insurance and workmen's compensation, as well as support/ supplementation.[11] Lalonde and Johnson, along with most of the non-NDP provinces, dismissed the omnibus approach as impractical, citing bureaucratic barriers to dissolving programs and the popularity of social insurance programs. Still, most provinces sympathized with Quebec's more moderate position that unemployment insurance and other social insurance measures should be adjusted to make them more compatible with the new reform package. By November 1974, however, it was clear that there would be no attempt to alter UI. Unlike the Review itself, the UIC had strong support in cabinet and a suspicious bureaucratic staff.[12]

The third conflict centred on competing designs for the income support/supplementation program. The Orange Paper – which comprised separate strategies for income support and supplementation, and paid little attention to the tax system – naturally gave the impression that the federal government was already committed to a two-tier model to be implemented through transfer payments to beneficiaries, not through the tax system. But Lalonde and Johnson insisted throughout 1973 and 1974 that they were open to alternative suggestions.[13] Indeed, the main item on the agenda of the November 1974 welfare ministers' conference was a discussion of alternative models for income support and supplementation that had been drawn up by federal and provincial officials; three of those models found champions among the various participants.

The first was a one-tier support/supplementation program in which all recipients, employable and unemployable, would receive the same minimum payment (guarantee level) and would be subject to the same incentive-creating tax-back rate. The two other popular options had two tiers, with employable and unemployable claimants being assigned to different categories. The guarantee level for the support tier (for unemployable recipients) was higher than that for supplementation (for employable recipients.) The guarantee level in the supplementation tier of the two-tier models was not intended to provide enough income for recipients to sustain themselves, whereas the one-tier model's minimum was intended to do this for everyone. The two-tier options were therefore much less expensive than the one-tier model. The difference between the second and third options was that the former would be delivered through transfer payments to beneficiaries, the latter through the tax system.[14]

The expensive one-tier option, predictably, was supported by the three NDP governments, but most of the other provinces expressed reservations about it. Nova Scotia and New Brunswick considered it too expensive. Reflecting its traditionally cautious position, Alberta strongly supported the two-tier approach, arguing that the one-tier option would encourage laziness. Quebec and Prince Edward Island made no specific choice, but Quebec appeared willing to accept a two-tier program. Of the provinces supporting a two-tier approach, only Ontario clearly favoured a tax-delivered system (the third option) – a position that had been approved by the provincial cabinet in 1973. But a number of provinces (including Quebec, British Columbia, Saskatchewan, and Nova Scotia) were concerned about the technical feasibility of delivering benefits through the tax system.[15]

Thus when the November meeting ended, there was no consensus on an appropriate model for income support/supplementation. The two-year planning phase of the Review was coming to an end without having produced any agreement on reform. But the lack of consensus was largely irrelevant in any event, as Lalonde was about to ask cabinet to approve the model of his choice – the two-tier, transfer-delivered option of the Orange Paper. Despite their avowals to the contrary, there is no evidence that Lalonde and Johnson ever seriously examined the alternatives proposed by the provinces. They considered the one-tier option both too expensive and, for technical reasons, undesirable; the tax option was not available, primarily because

Finance's Simon Reisman objected to it. In effect, Lalonde undertook a dialogue of little consequence with the provinces and simply waited for a year and a half after the release of the Orange Paper – until the time arrived to return to cabinet for authorization of his preferred design. But when he submitted his proposal to his cabinet colleagues in January 1975, he was unable to claim that it was supported by a federal/provincial consensus as LaMarsh and MacEachen had done when they had approached cabinet with the Canada Assistance Plan.

Cabinet debacle, January–February 1975. In addition to the two-tier, transfer-delivered model, Lalonde's proposal to cabinet also included financial and jurisdictional arrangements and a timetable for implementation. The federal authorities had largely avoided discussing these three items with the provinces in 1973 and 1974, in keeping with the plan of the Orange Paper. Since the primary intent of the support tier was to provide an adequate income, not to create work incentives, it would have a relatively high guarantee level (to be set by the provinces, within national limits), with a tax-back rate of 75 percent. The supplementation tier would have a lower guarantee level (set by the federal government) and an incentive-creating tax-back rate of about 33.3 percent. Support would be administered by the provinces, while supplementation would be administered by whichever jurisdiction had had the closest contact with the recipient in the past; this implied federal administration for most recipients, who would turn to supplementation after exhausting their UI benefits. The federal government would pay for 50 percent of the support level and a larger share of supplementation. Support could be implemented quickly, but supplementation would have to wait until 1976. The incremental cost of the package for the federal government would be about $1 billion annually.[16]

The proposal encountered immediate criticism from Finance, reflecting its historic market-oriented accumulation strategy. Reisman launched the offensive, but his views reflected the prevailing philosophy within the department and he was fully supported by his minister, John Turner. Reisman's views "represented a majority viewpoint within the Department, having more to do with the ideology of mainstream Western economics than with any kind of 'coerced consensus.'"[17]

In April 1973, Lalonde and Johnson had anticipated that their Review proposals would be financed "within existing levels of taxation." The needed money would arrive through automatic increases in government revenues. By early 1975, however, Finance had already taken a number of steps to achieve its goal of restraining the demand for greater federal spending by changing the tax system. Successive budgets had significantly reduced the tax burden on corporations, and Turner's first budget after the 1972 election indexed personal income tax rates – a move that eliminated the capacity of the income tax to generate automatic and substantial increases in revenues.[18] The budget of November 1974 continued these trends.[19] Coupled with the economic slowdown that began that year, these changes meant that government revenues were not growing nearly as quickly as anticipated.[20]

Even before the support/supplementation package went to cabinet, the potential consequences were perceived by Richard Gwyn, an Ottawa journalist. Writing immediately after the November 1974 budget, he argued that its tax cuts were a heavy blow to the Review: "In effect [John Turner] has preempted Lalonde's [social] security review for at least 18 months ... The peculiar process of budget-making made it possible for Turner to shape social as well as economic policy."[21]

Gwyn's analysis was prophetic. At meetings of a cabinet committee and the full cabinet in February, Reisman and Turner forcefully – and, by and large, successfully – attacked the support/supplementation proposal. Cabinet agreed that Lalonde could offer the provinces the income-support component of his proposal, to come into effect on 1 January 1976, but it did not authorize implementation of the supplementation tier, which was more expensive and – as Johnson and Lalonde admitted – far more important for the realization of the Review's objectives. Supplementation was endorsed in principle, but its introduction would be delayed for at least a year or two after the implementation of support, and it would "depend either upon a fiscal dividend from economic growth ... or indeed the reallocation of fiscal resources."[22] Since there was no guarantee that satisfactory economic growth would occur or that the government's spending priorities would change, the provinces realized that this meant an indefinite delay.[23] What was being offered was a modest reform of CAP that would permit the income-testing of assistance benefits.

The attack by Reisman and Turner on the support/supplementation package was a decisive victory in Finance's efforts to restrain public spending, as Reisman himself acknowledged: "For a while new programs were coming in so fast we felt like a pair of goalies trying to bat them away. Sure a lot went by. But we won the big one – the social welfare legislation that Marc Lalonde and his deputy were pushing. That was a multi-million dollar program and we really went to the trenches on that one."[24] It was also a victory for Reisman's contention that any form of GAI, if introduced, would erode the work ethic in Canada.[25]

Finance undoubtedly increased its influence in cabinet by successfully restricting growth in the tax base, but its task was made easier by Lalonde's isolation. Poverty had not been a high political priority for cabinet in 1973, and it had no more defenders there in February 1975. Although Trudeau had, in December 1975, sent Lalonde a memo in which he encouraged him to proceed with his plans, he did not intervene on Lalonde's behalf when Turner and Reisman launched their assault. Moreover, Lalonde lacked the skills or inclination to build support for his proposals among the other ministers. At least one of his colleagues who was sympathetic but had raised questions about the proposal at cabinet meetings, was sternly rebuked by Lalonde for doing so. Others had their own spending priorities – in transportation and energy policy, for example – and thus had their own reasons to side with Finance.[26] When Lalonde defended his proposal, he was therefore very nearly alone.[27] Without political allies, and challenged by Finance at a time when the economy was deteriorating, the Health and Welfare minister was defeated.

Provincial rebuff, February–April 1975.   Lalonde presented his reduced package to a federal/provincial welfare ministers' conference on 18 February: the federal government was prepared immediately to begin designing an income support program that could be introduced on 1 January 1976, but the design and implementation of supplementation would have to wait for at least two or three years, perhaps indefinitely.

The response of provincial ministers and deputy ministers, expressed at meetings held in February and April, was negative, thus ensuring the defeat of this limited package. This provincial hostility reflected the conflict in grand designs that had already become apparent in 1973 and 1974. But it also revealed a second, more strategic, kind of bargaining that now increasingly became a source of interjurisdictional conflict. The jurisdictional and financial components of the federal offer – i.e., the issue of who would administer the new programs and who would pay for them – were the focus of this strategic debate. The federal and Quebec governments, and those of the western provinces to a lesser degree, now fought to maximize their control over the administration of the supplementation tier.

While cautious about any program changes that implied increased costs for them, the Atlantic provinces responded positively to

Lalonde's meagre proposal. Ontario voiced general support but sounded an ominous note of caution about its willingness to undertake the reforms. The Ontario representatives at the February meetings doubted whether their government would be able to begin the support program the following January; and the minister said he could not commit his province to paying for supplementation. Alberta also generally supported the Lalonde proposal but, along with the other western provinces, preferred provincial administration of supplementation.[28]

But the most negative reactions came from the three provinces with NDP governments and from Quebec. They were incredulous that the federal government had offered so little. They pointed out that only the support proposal was firm and that this amounted to no more than a modest expansion in the existing Canada Assistance Plan. The NDP governments renewed their demand for a one-tier program, and Quebec now appeared to prefer this option. On a more strategic plane, they also argued that the one-tier program should be administered by the provinces.[29]

There were important differences between the NDP ministers and Quebec. The former were more emphatic in stressing their preference for an ambitious grand design but less determined to resist federal administration of supplementation. For Quebec, the priorities were reversed: jurisdiction over supplementation was more important than all else. The Quebec government was willing to accept a two-tier program if its structure remained flexible. But if support and supplementation were to be introduced gradually, the latter must precede the former.

Johnson and Lalonde reacted firmly and negatively to the demands for a one-tier approach, but Quebec's position appeared to offer a basis for compromise. They were prepared to abandon their proposal to implement support before a design for supplementation was agreed to. Instead, both elements of the two-tier program would be developed and implemented at the same time. And they said they were willing to reopen the issue of who should administer supplementation.[30] In fact, as will be seen later on, they never seriously contemplated alternatives to federal administration.

A communiqué issued during the February meeting suggested that a federal/provincial agreement was possible, based on the federal compromise.[31] But major obstacles remained. Not only did the NDP ministers continue to denounce the two-tier option,[32] but other crucial questions had not yet been agreed upon with the other provinces – such as which elements of the reform would occur first and when, and who would administer supplementation.

The one- versus two-tier debate was resumed at the meeting of welfare ministers at the end of April. Lalonde angrily attacked the position adopted by the NDP ministers. After a lengthy quarrel, they retreated somewhat and accepted a communiqué that strongly suggested agreement on the two-tier approach. At no time, however, did they indicate anything more than reluctant acquiescence.[33]

At the April meeting, Johnson and Lalonde announced details of the revised approach mooted in February in response to Quebec's position. For the first time, they also provided a detailed cost-sharing formula for both tiers. The federal government would pay for two-thirds of supplementation, and this proportion would also apply to a significant part of support. The senior government would share 50 percent of the remaining costs of the support tier, up to the national average benefit level. Beyond this, it would cover one-third of provincial costs. Johnson and Lalonde were less precise on other matters. They suggested that the thorny issue of who should administer supplementation should be studied by an independent body. In private discussions, however, federal actors remained as adamant that the federal government must retain an important role in administering supplementation as Quebec was determined to avoid it. Finally, the federal participants proposed that the two levels of government spend the next eighteen to twenty-four months designing the supplementation tier.[34]

The April welfare ministers' meeting was no more successful than its predecessor two months earlier. Ontario's minister was almost silent at the meeting, largely confining his remarks to an occasional repetition of his province's preference for a tax-delivered supplementation program – an option that had been abandoned by all other governments. The Atlantic ministers also had little to say; indeed, they preferred the February federal proposals to those offered in April, because the former promised an immediate and manageable improvement in income support. The NDP ministers never really accepted the two-tier option. Quebec again led the way in providing a detailed response to the federal proposals. Claude Forget complained that the federal supplementation design was too vague. He suggested that the design be settled as soon as possible, noting that the jurisdictional issue could not be resolved until this was done. He also questioned the utility of an outside study of jurisdiction, since Quebec would accept only a limited federal role in administering supplementation.[35] In the end, Quebec agreed to a communiqué that endorsed an independent study of the jurisdictional issue, but Forget made it clear that he would continue to insist on provincial jurisdiction.[36]

The only other significant point of agreement spelled out in the final communiqué was that "officials should be instructed to work out the details of an operational design for an income support and supplementation system" before the end of 1975.[37] In fact, however, these bureaucratic discussions were soon abandoned, and the proposed independent study of jurisdiction did not take place.[38] In June 1975, Johnson – who had played such a crucial role in driving the Social Security Review forward from the outset – left his position at Health and Welfare to become president of the Canadian Broadcasting Corporation. He was replaced in August by Bruce Rawson, until then the deputy minister for welfare in Alberta. By the end of the summer, it was clear that the federal government would have to redesign completely its proposal to the provinces and that little concrete federal/provincial discussion of income security reform would occur again until the following year.[39]

Employment

The employment strategy had an important place in the Orange Paper because of the liberal ideological assumptions of the document. Employment in the private sector was to be the primary foundation of social security; only when this avenue was impeded would other measures be justified. But many tensions undermined the strategy, not only at the design level but also as legislation was being drafted to implement it.

Intrajurisdictional conflict. The Orange Paper did not start with existing employment measures in describing an employment strategy; instead, it proceeded deductively to identify what job-creation initiatives were most likely to address poverty. Johnson's vision of the strategy reflected the persistently high levels of unemployment in Canada during the early 1970s. Unlike some non-liberal welfare states, Canada was not able to achieve full employment during the postwar era; its governments also made much less of a determined effort to achieve this goal.[40] Consequently, as Rachlis notes, "the Orange Paper ... rejected full employment as central to a comprehensive social security system," because that goal was seen as being unrealistic.[41] What was needed was a more modest and more selective approach that would reach a particularly disadvantaged target group. In the Orange Paper's own terms, "it is only realistic to recognize that there are bound to be people in parts of the country who cannot readily find jobs in the general labour market. And it is these people who become the concern of social policy." A long-term community training and employment program was needed for "people who have been unemployed for an extended period of time."[42]

Manpower rejected Johnson's definition of the strategy because it threatened its own programs. In effect, while Johnson's concept of an employment strategy was modest and characteristically liberal, it represented enough of a departure from Manpower's existing measures to be perceived as a threat. The Orange Paper did not specify how large the new community employment program should be, but Manpower officials wanted to scale it down, arguing that its implementation could be achieved by refining and coordinating existing programs administered by their department rather than by setting up a major new program.

Many NHW officials, along with their colleagues in provincial welfare departments, were convinced that Manpower had no real interest in the Review. During the spring and summer of 1973, Johnson had "violent" debates (the term used by some interviewees) with leading Manpower officials. The dispute subsided by early 1974, although there remained tensions about the relative lack of interdepartmental consultation. By then, Manpower had successfully redefined the employment strategy as a modest experiment aimed at refining existing federal and provincial manpower programs of relevance to the poor. Manpower was able to achieve this by neutralizing Johnson's main criticism of existing measures – that is, his belief, stated in the Orange Paper and even more emphatically in private memoranda, that these measures were far too preoccupied with reducing overall unemployment and with developing the skills needed to meet shortages in the labour market. This macroeconomic approach, Johnson argued, was unlikely to help marginal participants in the labour market or people without the skills to take advantage of job-training or other opportunities. Long-term programs were required to help these people, either because they would never be able to enter the regular work force or because it would take a long time for them to acquire the necessary skills.[43]

Indeed, Manpower's approach to employment policy traditionally focused on skill shortages in the aggregate labour market; in 1973 the ability of Manpower's programs to reduce overall unemployment was also invoked to justify their existence.[44] Among these programs were the Local Initiatives Program (LIP) and Opportunities for Youth (OFY), which were "client-oriented" but had a countercyclical and short-term focus.

When the Orange Paper was released in April 1973, Manpower minister Robert Andras submitted a memorandum to cabinet outlining his department's approach to the employment strategy. He related the strategy to the goal of lowering unemployment rates and suggested that the volume of community employment could be adjusted to meet the government's aggregate employment objectives.[45] Johnson subjected Andras' memo to a lengthy critique, which he passed on to Lalonde. He opposed the link with macroeconomic policy because it would prevent community employment from providing the needed benefits to its target groups. For this to be achieved, the government's commitment to employment for the disadvantaged had to be tailored to the needs of that clientele, and it had to be a long-term undertaking, independent of the seasonal fluctuations of the economy.[46]

The issue went to cabinet, which accepted Johnson's position that the employment strategy should be kept separate from aggregate employment policies. Accordingly, Manion explicitly divorced the strategy from these objectives in discussions with the provinces at the end of the summer. He also adopted Johnson's argument that community employment had to be designed to meet the special needs of its clientele.[47] While this change required Manpower officials to abandon their traditional focus on unemployment levels, it did not threaten their main, largely defensive, objective in the Review. By the autumn of 1973, Manpower officials were telling their provincial colleagues that community employment implied not a massive new program but the adaptation and better coordination of existing manpower programs.[48]

Once Manpower explicitly modified its approach to community employment along the lines preferred by Johnson, interdepartmental acrimony on the overall direction of the strategy subsided. Perhaps in deference to Manpower's expertise in this field, Johnson adopted the view that existing programs were compatible with his objective.[49] In any event, Johnson was undoubtedly aware that Manpower's jurisdiction over the employment strategy gave him only limited room for manoeuvre.

There remained other conflicts at the federal level, however. First, a widespread feeling persisted among NHW officials that Manpower was not allowing them to participate in the employment strategy. NHW was not involved in developing the operational proposal on community employment that went to cabinet in February 1974.[50] Internal Manpower memoranda stressed the desirability of proceeding with the strategy as independently of NHW as possible.[51] In the three months before Manpower took its design to cabinet, Johnson repeatedly complained to Manpower officials about their failure to involve other interested federal departments.[52] According to a leading Manpower official, "the manner in which Al Johnson,

Russell Robinson and Guy Fortier have, on occasion, chosen to become involved in the substance of the employment strategy [is] inconsistent with our Minister's general mandate to lead the development of that strategy."[53]

The second persistent conflict at the federal level transpired within NHW, although it also contributed to the department's marginalization within the employment strategy. The planning officials that Johnson had brought with him to NHW had no expertise in the manpower field. As a result, the department's contribution to the strategy was delegated to outsiders who had no commitment to the reform agenda. Foremost among these, in the early part of the Review, was Gail Stewart, the wife of an Ottawa "mandarin," who expounded an unorthodox view of employment issues. Stewart, along with some allies within NHW, produced a number of memoranda that departed radically from the liberal assumptions of the Orange Paper. They stated that the Orange Paper's target group was too narrow and that it should include all individuals not in the labour force who were able and willing to work. Furthermore, community employment should provide socially and personally rewarding alternatives to tedious and unrewarding jobs in the private sector. The point, Stewart argued, was not to change the people participating in the program but to alter the "opportunity structure" available to them. Stewart complained that Manpower officials ignored her suggestions.[54]

By February 1974, Stewart's views were in open conflict with Johnson's. He considered her approach completely impractical. The community employment strategy had to have a limited target group, he argued, if its costs were to be kept within bounds. Drawing on the liberal assumptions of the Orange Paper, he also strongly disagreed with Stewart's suggestion that alternatives to jobs in the private market should be provided. Restoring people to normal private employment was, as the Orange Paper made quite clear, the point of the strategy. After a heated exchange of memoranda in February 1974, Stewart's association with the Review ended.[55] Richard Van Loon was then hired by Health and Welfare to coordinate the department's role in the employment strategy. Because of this internal dissension, Johnson was not getting useful advice within NHW and was therefore unable to add to, or challenge, Manpower's deliberations.[56]

Federal/provincial conflict. Federal/provincial tensions about the employment strategy reflected the same two factors that impeded the parallel discussions on income maintenance. The NDP governments denounced the Orange Paper's liberal conception of the employment strategy from a broadly social democratic perspective. But this influence again made itself felt in the context of interjurisdictional relations and reflected the preoccupation with rival grand designs in that setting. The antagonism of the non-NDP provinces to the federal reformers was more purely strategic. Friction also developed because of differences in the professional profile of the participants in the employment strategy at the two levels of government. While labour market officials dominated the strategy at the federal level and in Ontario and Quebec, welfare officials were responsible for its implementation in several of the smaller provinces. Indeed, some provinces showed little interest in the strategy, and federal Manpower officials believed that this reflected the influence of welfare officials. There was a well-established pattern of hostility between the two groups.[57]

Two specific objections were raised by the provinces. Some – Ontario, in particular – wanted a much broader range of employment measures to be discussed by the working party than Manpower was willing to consider. Manpower officials were required to resist these pressures because the Orange Paper (and their mandate from cabinet) specified that the employment strategy must focus on a very narrow target group – those who experienced continuing difficulty in finding work.[58] But Manpower's resistance also reflected its defensive objectives in the Social Security Review: it did not want to allow the provinces to transform the employment strategy into a critical investigation of a broad range of its programs.

The grand designs for reform of the NDP governments – Saskatchewan's, above all – were a second focus of disagreement. The NDP governments envisaged an employment strategy in broadly social democratic terms, stressing the state's responsibility for maintaining full employment at adequate wages and under acceptable conditions. They argued that the strategy should be a substitute for undesirable, low-wage jobs in the private sector and that it should set full employment as its objective.[59] Similarly, some provincial welfare officials saw the strategy as an opportunity to "humanize" work rather than adjust its clients to the needs of the existing labour market.[60]

These provincial perspectives continued to impede federal/provincial agreement in the fall of 1973. The Ontario government was particularly aggressive and by September had convinced a number of other provinces to support its vision of a broad review of federal and provincial manpower policies. A meeting of the working party in November witnessed considerable dissension. Many participants used the meeting to expound their personal views on employment issues, which often differed substantially from the goals of the Orange Paper. It was not until December that federal/provincial negotiations made significant headway, when a meeting of deputy ministers agreed on a definition of the target group for community employment and also agreed that each government should draw up a concrete program proposal so that a specific design could be agreed upon the following February.[61]

But concrete agreement on a program proved elusive. In February 1974, the federal and provincial ministers responsible for the strategy received a bulky report from the working party, consisting of papers from each government on community employment, along with a covering document that was supposed to reflect a consensus of these perspectives. As senior Manpower officials freely admitted, no real agreement had been reached on the target group or the objectives of community employment.[62] Provincial statements in the report presented a wide range of contrasting design options. At the February meeting, the governments of Saskatchewan and British Columbia repeated their earlier views; Ontario was now more subdued but, along with Quebec and Alberta, demanded a program with only minimal national standards.[63] It was obvious that no consensus would emerge on community employment. Indeed, the design presented to cabinet by Manpower that month had not been previously discussed with the provinces.

A legislative framework. Manpower minister Robert Andras took his preliminary views on the community employment concept to cabinet on 5 February 1974. His memo informed the ministers that whatever the provinces may have thought, the federal government would only accept a narrow definition of the target group. The memo sought one important decision from cabinet – that "the Minister of Manpower and Immigration should be authorized to raise with provincial ministers the possibility of experimental projects under this Policy during 1974." By then, Johnson had stopped expressing major substantive reservations about Manpower's handling of the employment strategy; he and his minister accepted the experimental approach, and cabinet authorized its presentation to the provinces.[64]

At the welfare ministers' conference, later in February, Andras raised the possibility of using experimental projects over a three-year period. While the conference witnessed continued disagreement about the appropriate scope and purpose of community employment, most provinces responded positively to the experimental approach, though few were enthusiastic. Many observed that it was the most feasible option, given the persistent intergovernmental discord.[65] A notable exception to this consensus was Quebec, which emphatically opposed such experiments. Its welfare minister, Claude Forget, argued that enough was already known about community employment to proceed directly to a full program. Exhibiting considerable foresight, Forget was also apprehensive that the federal government might withdraw from the projects once they were well under way, leaving the provinces "holding the bag."[66]

After the February meeting, other provinces voiced scepticism about the federal government's ability to make a long-term commitment. They also wanted Manpower to specify how much money would be available for projects in each province.[67] By July, Andras had nonetheless secured the agreement of all provinces – including Quebec – to proceed with experimental projects. Thus when his detailed proposals about the design and financing of the experimental projects went to cabinet on 26 July, he was able to claim that they had provincial support,[68] but this consensus was very much led by the federal government, and provincial concurrence was unenthusiastic.

Andras' July memo made it clear that Manpower had extremely modest objectives in the community employment area. The three-year developmental period would only require the expenditure of $50 million, mainly to finance the evaluation of experiments and the extra staff needed to administer the projects. Interjurisdictional disagreement prevented a more ambitious undertaking: "It has been clear from the discussions with the provinces that it would be difficult to arrive at a consensus in the very near future on the design of a strategy." The memorandum was less forthright about Manpower's own reluctance to jeopardize its existing programs by adopting a more ambitious strategy. But there were hints of this reticence, as the memo repeatedly emphasized that the components included in the experiments would derive from existing federal and provincial programs. It also asserted the need for further efforts in "developing appropriate conceptual and administrative relationships with *ongoing job creation programs*, [and] with the rest of the social security system."[69]

The experimental approach was accepted by cabinet in August. During the rest of 1974, Manpower officials conducted bilateral discussions with their provincial counterparts about selecting communities for projects and establishing the administrative mechanisms to coordinate federal and provincial initiatives in the communities affected. In early 1975, Manpower was already claiming significant progress; its *Annual Report* announced that preliminary agreements on projects had already been signed with six provinces.[70]

In fact, however, the actual projects emerged only very slowly and were accompanied by considerable federal/provincial tension. Many at NHW experienced frustration at these developments. Johnson hoped to have his department participate in designing standards for the projects, and Van Loon's arrival in March 1974 was an effort to improve its policy advice in the employment field. Johnson approached senior Manpower officials to enlarge his department's contribution to the employment strategy, but they were suspicious of this move and never allowed NHW to play a meaningful role in the strategy.[71]

Social Services

The Orange Paper also cast social service reform in a liberal context: social services were depicted as being mainly concerned with restoring individuals to a place in the work force. This focus of reform was successfully challenged by welfare officials. At the outset, interdepartmental rivalries with Manpower at the federal level threatened the development of service reform as an independent strategy. Reform was also impeded by the contrasting professional backgrounds of leading participants from the two levels of government.

Participants in the April 1973 welfare ministers' meeting knew that there was a potential conflict between the mandates of the working parties on employment and social services, since both would have to be concerned with employment services. Because the employment strategy was entrusted to Manpower at the federal level, these conflicting mandates became a source of interdepartmental disagreement. When Johnson met Allen Gotlieb, the deputy minister of Manpower, in July 1973, the latter asked "whether it would be prudent to establish a Social ... Services Working Party. His concern, and Manion's, was the overlap between the work of the Working Party and that of the Working Party on Employment."[72] Johnson defended the notion of a working party for social services, and the issue was not raised again by Manpower. But Manpower remained suspicious of the service strategy and was able to constrain its development.

The federal planners wanted to avoid incremental reforms in social services, as they did in income maintenance, and for the same reasons: 1) incrementalism undermined the systematic nature of the Review; and 2) the political priority of other social programs meant that no money would be available for significant reforms until 1975. Moreover, service reform was a low priority for them. The career welfare officials who dominated the Review in many provinces, by contrast, wanted immediate changes in services and saw reform in this area as a high priority. These contrasting views resulted in debates about service reform during 1973 and 1974.

Attention to social services within the Review began in October 1973, but there was little progress in the first year. The major responsibility of the working party on social services was to draft a report on comprehensive reform. Professionally, this working party was more homogeneous than the other two: almost all of its members had a background in social welfare departments. As a result, there was little interjurisdictional acrimony, and members shared a philosophy that departed significantly from that of Johnson and his subordinates. They were unhappy with the Orange Paper's liberal focus on services as an adjunct to the objective of restoring people to a productive role in the economy. While they were not prepared to advocate a non-liberal ideology, they wanted services to help people realize their full potential as human beings; employment was only one aspect of this potential. The one significant accomplishment of the working party's interim report, completed in late 1974, was to broaden considerably the Review's focus on services.[73]

In other respects, the working party achieved little. Its interim report was discussed by the ministers in November and largely dismissed as vague and unhelpful.[74] Thereafter, social services were debated at the ministerial and deputy-ministerial level. By then, it was clear that most of the provinces saw service reform as a high priority. After the provincial ministers had expressed impatience with the slow pace of reform in September, Johnson convened a special meeting of deputy ministers of welfare in December to discuss social services. He asked them pointedly whether they wanted federal involvement to continue. They emphatically stressed the importance of federal cost-sharing; Quebec's representative even spoke of the need for the federal government's policy leadership and financial involvement in services. Only the two anti-reform provinces – Ontario and Alberta – were not enthusiastic about the federal role.[75]

Thus by the end of 1974, federal officials were well aware that the provinces wanted reform in social services. One even proposed to Johnson that the federal government, in effect, use its willingness to remain involved in the service field as bait to induce a positive response to federal proposals on income security: "I personally think that the provinces will support any federal proposed income support/supplementation scheme as long as they are assured that we will continue the cost-sharing of services. Cost-sharing, therefore, is probably the most formidable tool we have."[76] Johnson did not follow this advice, which was, in any event, based on an erroneous premise. Instead, in early 1975 he authorized senior welfare officials to draw up a legislative proposal for service reform. Unlike the other strategies, these proposals were to a considerable extent a response to the provinces' desire for reform.

The federal/provincial conference of welfare ministers held in April 1975 was a watershed for the Social Security Review. Each of The Review's three strategies had reached a crucial stage. Lalonde and Johnson's income security proposals were poorly received and would require substantial modification. The employment strategy was beginning its implementation phase, but very little had been achieved in terms of concrete program reforms. At the April conference, the federal government finally pushed social service reform to the top of its agenda and presented the provinces with a detailed proposal.

CONCLUSION

Launched in April 1973, the Social Security Review underwent fundamental changes in each of its key strategies as a result of cabinet decisions in the spring of 1975. Developments in the intervening period again reflected the societal and organizational context in which the Review took place. The pragmatic and ideological liberalism of the Orange Paper had an ongoing influence on federal reformers. The federal approach to each strategy reflected a liberal preference for the market and for the maximum possible attachment of individuals to employment. This liberalism, however, was contested during the Review. It was challenged by provincial governments with a different ideological complexion – social democratic in the case of provinces with NDP governments, more resolutely liberal in the case of Ontario and Alberta. Dissident federal bureaucrats (like Gail Stewart) also sometimes expounded divergent ideas.

At the same time, political interest in poverty reform remained minimal, again reflecting political class influences. Even when the provincial governments brought their ideology to the bargaining table, neither they nor their federal counterpart made poverty reform an issue of fundamental concern. Earlier policy commitments by the federal Liberals, reflecting the much greater political interest in the universal elements of Canada's welfare state under the influence of the NDP, continued to delay poverty reform and gave rise to acrimony. And functional class influences now became a decisive factor: in early 1975, the Finance department, pursuing its traditional market-oriented accumulation strategy, inflicted a devastating blow on the income maintenance element of the Review.

These societal influences were complemented by organizational ones, reflecting the impact of the institutionalized structure of public policy making. The broad scope and systematic design of the Review required the participation of many people with diverse professional backgrounds and contrasting interests and program loyalties, which fragmented the Review into three separate elements and created tensions and frustrations within each. These professional differences were complemented by other sources of friction in federal/provincial discussions that reflected competing systematic and supradepartmental objectives among the participating governments. There were competing "grand designs" on income maintenance and employment, reflecting the conflict-generating tendencies of intergovernmental relations in an institutionalized context. In effect, ideological conflict about the liberal orientation of the Review – a political class phenomenon – was reinforced by the institutionalization of the Canadian state and by its fostering of federal/provincial relations around systematic and government-wide objectives that potentially differed significantly between jurisdictions. As the Review proceeded, federal/provincial conflict became more purely strategic, focusing on who would pay for, and who would control, any new program. Each government wanted to maximize its autonomy from the other level of jurisdiction while minimizing program costs. The combined effect of all these influences was pervasive, debilitating discord.

CHAPTER SEVEN

Demise of the Social Security Review, 1975–78

The federal and provincial welfare ministers did not reach agreement on Lalonde's support/supplementation proposal in April 1975. Strategic bargaining, which had surfaced in February, became ever more prominent as the provinces sought to maximize their jurisdictional authority while limiting costs. As the economic situation worsened throughout 1975, even the more affluent provinces became unwilling to absorb any significant expenses associated with a new support/supplementation program.

Heightened sensitivity to costs was reinforced by new tensions between the federal government and the provinces in related areas of policy making. In 1975 the federal government reduced unemployment insurance coverage significantly, causing the provinces to protest that this decision increased their social assistance caseloads. In his June budget the Finance minister announced restrictions on federal sharing of health care costs, gave notice that the federal government would replace cost-sharing with a block grant in the health area, and curtailed equalization payments to the provinces.[1]

INCOME SUPPORT AND SUPPLEMENTATION

In this context, if the support/supplementation proposals were to survive, federal actors would have to respond to provincial sensitivities about these developments better than they had during the first two years of the Review. When Lalonde chose Bruce Rawson to replace Johnson as deputy minister of Health and Welfare, the Review acquired some needed flexibility. The revised federal proposal that emerged in early 1976 departed significantly from those which had preceded it. But continued federal intransigence on some key issues, along with the linked deteriorations in economic and federal/provincial relations, precluded a successful completion of income maintenance reform.

A Revised Proposal

After the April 1975 conference, Lalonde wanted to solve any outstanding issues quickly; the deepening recession meant that time was working against reform. Rawson convened a meeting of provincial deputy ministers in August. The result was not encouraging; by the close of the meeting, Rawson knew that only modest results were now possible. With increasing success, provincial treasury departments were espousing the same restrictive economic agenda as Finance articulated at the federal level. While Ontario had always been a cautious participant in the strategy, its welfare deputy minister brought a particularly pessimistic view to this meeting: his government was planning large budget cuts and could not implement supplementation in the short term. Quebec's views changed even more dramatically: its deputy minister said that the first two years of the Social Security Review had been a waste and that the Quebec cabinet was no longer willing to spend new money in this area. The most sensible step, he added, would be to develop improvements in income support through the Canada Assistance Plan.[2] Thus the province whose social security concerns, more than those of any other jurisdiction, had led to the launching of the Social Security Review, could no longer proceed with anything more than modest reform. Other provinces also announced they could no longer afford ambitious reform projects.[3]

Rawson now began to draft a completely new proposal. The resulting memorandum, which went to cabinet in early February 1976, came closer than any previous federal effort to responding to provincial concerns; it also recognized the constraints imposed on both levels of government by the economic recession.[4] The proposal offered a detailed program outline, as the provinces had requested. Specific ceilings for the federal government's cost-sharing responsibilities were given for each category of recipients. To please those who wanted a one-tier program, it offered each province two options – a two-tier program and a "unitary" one. In response to provincial concerns about jurisdictional issues, Rawson's proposal also allowed the provinces to administer the entire program. Finally, to accommodate growing concerns about costs, the program was much more modest than the 1975 proposal. While the cost of the earlier proposal was estimated at about $1 billion, the new proposal would cost between $225 million and $365 million. Most dramatically, almost all of the incremental expenditures would be absorbed by the federal government. To counter possible opposition in the federal cabinet, Rawson's memorandum proposed a gradual implementation schedule, beginning in 1978.[5]

Some provisions of the offer did not respond to provincial demands, but on these points the federal authorities refused to bargain. First, the "unitary" option would essentially amount to an extension of income support. It would be less generous than the two-tier proposal, and it was far removed from the one-tier, integrated support/supplementation program preferred in 1975 by the three NDP governments. To keep costs to a minimum, federal officials were also determined to impose severe restrictions on access: supplementation would only be available to adults with dependent children, single persons over the age of 54, and childless couples whose breadwinner was at least 54 years old. Finally, the tax-back rates were 70 percent for support – a high figure – and 35 percent for supplementation. Each of these provisions would occasion conflict with the provinces, but the federal authorities, which had already made a number of significant concessions to them, would go no further.

The new income support/supplementation proposal went to the cabinet committee on 14 January 1976. There it was attacked by Donald Macdonald, who had assumed the Finance portfolio the previous September. His position was based on a memorandum prepared by Thomas K. Shoyama, his new deputy minister. As in the past, the memo embodied the department's view that new social security expenditures would undermine economic growth. The memo acknowledged that because of its modest costs, "the new proposal of Health and Welfare is ... much closer to the view we held last year," but because the economic situation had deteriorated rapidly in recent months, there was a need for even more severe restraint than was anticipated in 1975. Shoyama therefore recommended that "given that the Government is committed to restraining its expenditures, we believe that the reforms contemplated in this document can, and should be absorbed from existing welfare budgets by reallocation of existing finances. For example, the permanent de-indexation of Family Allowances would free sufficient funds from which to pay for the proposed Unitary System. As for the more expensive two-tier option, it should be rejected altogether."[6]

Finance did not convince cabinet to pay for the proposals out of savings in other programs or to jettison the two-tier option. But its opposition restricted the proposal in one important way: Lalonde could not offer the provinces even the very cautious implementation schedule mentioned in the memorandum. Instead, he had to give the same kind of vague assurance as in February 1975: implementation would "occur when our capacities and disposable financial resources permitted."[7] Such an ambiguous promise could only have the same effect as it had had a year earlier – to increase the provinces' scepticism about the federal commitment to reform.

Lalonde submitted his new plan to the provinces at a meeting of welfare ministers in early February 1976. In preparation, his officials contacted their provincial counterparts to get a preliminary assessment of their ministers' views. The position that stood out most clearly was that of Ontario. By early 1976, political tensions between Ontario's Conservative government and the Liberal government in Ottawa had reached a high point. During their visit to Toronto, the federal officials were told that they could expect a very negative view from the Ontario welfare minister.[8] In fact, his objections would make agreement virtually impossible and were presumably designed to achieve that end. Thus on the eve of the February meeting, Lalonde and Rawson already knew that the income maintenance strategy was unlikely to survive.

Federal/Provincial Discussions,
February–May 1976

At the February meeting of welfare ministers, financial considerations overshadowed all others; the tone of the discussions was frequently shrill, especially between Ontario and the federal government. All of the provinces abandoned the positions that they had taken throughout the first two years of the Review. Neither of the western provinces that still had an NDP government, for example – Saskatchewan and Manitoba – continued to propose the introduction of a comprehensive one-tier proposal.[9]

Ontario's minister objected both to the design of the federal proposal and to its potential costs. But as John Grey pointed out in *The Ottawa Citizen*, Ontario's position was far removed from those which it had taken in recent times along with other jurisdictions, and it could only be interpreted as an effort to undermine the Review.[10] Ontario's minister complained that the support/supplementation proposal departed from the Review's objective of rationalizing the social security system. He added that his province would only accept a program delivered through the tax system and that even if Lalonde acceded to its demands, Ontario could not afford to implement reform in the foreseeable future.[11] Quebec's minister was more positive, but for fiscal reasons his government was equally unable to make a commitment. The implementation of reform would only be possible when economic conditions improved. Other provinces also worried about costs, and no minister could commit his province to implementing reform.[12]

Lalonde told the provincial ministers that they would have to make a final decision on the government's proposal by June. The federal authorities would then consider the Social Security Review to have ended, and the proposal would be withdrawn. The results of the February meeting were not encouraging, but federal officials spent the next few months in bilateral discussions with their provincial colleagues, attempting to increase the chances of success in June. These discussions led some observers to believe that the proposal might be accepted after all,[13] but this hope proved to be illusory. When the provincial welfare ministers arrived at the June conference, they were often much less positive than their welfare officials had been, as most of them had just consulted their cabinets about the proposal. While the officials apparently wished to proceed with reform, they were thwarted by provincial cabinets, acting under the influence of their increasingly restrictive treasuries.

The oppositional role of the provincial treasury was particularly prominent in Ontario. One of the most heated exchanges of the entire Review occurred at an April meeting of federal and provincial finance ministers. Darcy McKeough, Ontario's treasurer, delivered a sweeping and uninformed denunciation of the federal proposal. Apparently unaware that the support/supplementation design now under discussion had been considerably scaled down since the previous year, he attacked the federal government for proposing a new program that would cost $1 billion (the estimated cost of Lalonde's 1975 proposal). He stated flatly that "Ontario cannot ... support this guaranteed income scheme" and concluded by saying that he found it "difficult to believe that the federal government would ... place another expensive burden on Canadian taxpayers."[14] When federal officials later contacted officials in Ontario's Community Services ministry, the latter said that they had not been consulted about the statement and that the provincial deputy minister, who sided with Lalonde, felt "terribly embarrassed."[15] From the beginning, Ontario's participation in the Review was strongly influenced by its treasury ministry; by 1976, the treasurer was actively and publicly attacking income maintenance reform, apparently without consulting the provincial ministry responsible for the policy field.

The End of Federal/Provincial Reform, June 1976

At the June meeting, Lalonde reiterated that this gathering represented the end of the Review process. The provinces could either accept or reject the federal proposal on income maintenance; there was no room for major changes.[16] Lalonde, who had been warned about developments in Ontario and elsewhere, already knew that those present at the conference would not reach agreement.[17] The cost of the federal proposal and the sharing arrangements were, once again, the main objects of dispute.[18]

Provincial anxieties about cost were aggravated by federal efforts to reduce expenditures in other areas of social policy, as the June conference made abundantly clear. Many provinces demanded an assurance that the federal government would not use the new support/supplementation proposal to reduce its share of expenditures on income maintenance. Lalonde responded angrily that he would give such an assurance only if the provinces agreed to do the same.[19]

Two recent developments, above all, accounted for this mood of suspicion. The provinces continued to face rising social assistance caseloads, citing the 1975 UIC cutbacks as the main cause. Many of them were also suspicious of the federal government's intentions in transforming cost-shared programs for postsecondary education and health into unconditional block grants. They feared that Ottawa might want to transfer the financial burden of these programs to them. And since a first ministers' meeting on fiscal relations was planned for mid-June – two weeks *after* the welfare ministers' conference – some provinces said that they could come to no firm conclusions about Lalonde's proposal until they knew what would transpire at that meeting.[20]

A communiqué released at the end of the welfare ministers' conference stated that "with the exception of New Brunswick and Prince Edward Island which did not express an opinion on the program designs pending the outcome of the first ministers' meeting later this month, and Ontario which stated that it was not prepared to accept the basic program as presently designed ... all provincial ministers expressed their provinces' agreement in principle with the Income Support and Supplementation proposals jointly worked out during the course of the Social Security Review."[21] In fact, New Brunswick and Prince Edward Island made it clear that their participation in the program was very unlikely under any circumstances. Nova Scotia and Newfoundland endorsed the proposal in principle but also stated that they could not afford to implement it soon. Alberta and Manitoba wanted to settle broader issues of federal/provincial fiscal relations before making a commitment to support/supplementation. While Quebec seemed interested in the federal proposal, it could not afford to put it into place immediately and expressed a number of technical reservations. Only British Columbia, now under a Social Credit government, and Saskatchewan had genuinely positive comments to make at the meeting, but even those two provinces had reservations, which, they hoped, would be addressed over the next few weeks.[22] Thus when the June welfare ministers' conference ended, no agreement had been achieved on income maintenance reform.

After the conference, Lalonde still hoped that the provinces, with the anticipated exception of Ontario, would eventually accept his proposal. Over the next twelve months, he corresponded with his provincial counterparts, many of whom made encouraging statements about the proposal's design.[23] But only Saskatchewan's minister was able to commit his province to implementing it, and on 8 August 1977 Lalonde withdrew the proposals.[24] This effectively brought to an end the income maintenance element of the Review.

Towards a Unilateral Solution, July 1976–January 1978

The federal government then turned its attention to unilateral initiatives, which would have to be very modest in scale. After mid-1976, policy making within NHW took quite separate paths for support and supplementation. The federal authorities recognized that support could only be reformed in conjunction with the provinces. Officials in NHW prepared a modified support proposal in September 1977, but this document generated controversy within the department and was quietly dropped in 1978 without ever having been presented to the provincial ministers.[25]

On supplementation, by contrast, the federal government was willing to proceed on its own. Lalonde had warned the provinces in June 1976 that if agreement was not reached, the federal government would consider developing its own supplementation program and delivering it through the tax system.[26] An important precondition of unilateral action was that Finance and Taxation officials had to agree that such a scheme was technically feasible. Reisman's refusal to let the tax system be used for supplementation purposes at the beginning of the Review had led to the exclusion of tax delivery from serious consideration before 1976. Only the support, or at least the acquiescence, of Finance could remove this roadblock.

Thus the creation of an Interdepartmental Task Force on Tax-Transfer Integration in July 1976 was a major step towards a unilateral federal program. Chaired by Mickey A. Cohen, a Finance official, the group included officials from the departments of Health and Welfare (including Robinson) and Revenue. Its mandate was to assess whether tax delivery of various government programs (including income supplementation) was feasible.[27] NHW officials hoped for, and obtained, an affirmative result when the task force reported to cabinet in July 1977.[28] Finance now acknowledged that tax delivery was possible, but it still did not see it as desirable. It continued to resist NHW's supplementation program for the same reason as in 1976: the proposal simply could not be afforded unless it was financed from savings in other social programs. Some senior Finance officials also expounded what others called a "purist" view of the tax system – namely, that it should be exclusively a mechanism for collecting revenues, not for delivering social programs.

Cabinet's response to the task force report satisfied NHW's desire to investigate tax delivery of supplementation further, while accommodating Finance's resistance. The cabinet instructed the ministers of both departments to continue their joint work by preparing "a memorandum identifying and assessing specific policy options for ... Supplementation."[29] Health and Welfare could now hope that a unilateral federal supplementation program might be implemented. But Finance's objections to the idea were also reflected in the mood of cabinet. First, it only authorized a study of the concept: no commitment was made to actually introducing tax credits. Second, NHW officials were made aware that a basic condition of any new initiative was that it must be funded from savings in existing programs and that it must be an even more modest initiative than that proposed by Health and Welfare in 1976. That this was clearly understood is evidenced by an internal memorandum written several months later: "It is our belief that rearranging some current tax provisions and expenditure programs could free up sufficient funds to finance some kind of refundable tax credit for the working poor. Of course, with this kind of financing constraint, the initiative might have to be *very* modest, certainly much more modest than even the June 1976 proposals."[30] And it was equally clear that the most likely rearrangement of existing expenditures would involve the transfer of funds away from universal family allowances, either by income-testing them or by preserving their universality but reducing their value.[31] This, of course, was the avenue recommended earlier by Finance deputy minister Shoyama.

Monique Bégin replaced Lalonde as minister of Health and Welfare in September 1977. Early in 1978 her officials were still working on the supplementation options with their counterparts at Finance. Leading officials at NHW had accepted the necessity of curtailing family allowances in exchange for a modest supplementation program. They still had to overcome Finance's resistance to tax credits, and this would only happen in the context of an extraordinary budgetary exercise later in the year. Subsequent events would also be shaped by Bégin's policy preferences. In any case, both the objective of conducting income security reform jointly with the provinces and the desire to conduct poverty reform systematically had been abandoned.

The Child Tax Credit

As noted in chapter 5, Bégin proposed the introduction of a taxable cash allowance for children in the report of the Royal Commission on the Status of Women in Canada in 1970. After her appointment as minister of Health and Welfare, she again became interested in this possibility and saw tax credits as a way to introduce such an allowance.

It was not until August 1978, however, that the cabinet became receptive to the introduction of tax credits. This change of mind took place, paradoxically enough, in conjunction with a severe spending restraint exercise launched by the Prime Minister. Trudeau announced his plan for a substantial reduction in government expenditures in a speech on 1 August, shortly after returning from an economic summit in Bonn. The announcement was inspired by discussions with other national leaders at the summit and was not the product of consultations with any of the cabinet ministers (not even the minister of Finance).[32] The fiscally restrictive philosophy that had long prevailed at Finance and that had become more influential in cabinet since 1976 was now actively and independently adopted by the Prime Minister and his closest advisers.

Trudeau announced that his ministers would be called back to Ottawa immediately to discuss how the cuts, totalling $2 billion, were to be distributed among departments. Bégin was completely surprised by the initiative; when the cabinet met, she was told that one of the programs singled out for reductions was the universal family allowance. Both she and Finance minister Jean Chrétien understood that this cut would be very unpopular.

It was in this context that the idea of a very modest tax credit, targeted exclusively at families with children, was raised in cabinet discussions. The credit would be introduced to divert attention away from the many reductions that were being made in family allowances and other programs and to present the entire package in a more positive light. The cuts, in the words of Treasury Board president Robert Andras's, "would not touch payments and services ... to many unfortunate Canadians who are least able to protect themselves against inflation and economic hardship." Using this fundamentally liberal argument, the government could argue that it was showing compassion while responding to the rigorous requirements of economic renewal.[33]

The introduction of the credit was agreed to by Bégin and Chrétien. Finance officials either accepted – or could no longer overrule – the use of credits, and Shoyama even contributed to the drafting of a preliminary outline of the credit for cabinet. Details of the legislation were worked out subsequently by officials in Robinson's branch at Health and Welfare.

The program cuts included a reduction in the monthly family allowance payment from $25.68 in 1978 – and a projected $28 in 1979 – to $20. The saving realized from this reduction (approximately $690 million per year) would be channelled into the tax credit, which would apply to families with children whose income was below the national average. A smaller sum of money would come from reducing the tax exemption for children and eliminating the $50-per-child tax reduction. The overall impact of the cuts and of the new credit was "revenue-neutral" – that is, in the family benefits area, the government was neither spending more money nor saving any. The credit's value to a family of four was less than half that of the very modest 1976 supplementation proposal. A maximum credit of $200 annually per child was available to families with an income of less than $18,000 per annum.[34]

The Child Tax Credit of 1978 was the Social Security Review's only concrete by-product. Because it had become impossible to develop any new income maintenance program through federal/provincial discussions, the credit was implemented unilaterally by the federal government. In addition, the program was primarily financed from savings in the existing family-allowance demogrant and thus represented a modest and incremental response to poverty rather than an ambitious and systematic one; it also represented a move towards a more selective income security system in Canada rather than a simultaneous improvement in universal and selective measures. Its unilateral development, along with these design features, meant that the credit failed to reflect the objectives of the Orange Paper.

SOCIAL SERVICES

By February 1975 the social service strategy was moribund. The working party on social services was inactive, and no effort was being made at the federal level to prepare new legislation in this area. Most provinces, however, continued to see reform in social services as a priority. Recognizing that he could count on provincial support, at least in general terms, Johnson directed his officials to draft a memorandum to cabinet on a new Social Services Act. The rejection of NHW's ambitious support/supplementation proposal in February had provided its senior officials with an opportunity to seek cabinet approval of service reform: having already won such a major victory on income security, Finance would find it harder to attack the proposal on social services.

Of the three major components in the Review, the service strategy was alone in being conducted largely by career officials within NHW. Under Johnson's general guidance, the cabinet memo was prepared by John Osborne and Del Lyngseth, career officials in the department. Later, when work the details of a legislative outline began, Brian Iverson and his Social Services Program Branch assumed responsibility for drafting the legislation. At the provincial level, the services strategy was also largely conducted by career welfare officials, many of whom had a background in social work. This strategy came much closer than the others to benefiting from the kind of shared professional experience and norms that characterize federal/provincial relations under a departmentalized cabinet structure and foster successful interjurisdictional policy making.

Like the support/supplementation package, social service reform was nonetheless unsuccessful, for similar reasons. Cooperative policy making was impeded by discord within the federal government between officials with different professional backgrounds. It was also undermined by strategic bargaining between the two levels of government over who would finance and control reform. Thus service reform was crippled by the deleterious economic and intergovernmental developments that surrounded it.

Johnson excepted, planning officials at NHW remained uninterested in social services. Robinson argued that any new legislation should include only modest changes from the existing provisions of CAP and that two years of painstaking research should be conducted to assess future needs before a more comprehensive reform was contemplated. Van Loon made similar arguments.[35]

But Johnson had already decided upon his course, and the memorandum went to cabinet in early April; on the 15th, the document was largely accepted by cabinet as a basis for negotiations with the provinces.[36] It was further discussed at a series of federal/provincial meetings later that month and again accepted by the provinces as a basis for negotiation. But the federal package was discussed only in very general terms at these meetings. When the provinces finally focused on its details in the summer and autumn, they found much ground for complaint.

Federal/Provincial Conflict

The federal proposal was designed to allow greater flexibility in the delivery of social services than was present in CAP, which restricted cost-sharing to services made available to clients on a needs-tested basis. The new legislation envisaged a range of different formulas – from universal availability at no cost, through universal availability with the selective application of user charges, to income-testing and needs-testing. In addition, the new legislation would cover some services (for rehabilitation and prevention, for example) not included in CAP. It would therefore move well beyond CAP in both the range of delivery options available and the number of services covered.

But the federal proposal included other features less likely to appeal to the provinces. In internal discussions, federal welfare officials often referred to the need for federal leadership in the area of social services; to secure what they saw as important national objectives and to constrain costs, their proposals specified which mode of delivery would be available for each service. Services were listed in five categories, each of which set the conditions that clients must meet if a province wished to qualify for cost-sharing.[37] Services could only be added to any of the categories, or moved from one to another, by federal order-in-council. The provinces would be consulted before such a change was made, but there was no requirement that the federal government abide by their wishes. The federal authorities could also terminate their participation in the legislation after a one-year notice period.[38]

Federal officials spent the summer drafting a detailed legislative outline based on the April proposals, and this was presented to the provinces in the fall.[39] NHW officials were unpleasantly surprised by the provincial response. As one of them put it, they had "seriously misread" their provincial counterparts. In contrast to the federal desire to exercise policy leadership, the provinces wanted a very limited role for the federal government beyond sharing the costs of provincial services. The issue of national standards, which had proved a minor irritant in the creation of CAP, became a fundamental point of disagreement between federal and provincial officials in the context of the acrimonious interjurisdictional relations of the mid-1970s.[40]

Some provinces went so far as to question the appropriateness of the federal authorities' setting any conditions for cost-sharing, implying that they would prefer a block-funding approach. In a communiqué the provincial ministers "unanimously expressed grave concern that federal legislation in the cost sharing of social services

not pre-empt the right and duty of each province to fulfil its constitutional responsibilities in this important field."[41] Their concerns were
elaborated in a joint letter to Lalonde: "For the legislation to include
detailed program description, and listing of existing services under
each grouping, would be to defeat the very purpose of the new
legislation and our shared goals." As an alternative, the provinces
proposed that services be divided into only two very loose categories,
that provincial acquiescence be formally required for any changes in
program structure (as was the case with the Canada Pension Plan),
and that the notice period for termination of cost-sharing be five
years.[42]

Federal officials now modified their proposals and presented the
provinces with a revised outline in February 1976. The number of
service categories was reduced from five to three, and the document
explicitly affirmed provincial jurisdiction over social services. The
period required for a notice of termination was augmented to three
years, but the federal government refused to extend it beyond this;
it was also unwilling to abandon its unilateral right to alter the
conditions of cost-sharing.[43] At the February welfare ministers' conference, the provinces seemed to be satisfied with the changes; a
conference communiqué announced that the federal and provincial
governments had agreed on a legislative draft for a new social services act and that after each minister had obtained the consent of his
or her cabinet, a further meeting would finalize the agreement.[44]

But when the deputy ministers met in April to clear up any
remaining details, the mood had soured considerably. As in 1975,
once they had studied the federal proposal in some detail, the provinces became apprehensive about its implied restrictions. Quebec was
particularly insistent that the federal outline was still too complex;
Ontario and Manitoba wanted an assurance that federal contributions
to services would meet a guaranteed minimum. A plethora of other
objections to details in the outline were raised.[45]

At the next meeting, held in June, Lalonde expected to reach final
agreement on the legislation, but there was no consensus. In part,
the provinces hesitated to commit themselves because they continued
to have technical reservations. But the most important reason for
their hesitation had to do with the rapidly deteriorating situation of
federal/provincial fiscal relations. Many provinces complained that
they could no longer count on continued federal financial participation in shared-cost programs; this made them reluctant to commit
themselves to undertaking a new one. Ontario refused to endorse
the social service package before the meeting about fiscal arrangements scheduled for later that month, and other provinces said that

while agreeing in principle to the federal offer, they would not make a final decision until they were apprised of the extent of future federal participation in shared-cost programs.[46] The June 1976 meeting thus ended without a firm agreement on social service reform.

Interdepartmental Conflicts

Johnson's initiative in the social service area also encountered opposition within the federal government itself. The department of Manpower and Immigration, which had opposed the creation of a working party on social services in 1973, now vehemently attacked Health and Welfare's effort to include employment-related services in the proposed new act and was able to reduce the scope of the legislation. As for Finance officials, when they saw an early version of the first legislative outline, they became concerned about its financial open-endedness and persuaded Health and Welfare to include explicit financial ceilings in later versions. Finance's concern was premised on its restrictive fiscal agenda and reflected the ongoing impact of the new economic circumstances on service reform. Both of these developments restricted its scope and exacerbated the federal/provincial tensions discussed above.

The conflict with Manpower proceeded in three stages. The first was the discussion of Johnson's memorandum in cabinet in April 1975. Robert Andras and Allan Gotlieb complained to their colleagues at NHW that by proposing to share the costs of employment services delivered by the provincial governments, the cabinet memo might provide federal money to provincial programs that duplicated services already provided by Manpower. Gotlieb demanded that the cabinet document include an "iron clad guarantee" that no duplication would occur.[47] On Johnson's advice, Lalonde refused to include such a guarantee, but the cabinet decision authorizing Lalonde to proceed with the initiative attempted to accommodate Manpower's fears: no provincial service funded under a Social Services Act could duplicate an existing federal service, and the Health and Welfare minister would have to consult with his colleague at Manpower to ensure that this did not happen.[48]

The dispute with Manpower reignited at the end of the summer, as NHW officials were finalizing their first legislative outline. Gotlieb referred to the outline as "totally unacceptable" and proposed a very sweeping exclusion of provincial employment-related services from the proposed legislation. The exclusion would cover services duplicating those already available through existing federal programs, but it would also extend to those which *could be provided* under an existing federal program or service."[49] In Gotlieb's opinion, "nearly all" of some categories of employment services mentioned in the outline were provided, or could be provided, under a Manpower program.[50] Manpower officials asserted that if there was any money available in the federal treasury for employment services, it should be directed towards programs administered by their department, not by provincial social service departments.[51] NHW officials replied that the provinces had a legitimate interest in employment services and could coordinate them more effectively with their other services.[52]

The final and decisive round in the conflict occurred in November and December, as NHW was revising the September outline. This time, the dispute dragged on for six weeks and ended only on 29 December, when the two departments worked out a compromise. The new outline allowed NHW to include employment services in the legislation, but it also included a substantial restriction aimed at meeting Manpower's objections: no services would be financed under the legislation that created jobs, unless this happened only incidentally. More importantly, no existing Manpower service could be duplicated unless the provincial alternative was being provided in a geographic area where Manpower's service was not available or unless there was a need in the community for both services.[53] As many provinces quickly realized, this implied that if Manpower expanded access to a service, the provinces could lose cost-sharing for their employment service if it was seen as an alternative.

This settlement ended Health and Welfare's troubles with Manpower, but it created additional conflicts with the provinces. From 1975 to 1977, they often complained that the cost-sharing provisions were far too restrictive for employment services. Many provincial welfare officials did not trust federal Manpower officials to provide adequate employment preparation for traditional welfare recipients, and they argued that Manpower programs were no substitute for their own.[54]

The department of Finance did not attempt to derail the social service proposal when the latter went through cabinet in April 1975. But when the first legislative outline was taking shape, Finance balked at its open-endedness. While the outline burdened the provinces with numerous conditions, it did not set any explicit ceilings on the level of federal cost-sharing. If federal program conditions were met, the provinces could count on federal coverage of 50 percent of their costs.

At the end of August, Lalonde and his senior advisors met Finance minister Macdonald and senior officials from that department, the Treasury Board, and the Privy Council Office to discuss the outline.

Macdonald asked that explicit cost controls be put into the document. On 23 September, Cohen, the assistant deputy minister of Finance, again pressed Rawson to add to the document explicit upper ceilings on federal contributions. Cohen asserted "that the need for cost control is even more pressing now than it was earlier this year in the light of economic and fiscal developments. The last Budget accentuated the thrust of fiscal policy towards expenditure restraints as evidenced, for instance, in the measures to contain the growth rate under both medicare and hospital insurance."[55]

In his reply, Rawson argued that costs in the planned Social Services Act would not spiral out of control without explicit ceilings. But he also hinted that the revised version of the legislative outline might include tighter financial controls.[56] In fact, Health and Welfare was already working on alternative options for including ceilings in the revised outline.[57]

The revised legislative outline did include such ceilings. It specified that "a ceiling on contributions towards costs of residential services for adults [the most open-ended class of services in the outline] will be established after a three year period following proclamation of the legislation." The federal government would continue to share in half the costs for the first three years only if the provinces submitted detailed information that would "yield the data required to determine comparable costs across Canada to serve as a basis for considering the nature of the ceiling to be introduced in the legislation."[58] This restriction appeased Finance, but pressure to include even more radical constraints on federal fiscal commitments to the new shared-cost program were to emerge later in 1976 and in 1977.

As with the Manpower dispute, the resolution of the conflict with Finance led to a deterioration in Health and Welfare's relationship with the provinces. Provincial welfare officials understood that their federal counterparts were under pressures to restrict costs, but they now complained that the federal authorities were restricting cost-sharing for services that often experienced unpredictable growth in demand.[59]

The Demise of Cost-Sharing, June 1976–September 1977

The June 1976 federal/provincial conference did not eliminate all of the remaining disagreements on details of the social service proposal. Nevertheless, once the provinces were assured that developments in other areas of fiscal federalism would not affect service reform, it became possible to move forward with a detailed legislative proposal.

Federal and provincial officials worked on the details of the legislation during the remainder of 1976 and the early months of 1977.

Bill C-55, the final version of the Social Services Act, was introduced in the House of Commons on 20 June 1977. It proposed a radical reform of the federal sharing of provincial costs. A range of delivery options were provided, including universality, to replace CAP's requirement of a needs test, and more services were covered than in the existing legislation. But the bill was withdrawn almost as soon as it was tabled. On 15 September, in his last act before leaving the NHW portfolio, Lalonde announced that the cost-sharing proposals would be replaced with a "Social Services Financing Act" that would finance provincial social services on a block-funding basis.[60] This development reflected the ever-increasing impact of the forces that had been shaping discussions on the social service legislation since their beginning in 1975. Lalonde and his officials continued to experience frustrations in negotiations with the provinces as they finalized the details of the legislation. As a departmental memo put it at the time, "the provincial desire to respond to the needs of their citizens as they see fit, with little or no federal involvement, is incompatible with cost-sharing as a funding instrument."[61] Relations with Quebec and Ontario were particularly difficult during this period. In Quebec the *Parti Québécois* had won a provincial election in November 1976. Its Social Affairs minister, Denis Lazure, took a far more strident position in negotiations with the federal authorities than had his Liberal predecessors. Lazure stated flatly – and very publicly – that Quebec would consider any new cost-sharing arrangement an invasion of provincial jurisdiction; he specifically rejected Bill C-55. More privately, during the following summer Ontario also began to raise emphatic objections to the cost-sharing approach and to suggest a block grant as an alternative.

The introduction of block funding for hospital and medical services in April 1977 was a landmark result of the prevailing desire of the federal government and the provinces to achieve autonomy from each other's priorities. Because block funding gave the provinces access to federal money with very few strings attached, it whetted their appetite for more of the same.[62]

In the face of these mounting obstacles, even such long-time welfare officials as Brian Iverson, who had long championed cost-sharing, abandoned any hope that this formula could work in the area of services. Iverson drew up a cabinet memo proposing that Bill C-55 be replaced with a block-funding proposal. Lalonde was also frustrated with the provinces and supported the proposal.

The Eclipse of Social Service Reform,
September 1977–November 1978

The block-funding proposal sought to replace the sums that the provinces would receive for social services under CAP and the Vocational Rehabilitation for Disabled Persons (VRDP) Act with a block grant, using 1977–78 as the base year. The grant would be escalated in subsequent years "on the basis of the three-year moving average of GNE per capita."[63] The proposal also included provisions designed to make it more appealing to the provinces – especially the poorer ones, which traditionally supported cost-sharing – and to accommodate what remained of the desire by federal welfare officials to stimulate improved services in the provinces. The formula included a "levelling factor" designed to equalize per-capita payments to each province over a period of ten years; this, in effect, would transfer resources from those provinces which spent more on services – usually the richer ones – to poorer ones that spent less. In addition, the formula included a sweetener: in the first year of the new legislation, the provinces would receive $150 million in excess of the sum that they would qualify for under the existing CAP and VRDP legislations. This money, it was hoped, would be spent on improving services.[64]

Although these provisions obviated the mounting attacks by the provinces on federal interference in their affairs, their initial response was not enthusiastic. A conference of provincial welfare ministers condemned Lalonde's announcement a week after it was made, because the federal government had not consulted them in drawing up the proposal.[65] With the exception of Saskatchewan, Prince Edward Island, and (less emphatically) Nova Scotia, all provinces supported the move from cost-sharing to a block grant, but many had reservations about specific features of the federal proposal. Both Quebec and Ontario – the provinces most anxious to terminate cost-sharing – would have preferred a simple transfer of tax points; and British Columbia opposed the levelling factor, which would disadvantage it as a high-spending province. But most provinces accepted the block-funding proposal.[66]

This support was dampened, however, when Bégin announced in December 1977 that the $150 million sweetener would have to be deferred for one year because of budgetary restraint within the federal government.[67] But at a federal/provincial meeting of welfare ministers on 7–8 March 1978, all of the provinces except British Columbia agreed to the principles of the block-funding package. With the sweetener gone, however, no province showed much real enthusiasm for the legislation.[68]

The Social Services Financing Act was introduced in the House of Commons on 12 May, but it had not yet been passed when the House recessed for the summer in July. Rawson assured the provinces that the legislation would be reintroduced in the autumn,[69] but Trudeau's economic statement of 1 August signalled an even more vigorous period of fiscal restraint in the federal government. This, combined with the evolving attitude of the new Health and Welfare minister about unconditional transfers to the provinces, precluded passage of the legislation.

The social service legislation was not included in the list of program reductions drawn up within the federal government in August, but it was very much affected by the atmosphere of severe restraint that now prevailed. Finance played an important role in transmitting this influence. On 8 September, Chrétien and the president of the Treasury Board made a joint statement announcing a significant reduction in the rate of growth that the federal government would permit for the health and postsecondary-education block grants included in the 1977 Established Programs Financing (EPF) Act. Later, Chrétien notified the provinces that he would lower the level of equalization payments to the poorer provinces.[70] Not surprisingly, this evoked a storm of protest from the provinces.

At a meeting with provincial treasurers in November, Chrétien effectively induced the provinces to terminate service reform. He told them that he would reconsider the EPF cuts, but only if the provinces agreed to give up the Social Services Financing Act. The provinces preferred to maintain EPF levels rather than demand passage of the act – which now offered them little anyway – and so the federal government withdrew the legislation.[71] Thus the death of service reform was largely a by-product of the atmosphere of severe fiscal restraint instigated by the Prime Minister in August and implemented with considerable zeal by the department of Finance.

Had Bégin chosen to defend the service legislation, Chrétien could not have succeeded in having it withdrawn without a struggle; however, no such struggle took place. After spending a year in the Health and Welfare portfolio and witnessing the deterioration in federal/provincial relations, Bégin became convinced that the provinces could not be trusted to maintain an adequate financial commitment to social programs without the inducement of federal cost-sharing arrangements. In her view, block funding in the health sector had eroded standards there, and the existing cost-shared Canada Assistance Plan was therefore better than block funding as a guarantee of service standards. In an atmosphere of mutual suspicion between the two levels of government, Bégin could no longer support legislation that would reduce federal program controls.

EMPLOYMENT

By 1975, NHW had long abandoned any effort to control the community employment program, but some interdepartmental tensions remained over the strategy. In November of that year, Manpower had trouble obtaining financing for the experimental projects and sought from cabinet a long-term commitment of $50 million to complete them. In advising Lalonde on what position to take on the matter, Rawson was cool, suggesting that "we may not want to encourage the full commitment asked for by Manpower and Immigration." One reason for this was that, as Rawson flatly stated, "from the time that formal responsibility for CES passed to M&I, we were *never* consulted in advance about any substantive questions relating to CES ... At the bureaucratic level, there is now no special relationship between M&I and H&WC concerning the Community Employment Strategy."[72]

The implementation of the community employment projects aggravated the already considerable friction between provincial welfare officials and federal Manpower bureaucrats. At a meeting in September 1975 – well into the implementation phase of the community employment strategy – provincial welfare officials vented their anger to their federal colleagues. As Rawson described the mood of the meeting, most provincial officials were quite cynical about the projects: "Virtually all provinces felt this way and some were bitterly hostile ... the picture was overwhelmingly negative."[73]

The frustration of the provinces was understandable. As Manpower's own published accounts show quite clearly, the projects were slow to develop; often, they were never begun at all. Where they were, they were frequently the subject of considerable disagreement between federal and provincial officials. A 1977 Manpower publication claimed that the employment strategy had made considerable progress, but the document also referred to "misconceptions and unrealistic expectations that were held about the CES by the provinces" as a factor that had earlier slowed the pace of implementation. When the results of the strategy are examined more closely, it becomes clear that after almost three years the projects were only just beginning to get under way. In many cases, for example, mechanisms were still not in place to evaluate projects; in some provinces, important changes of direction were made very late in the day, requiring a major overhaul of projects.[74]

Finally, in the wake of Trudeau's August statement on cost-cutting, the Treasury Board began to draw up a list of programs to be eliminated; the community employment projects were included. Andras – who, as Manpower minister, had earlier overseen the creation of the projects – was now the president of the Treasury Board. According to a former Manpower official, Andras used the cut as a "sacrificial lamb" to prove that he could give up "one of my babies" to the restraint exercise. Given that community employment had never been pursued with much zeal at Manpower, the infant could hardly have been truly missed.

CONCLUSION

During its last three years, the Social Security Review was crippled by the societal and organizational forces that had shaped it from the outset. The most distinctive feature of the Review's last phase was the decisive role played by functional class influences. While the federal department of Finance, pursuing its market-oriented agenda, had been able to impose restrictions on the Review in 1973, it had not succeeded in preventing it from taking place. But by 1975 Canada's economy had deteriorated precipitously; provincial treasuries, pursuing market-oriented strategies similar to that of the federal Finance department, opposed new social expenditures with growing determination. The recession also strengthened the desire and the ability of Finance officials in Ottawa to scuttle the Review in an effort to restore a prosperous private economy. In early 1975 Finance scored its first major victory in the Review, effectively killing the relatively ambitious two-tier income security proposal that had originated in Health and Welfare. Thereafter, the core anti-spending assumption of Finance's accumulation strategy was advanced more aggressively and successfully both by provincial treasuries and by Finance itself. This assumption was also increasingly adopted on faith by first ministers at both levels of government; at the federal level, this culminated in the restraint exercise of the autumn of 1978, which created the Child Tax Credit and terminated social service reform and what was left of the employment strategy. No government apparently challenged the conventional economic orthodoxy in Canada that in economically troubled times, the best policy was restraint and retrenchment.

The demise of reform also bore the mark of the state's institutionalized structures. The supradepartmental initiatives fostered by these structures typically involved a variety of professional interests between and within governments. Conflict caused by this heterogeneity continued during this period, especially in the social service and employment strategies. The institutionalized structures also encouraged interjurisdictional relations based on government-wide objectives that frequently conflicted. In its last phase, government-wide conflict based on strategic considerations – who would control and pay for reform – became central to the Review. Here again, organizations refracted societal pressures.

CHAPTER EIGHT

Parties, Interest Groups, and Poverty, 1968–78

The political parties did not exercise significant influence on poverty reform in the executive settings examined in the last three chapters. Here, we examine the role of parties in election campaigns and within federal and provincial legislatures. During the Review period, the main parties continued to prefer social security measures broader than those contemplated by welfare officials; this was particularly true of the NDP. None of the parties made poverty reform an important electoral or legislative issue before or during the Review – thus continuing a pattern observed during the 1960s. Economic class organizations – labour unions and business federations – also had no apparent impact on poverty reform. This reflected the broader interests of these groups, as well as labour's limited capacity to influence government.

Non-class, non-governmental interests were similarly inconsequential. During the 1970s organizations of the poor gained prominence in the social security field. While the emergence of these groups was the most important change in the extragovernmental environment of poverty policy making since the 1960s, neither antipoverty groups nor middle-class organizations involved in similar work had a major impact on policy making. Among the main reasons for this were their modest material and intellectual resources, their limited capacity to mobilize their respective constituencies, and their financial dependence on the federal government. The pervasive impotence of non-governmental actors was reinforced by the barriers erected by governments against meaningful involvement in the Review by outside interests. Non-governmental involvement was considered likely to aggravate the fragmentation and acrimony that already characterized the Review process.

POLITICAL PARTIES

Despite the high public profile of poverty issues during the 1970s, none of the national political parties gave poverty reform a major place in its program. In general, they were not strongly motivated to reform policies that were mainly of interest to politically and socially marginal citizens. The parties of the right, which subscribed to a liberal, market-oriented ideology, were the most willing to use the mechanism of a guaranteed annual income to alleviate poverty – a pattern that conformed to the hypotheses set forth in chapter 1. The ideological appeal of the GAI concept in a liberal environment nevertheless only partly compensated for the lack of electoral incentives to reform poverty measures. The NDP, as a social democratic party, was particularly sceptical of the market dependency implied by a GAI.

The GAI did receive some attention in the 1968 election campaign. In a speech on 4 May, Conservative Party leader Robert Stanfield promised to consider establishing "a guaranteed annual income for all those Canadians who cannot earn for themselves." A later statement revealed the quintessentially market-oriented basis for Stanfield's preference: "We must reform the welfare system which in many instances discourages people from working and adopt a plan that encourages rehabilitation and initiative." Stanfield did emphasize, however, that his support for a GAI reflected his personal views, not party policy. The NDP's T.C. Douglas endorsed the GAI concept, but this was done after Stanfield had injected it into the campaign, and Douglas did not give it much attention. The NDP's foremost social policy planks remained more inclusive, with promises to increase the monthly OAS pension,[1] achieve full employment, and provide inexpensive public housing. Trudeau and the Liberals were silent about a GAI and said little about poverty. Despite Trudeau's promise to foster a "just society," social security reform was not a high priority: "Another aspect [of a just society, besides individual freedom] is economic, and, rather than develop that in terms of social legislation and welfare benefits ... I feel that at this time it is more important to develop in terms of groups of people ... defined territorially ... like the Atlantic provinces." Trudeau persistently warned against excessive spending commitments.[2]

Thus the Liberal majority victory in June 1968 did not bode well for significant poverty reform over the next four years; and in 1969 and 1970 Trudeau publicly dismissed the GAI as too expensive to be considered in the foreseeable future. Shortly after one such pronouncement, in November 1970, the Liberals adopted the GAI as party policy at their convention,[3] but this had no noticeable effect on the government. Munro's incremental and frugal FISP proposal, launched only a week later, was justified with an allusion to the putative expense of a GAI. This remained the federal government's position until the 1973 throne speech.

Stanfield continued to express interest in the GAI in 1969, and he remained far more enthusiastic about the concept than did any prominent Liberal or New Democrat. He argued that a GAI could be financed by eliminating some existing universal income security measures and reiterated its value for creating work incentives. At a party policy convention, however, rank-and-file Conservatives rejected a resolution supporting a guaranteed income.[4]

With the end of Conservative support for the GAI and with the Liberals proceeding cautiously, it was left to the two smaller parties periodically to raise poverty concerns – and to propose the GAI as one possible solution – throughout the remainder of the 28th Parliament. The strongest commitment to a GAI during this period was, again, by a party of the right. Réal Caouette's *Ralliement des Créditistes* frequently proclaimed the merits of a GAI;[5] its argument was grounded in the market-oriented assumptions that had attracted Stanfield. The NDP also recommended a GAI, but it did so less frequently, and its position was more complex than that of the *Créditistes*. The NDP was anxious to reconcile its desire to alleviate poverty with its traditional preference for universal income security payments. The party's October 1969 policy convention adopted a GAI proposal but strongly emphasized that the GAI "must be supplemented by complementary programs in many fields if it is to be effective in eliminating poverty." It would be established alongside existing contributory and universal measures, and would be predicated upon efforts to create full employment.[6] In the Commons, the New Democrats were challenged by Munro about their support for a GAI; he wondered whether it was compatible with their defence of universality. Stanley Knowles, the NDP's social affairs critic, saw no contradiction: "Some of us are strong advocates of a guaranteed annual income ... I certainly do not mean by a [GAI] the kind of incremental addition that the Minister of National Health and Welfare has in mind. I have in mind rather something in the nature of a demogrant."[7]

Despite this, poverty issues received only intermittent attention in Parliament before the 1972 election; there was even less discussion of the poor during the campaign itself, although a number of social security issues were hotly debated. The Conservatives launched a strongly market-oriented attack on the Liberal government, criticizing the recent UIC changes as expensive and likely to encourage sloth, and promising to index income taxes to prevent automatic, inflation-induced increases in federal tax revenues. Stanfield referred to the "welfare jungle" as something requiring remedy and assailed the "chicken socialism" of the Liberal government, which was said to be undermining the work ethic. Along with their famous attack on "corporate welfare bums," David Lewis and the NDP championed the traditional social democratic goal of full employment, promising to achieve it simultaneously with important social security objectives by initiating a massive public-housing program, subsidizing mortgages, and funding urban transportation and day care. The NDP also promised to raise OAS payments to $150 a month, in part because that would substantially reduce the number of elderly Canadians requiring the selective (and therefore undesirable) GIS.[8] Lewis said little about his party's GAI policy. None of the three national parties focused attention on poverty-oriented reforms.

The guaranteed annual income nevertheless became an issue in the 1972 campaign debate. As in 1968, interest in a GAI came from the political right. Indeed, Caouette made it the cornerstone of his program. The GAI would replace all existing universal measures, thus resulting in a net saving in expenditures, and it would eliminate work disincentives from the social security system.[9] But the *Créditistes* did not campaign significantly outside Quebec, and their focus on the GAI concept did not give it a high national profile during the campaign.

Thus when the Social Security Review was launched in the January 1973 throne speech, it did not benefit from political momentum generated in a legislative or electoral context. And as was argued in chapter 5, there is little evidence of discrete pressure from the NDP, in the two months following the election, that would have caused the Liberal minority government to embark on a substantial program to reform poverty policy. The political atmosphere of the minority government contributed to the Review, but only in a general and indirect manner. The impetus towards reform emanated from federal and provincial bureaucracies, and thus the Review reflected the prevailing institutionalized state structures in a generally liberal ideological and policy climate.

After the Review was launched and during the election campaign of 1974, there were also few influences within the House of Commons that encouraged the Liberal government to push the initiative forward. Both the throne speech announcement and the subsequent tabling of the Orange Paper were greeted with surprisingly little comment from the opposition benches, at least with regard to the poverty reforms that the Review promised. One NDP Member of

Parliament did make a passing reference to the antipoverty element in the Review shortly after the January throne speech, but neither the Conservatives nor the New Democrats said much about the poor when the Orange Paper was tabled in April. Heath MacQuarrie, speaking for the Tories, greeted the paper positively but referred only to its family-allowance and Canada Pension Plan provisions. Knowles did mention poverty reform in his statement, but he mainly emphasized his party's strong preference for universality and discussed at length the abandonment of FISP and the preservation of the universal family allowance. His remarks on the antipoverty elements of the Review suggested approval, but they also indicated that the NDP had had little to do with inspiring them: "The idea of a guaranteed annual income, the right to live and to enjoy what our society can produce, is something we must establish if we are going to build on a good foundation the kind of social security system we can build. I agree completely with the minister *in his innovativeness and newness of ideas in this area.*"[10]

There was little discussion of the three Review strategies in the Commons from April 1973 until the defeat of the minority government in May 1974. Of course, the strategies – especially those on income security and services – were embroiled in fractious federal/provincial negotiations during this period; Lalonde and his parliamentary secretary deflected the very few questions asked about the Review by observing that matters were still under discussion with the provinces.[11] Following the NDP's policy convention in July 1973 and an *in camera* strategy meeting held a month later, a number of new demands were aimed at the Liberal government, but nothing was said about the Review or a guaranteed income.[12]

The 1974 election campaign revealed that with the deepening recession, social security issues of any kind were receding in political importance; inflation and Stanfield's fateful promise to stop it with mandatory controls were the main issue.[13] Most social policy debates centred on policies of interest to middle-class voters. The Conservatives promised a modest expansion of OAS coverage, while the NDP promised a more ambitious extension of coverage and a near doubling of the pension's value. All three major parties proposed measures to reduce the cost of home ownership, but the ongoing Social Security Review received no attention. Only the *Créditistes* again trumpeted their GAI proposal, making no reference to the Review.[14]

After the election, there was little protest from the opposition parties as the Review unravelled. During the month following the February 1975 welfare ministers' meeting, where Lalonde had announced that supplementation would be postponed indefinitely, only two questions were asked about the debacle in the Commons. When the support/supplementation discussions finally collapsed in June 1976, only one question was asked about the outcome of the Review in the Commons, and only the *Créditistes* continued their demand for a GAI, again failing to comment in any detail on developments at the federal/provincial level.[15]

LABOUR AND BUSINESS

Labour and business federations reflect class interests in the economy, just as the party system embodies class interests in the political arena. During the 1970s, economic class organizations continued to play a secondary role in the poverty sector, for largely the same reasons as in the preceding decade. The concerns of the poor were generally peripheral to the interests of class organizations, and labour organizations continued to have only modest capacities to achieve their policy goals.

Organized Labour

By international standards, Canadian organized labour remained relatively weak during the 1970s. This reflected the persistently modest levels of unionization in Canada, as well as the minor party status of the NDP, labour's political arm. While no resolutely anti-labour policy was adopted at the federal level during that period, the Trudeau government did not invite labour into the decision-making process. Organized labour's influence eroded significantly after 1975.[16]

As in the 1960s, labour's weakness was reflected in the discrepancy between the social democratic content of its social proposals and the predominantly liberal design of Canada's welfare state. This divergence continued to shape labour's approach to poverty issues, especially the GAI. The typically social democratic objectives of full employment and universal social security remained the core of labour's social agenda. While it accepted the GAI, the Canadian Labour Congress never became one of its foremost advocates. Organized labour thus had a negligible role in the Social Security Review.

A guaranteed income was first discussed within the CLC in 1966, and it remained a subject of controversy for some time. Andy Andras, the congress's director of legislation, was sceptical about how a GAI would be integrated with existing non-selective measures. By contrast, Gordon McCaffrey, another congress official, was enthusiastic and even suggested in a private memo that some existing universal measures could be replaced by a GAI.[17] The CLC's annual memo to cabinet for 1969 expressed approval of the GAI,[18] but it was not until the following year that the congress officially committed itself to the concept of a guaranteed income. Several policy statements made in 1970 recommended the idea, at the same time linking it firmly to the CLC's traditional social democratic agenda.

The most comprehensive expression of the CLC's policy in 1970 was a resolution passed at its national convention in May and submitted to Senator Croll's committee on poverty in November. The congress endorsed a GAI, but only as a third and final tier in the social security system; alone, "the provision of a minimum income, however adequate, is not enough." The first defence against poverty was that the poor must be given "opportunities to provide for themselves. This requires a policy of full employment, supplemented by adequate minimum wage legislation, strong labour market and manpower policies and ... regional development." The second defence would be universal and contributory social security measures. There must be "far-reaching improvements in Canada's system of social security," including "higher unemployment insurance benefits, improved benefits under the Canada Pension Plan and the Old Age Security Act, family allowances not only higher in amounts but more realistic, ... the introduction of a cash sickness benefit program and of a maternity benefit program." The GAI would be a "backstop," meeting whatever need was not accommodated by the first two tiers.[19] The congress was again reconciling its social democratic objectives with its liberal environment: no foreseeable change in government policies affecting the first two elements of Canada's welfare state could eliminate the need for significant measures targeted at the needy.

At the Croll Committee hearings in 1970, some of the participating senators attacked the CLC for devoting too little energy to policies primarily relevant to the poor; Andras conceded that this was the case.[20] The leading congress actors during those years did not see the CLC as a dominant force in shaping federal policies for the poor, and this perception was very much shared by officials within the federal government and in other non-governmental organizations. Similarly, during the period immediately preceding the Orange Paper's release in April 1973, the CLC exercised no direct influence over the federal government that could have contributed significantly to launching the Review; nor did prominent actors in the Review, both within and outside the federal government, attribute to organized labour a significant influence on the Review after it was launched.

Federal reformers did not meet CLC representatives about the Review until July 1973, and the poverty components of the Orange

Paper were not discussed until much later. Because most federal objectives in the Review were clearly established at the outset, especially in the income security field, these consultations are unlikely to have influenced policy making at Health and Welfare. The July meeting dealt exclusively with the views of the congress on the Canada Pension Plan proposals in the Orange Paper. At the end of the meeting, Lalonde complained that he had not yet heard from the congress about the poverty-oriented elements of the Orange Paper. He pointed out that "if we want to have any impact on the proposed changes to the social security system, we should present our views to the government 'before the federal government's own position has hardened'," implying that such a hardening had not already occurred. A congress official at the meeting inferred from this that the CLC should present its views to the government by mid-fall to have any effect.[21] In fact, it was not until some time later that the congress met Lalonde to discuss any subject other than pension issues. Internal discussion about the merits of the poverty elements of the Orange Paper had begun soon after the document's release, but in December 1973 internal memoranda still advocated further refinements in CLC policy.[22] As a consequence, the federal reformers were not fully apprised of labour's position on poverty reform until 1974. The CLC's eventual response to the Orange Paper reflected the GAI policy it had developed in 1970. It approved of support/supplementation but wanted benefit levels to be high enough to remove recipients from poverty. The CLC was adamant that income security reform should be complemented by higher minimum wages, which would prevent support/supplementation from being used by employers to subsidize low wages. Income security reform must also leave in place existing social insurance programs. The CLC was more ambivalent about the employment strategy. While supporting efforts to reintegrate the socially marginal into the labour market, the congress wanted a much more ambitious approach to employment – in effect, a full-employment policy. Apprehension was also expressed to the federal authorities about the possibility that a community employment program might pay less than prevailing market wages. The CLC paid little attention to the social service strategy.[23]

Business Federations

Business organizations had more opportunities to be involved in the Social Security Review than in the creation of CAP, and these were used to express caution about income security reform. In interviews conducted for this study, however, senior governmental and non-governmental actors in the Review expressed the opinion that business groups had no significant influence on the reform process. This marginal role reflected the same factors that were at work during the 1960s. The GAI concept was more compatible than most other social security measures with the liberal objectives of business, and thus objections to the GAI were milder than were those against other social programs. During the 1970s, the liberal image of the welfare state in the business community led to vigorous attacks on universal and public contributory programs; the GAI evoked a less hostile response. On the other hand, because of its potential cost and negative consequences for work incentives, business groups never actively supported proposals for a guaranteed income. After 1975, their views were distinctly negative, on balance.

Of the leading business federations, the Canadian Chamber of Commerce was the most active in the Review process; the Canadian Manufacturers' Association also periodically approached the federal government with its views, while the Canadian Bankers' Association played only a very modest role. The views of all three organizations paralleled the accumulation strategy pursued by the Finance department, but the latter, as an agent of capitalist class interests in the halls of power, played a much more crucial role.

The Chamber of Commerce developed a GAI policy in 1970, but its involvement in the Review did not begin in earnest until the spring of 1974. Since federal objectives on support/supplementation were firmly established well before this, the Chamber is unlikely to have had any influence on them; if it did, it was to assist, in a minor way, in the Review's destruction.

In a 1970 submission to the Croll Committee, the Chamber did not reject a GAI but argued that it could only be afforded by reducing expenditures on other social programs. The primary issue in considering new social programs was "the nation's ability to provide the physical as well as the financial resources needed ... It does not seem reasonable for public authorities to encroach further upon incomes, thus endangering private initiative." Meeting need within levels of taxation that did not hinder the market economy would have been easier "had we relied on selectivity instead of universality in drafting our social welfare plans." Furthermore, another "of the most serious problems of extensive social security is the incentive or disincentive to work which it may create in the recipient." These three objectives – limiting expense, increasing selectivity, and maximizing incentives – all reflected liberal goals; they all suggested to the Chamber that the GAI concept might have some merit. On the other hand, the Chamber refused to commit itself to that idea because it was unsure that a GAI could be financed from savings in other social programs and because its potential impact on incentives was still unclear.[24]

In April 1974, the Chamber made a formal submission to the federal government about the Review, apparently the first non-governmental organization to do so.[25] The brief repeated the Chamber's concern that the "overall costs" of the social security system might become an impediment to economic growth. While expressing approval of the focus on work incentives in the Orange Paper, the brief argued that "this principle seems to have been overlooked in some ... parts of the Orange Paper." In particular, a community employment program might dissuade people from accepting undesirable labour; and the "guaranteed annual income for everyone," which the Chamber thought was implied by propositions 7 and 8 of the Orange Paper, represented a "repudiation of the currently accepted work ethic." The Chamber's objections to a GAI therefore paralleled those of Reisman at Finance: although the guaranteed income was designed to enhance work incentives, it would, in fact, undermine them. For this reason, and because the Chamber still did not envisage that support/supplementation could be implemented without a significant increase in public spending, it did not encourage the federal government to proceed with the major propositions in the Orange Paper.[26]

Lalonde was slow to respond to the Chamber's brief. His January 1975 reply initiated an intermittent dialogue between actors at NHW and at the Chamber of Commerce about the merits of the Review.[27] Lalonde and his officials did not challenge the Chamber's liberal presuppositions. On the contrary, federal actors were anxious to point out the Orange Paper's stipulation that any new program was to be financed within existing levels of taxation and that support/supplementation was, after all, a selective measure. The federal authorities also insisted on the incentive-creating potential of the two-tier support/supplementation proposal, and Lalonde assured that no new income security initiatives of a universal kind were being considered by the federal government. When the exchange became acrimonious, it was not over the merits of a liberal image of the welfare state, but over the appropriateness of the Orange Paper's proposals in this liberal context. Federal actors defended support/supplementation in liberal terms: it would enhance, not erode, the market orientation of its recipients. Lalonde also insisted that in the inflationary times alluded to by the Chamber, it was all the more necessary that government protect the least advantaged citizens; he argued that there was a consensus in Canadian society that government should redistribute the nation's wealth towards the disadvantaged. The liveliest moments in the exchange resulted from the Chamber's disagreement with Lalonde on these points; the Chamber argued that redistribution was not justified in principle and was not supported by public opinion.[28]

There is little evidence that the Chamber's increasingly negative disposition towards the Review contributed significantly to the latter's demise. Admittedly, in a February 1976 meeting with officers of the Chamber, Lalonde attributed to the latter an important role in convincing NHW to scale down its support/supplementation proposals: "Some of your representations have led us to conclude that we should limit [the] extent of coverage." It was for this reason, he said, that the revised supplementation proposals would only cover families with children and those 55 years of age and over.[29] Nevertheless, none of the major Review participants interviewed for this study attributed such influence to the Chamber; the evidence cited in chapters 6 and 7 suggests that it was the representation of a market-oriented accumulation strategy *within* the federal and provincial governments – by the Finance department initially, and later by provincial treasuries and others – that destroyed the Review. Of course, this accumulation strategy very much paralleled the agenda of the Canadian Chamber of Commerce.

The position of the Canadian Manufacturers' Association, though stated less frequently, was similar to that of the Chamber of Commerce. A November 1973 memo from the CMA on social policy expressed concern about the growing problem of inflation and its negative consequences for industrial activity. It contended that rising government spending on social security was a major cause of inflation and should therefore be curtailed. In correspondence with Lalonde, the CMA's executive director criticized the Review. Referring to the scaled-down support/supplementation proposals in 1976, he wrote that "there is a strong and pervasive view that the proposals, on top of existing programs could be highly inflationary in nature ... we do not believe that without an equivalent ongoing reduction in outlays in other existing programs the country can afford this new program." The CMA also shared the Chamber's preoccupation with incentives: "We wonder ... whether income supplementation would prevent upgrading of skills by removing the motivation of people to move into a more productive job when they are content with current income because of income supplementation."[30]

These views were repeated at private meetings with Lalonde and his officials in the same year. Health and Welfare responded to the CMA in the same way as it had to the Chamber: the costs of a new program (especially the modest proposals of 1976) would be minimal and would therefore add little to inflation; and supplementation made ample allowance for incentives.[31] While the CMA was less active than the Chamber in the Review, its views were similar and do not appear to have had any more direct influence on the failure of the reform process.

There is no record of direct involvement in the Review by the Canadian Bankers' Association, but its statements on social policy during the 1970s reflected the liberal, market-oriented arguments expounded by the other business federations. Editorials in *The Canadian Banker* compared the merits of a negative income tax with those of existing social security measures, but they also expressed concern about how this approach might work in practice; they extolled the virtues of private and selective alternatives to such universal programs as medicare. By 1975, leading bankers were pointing the finger at government expenditure as the "engine of inflation," arguing that "the work ethic is not as widely accepted as it used to be and ... the economic disadvantages of not working have been notably lessened by the expanded welfare system."[32]

During the Social Security Review, economic class organizations expressed views that reflected their class interests. These interests account, in part, for the marginal role that these organizations played in the Review. Organized labour's social democratic agenda did, in the liberal context of Canada's welfare state, find a place for the GAI and other reforms considered during the Review, and it also made room for greater sensitivity to the needs of poor people; but universality remained the major preoccupation of the CLC's social policy. Similarly, because of their naturally liberal agenda, business federations objected less to selective reforms than to other types of social security reforms; but their interrelated concerns about government expenditures, inflation, and incentives all reflected a market-oriented view of capital accumulation and thus precluded eager acceptance of *any* reforms considered during the Review.

NON-CLASS ORGANIZATIONS

During the late 1960s, organizations claiming to represent, or speak on behalf of, the poor emerged in Canada. Local poverty organizations were rare before the mid-1960s but by 1971 had become quite common.[33] The early 1970s also witnessed the formation of national organizations of the poor. These developments reflected Canada's "rediscovery of poverty" in those years; they were also part of the increased focus on civic activism and participation in Canada and other capitalist democracies in the late 1960s.

Poverty Organizations

A report commissioned by the federal government in 1970 identified 215 noteworthy local and regional poverty groups across Canada.[34] Their emergence no doubt reflected some self-mobilization among socially disadvantaged people during the late 1960s, but as Lawrence Felt observes, the "proliferation of militant poor community groups" also owed much to "federal funding"; as fiscal resources became scarcer in the mid- to late 1970s, the number of local poverty organizations dwindled.[35] These groups never developed adequate independent financial or analytical resources, nor did they have a significant capacity to mobilize disadvantaged Canadians. In addition, while the federal government did not set explicit limits on political activism by groups receiving funds, its response to perceived radicalism suggests that implicit limits did exist. For all of these reasons, and because of the impediments to non-governmental participation in the Review (documented later on), poverty groups had no significant impact on poverty reform.

A number of departments in the federal government sponsored poverty organizations during the late 1960s.[36] The most active was Health and Welfare, which funded them through its National Welfare Grants (NWG) program.[37] This initiative reflected a commitment to the concept of citizen participation among some officials in Ottawa after 1968, especially among NHW minister Munro's political staff.[38] But the fear of potentially disruptive mobilization among poor Canadians played a role as well. The first poverty group to benefit from the NWG program, in 1969, was the Black United Front of Nova Scotia.[39] A cabinet memorandum from Munro and Secretary of State Gérard Pelletier recommending the funding referred to the Front as "the constructive and moderate elements within the black community of Nova Scotia" and argued that "the failure of this organization will result in the discrediting of these elements and the shift of power to more extreme elements."[40] When groups proved to be too radical, funding could be withdrawn. Thus when Munro halted a grant to the confrontational Hamilton Welfare Rights Organization in December 1971, he justified his action by referring to "the continuing alienation of the larger Hamilton population by the use of radical rhetoric."[41] Even activist organizations that avoided government financing were not immune to coercion by anxious officials. The Praxis Corporation, a largely middle-class organization that helped to sponsor activities among poor people during the late 1960s and early 1970s, did not benefit from government funding for its operating costs but was nonetheless the object of considerable suspicion among Liberal backbenchers during the early 1970s.[42] This apprehension also existed in other parts of the federal government. While organizing the Poor People's Conference in 1970, the corporation's files were clandestinely removed from its offices, and the premises were burned. The RCMP later acknowledged that it had the missing files and returned some of them.

Even when local groups managed to avoid the ire of their governmental sponsors during the early 1970s, the resources available to them for lobbying government on major policy issues were limited. Not only were they ill-equipped to comment on the technical details of government policies, but they also had little money.[43] Even during the height of activism among poor people in Canada, poverty organizations experienced an "inability to mobilize organizational membership, develop issue-oriented coalitions and stimulate public concerns and/or support."[44]

Because of these constraints, poverty activists did not participate actively in the Social Security Review. Henry Chapin's survey of 200 non-governmental social agencies and welfare interest groups found that "most of the organizations had either no involvement [in the Review] or could not recall what the nature of their involvement had been." Reflecting their dependent financial position, most accepted a "limited participation role in public policy-making." And because of their "lack of human and financial resources," they were unable to understand, let alone critique, technical details of the support/supplementation proposals.[45]

In the United States, mobilization among the poor had led to the formation in 1966 of a nationwide non-governmental organization – the National Welfare Rights Organization – but no similar group existed in Canada. In 1970, the federal government reorganized its National Council of Welfare (NCW), a public body providing advice to the minister of Health and Welfare, and consisting of interested citizens, a number of whom were poor. (The National Council of Welfare is not to be confused with the Canadian Welfare Council, a private body whose activities were discussed in chapters 2 and 3.)

The NCW was to be a spokesman for the poor during the Social Security Review.[46] Its first director, Leonard Shifrin, was a close friend of Munro's and had previously been a zealous advocate of citizen participation within his ministerial staff. Although its members were appointed by order-in-council, the NCW was not considered a partisan Liberal institution in its early years. Nevertheless, it had limited credentials as a representative of the poor: only about 40 percent of the NCW's members were poor; the others were from the middle class, often from the voluntary service sector. There was a feeling among the council's members, especially those who considered themselves more radical, that they had little impact on the content of its policy statements, the preparation of which was its main activity. In their view, the council's statements were controlled by its director.[47] Throughout the Review, the council's policy recommendations supported the federal government's approach, and federal officials saw the NCW as a friend.[48] The council's November 1973 commentary on the Orange Paper, for example, expressed approval of the outlines of its employment and service strategies, while asking for more specific information about them; it also accepted a two-tier approach to support/supplementation.[49] Similarly, when Lalonde was publicly criticized by the Ontario welfare minister at a conference held shortly after the fateful meeting of June 1976, Shifrin (among others) "at the discrete urging of some [federal officials], made timely and positive interventions supporting the federal proposal. [A] resolution supporting the federal position was strongly endorsed."[50] While Lalonde lauded the council's participation in the Review in 1976, this was probably more in recognition of its positive approach to federal positions than of any real influence on the reform process: none of the federal or provincial policy makers interviewed for this study attributed a significant role to the council as a conduit of policy input for the poor (or anybody else) in the Review.[51]

A Poor People's Conference took place in Toronto in January 1971. It had been conceived by NCW members "with the intention of providing representatives from local community action groups with an opportunity to assemble on a national scale."[52] The main achievement of the conference (which had been financed by federal government departments, led by Health and Welfare) was the creation of a nationwide coordinating committee that scheduled a number of rallies by poor people and, later that year, formed the National Anti-Poverty Organization (NAPO).[53]

The new organization relied heavily on government funding from the beginning.[54] As with similar bodies in the poverty sector, neither governmental nor non-governmental participants in the Review attributed any significant role to NAPO in stimulating or shaping poverty reform in the 1970s. This was, in part, because in its early years NAPO decided not to concentrate its resources in the national headquarters or to use them to advocate policy innovations. Instead, it saw itself as a loose confederation of local groups and preferred to engage in grass-roots activity.[55] This reluctance to take part in Ottawa-based lobbying no doubt owed much to NAPO's financial ties with the government, but there were other reasons. The organization's first director, Marjorie Hartling, was herself poor and could not call upon the professional resources necessary to make detailed technical commentaries on evolving policy debates during the Review. Her analysis of the Orange Paper was a sometimes confusing attempt to explain the document to NAPO's members, concluding that they must decide for themselves what to do in response to it.[56] When NAPO occasionally did take an advocacy approach, it did not adopt a clear and consistent position that could have contributed to poverty reform. For example, while leading figures in the organization condemned the implied two-tier design of the Orange Paper,[57] Hartling said the following year that she supported the Orange Paper's design for support/supplementation. At the same time, she rejected as inadequate the limited offer that Lalonde had made at the welfare ministers' meeting in February of that year.[58] But when the reduced support/supplementation proposals were abandoned after the June 1976 federal/provincial meeting, NAPO took a stand similar to that of the NCW and other federally sponsored groups in the public quarrel between the Ontario and the federal ministers: it sided with Lalonde, accusing Ontario of scuttling the Review; the Ontario Anti-Poverty Organization, a provincially funded entity, took its benefactor's side.[59]

Middle-Class Organizations

Middle-class non-governmental organizations were active in the poverty sector during the 1970s, as they had been in the previous decade. But they were no more effective than poverty groups in influencing the Review. Organizations of disabled persons – the old categorical groups – continued to take some interest in poverty issues during the 1970s, but the elimination of their special assistance programs in 1966 had substantially reduced their influence. In 1974, the Canadian Rehabilitative Council for the Disabled prepared a policy statement on the Orange Paper, largely endorsing its recommendations, especially on income support/supplementation;[60] but the council's views were vague and not actively pursued. The United Church of Canada was one of the most active middle-class participants in the Review. Its involvement was respected, but its preference for universal demogrants as the main line of defence against poverty was considered idiosyncratic in the substantially liberal atmosphere of the Review and received very little attention among policy makers.

During the early 1960s the Public Welfare Division of the Canadian Welfare Council had increasingly questioned the role it could play in policy making in federal and provincial governments. This questioning continued later in the decade, as the division sought a new mission for itself after achieving almost complete success in the creation of the Canada Assistance Plan.[61] At the same time, the council as a whole debated its traditional reliance on narrow professional groups within each of its divisions as the source of its policy recommendations. The structure was challenged for two reasons. First, reflecting the popularity of broad-based "social scientific" knowledge during the 1960s, many council members desired a more "integrative" approach to social policy. Social security proposals should, in their view, transcend traditional professional and program boundaries, and extend to previously neglected aspects of economic and manpower policy. Second, reflecting the increased attention that was being paid to the theme of participation, the council's members wanted to foster the involvement of program clients, including welfare recipients, in its policy making.[62] These themes underlay the recommendations of the Carver Report, submitted to the council's board of governors in 1969 as a blueprint for overhauling the cwc's structure. The report recommended that the council abolish its divisions, involve ordinary citizens in its deliberations, and add more of a research orientation to its work.[63] With the reluctant approval of the PWD, the board accepted the report, and in 1970 the Canadian Welfare Council became the Canadian Council on Social Development (CCSD).[64]

The CCSD's capacity to participate in social reform depended on the cogency and originality of its research and policy analysis, and on its capacity to serve as a forum for welfare-state clients. The CCSD acquired a modest expert research staff during the 1970s; this, and the greater financial resources available to it, meant that it was a far better candidate for effective participation in the Review than any other organization with an interest in the field. And yet, the council played only a minimal role. Neither its research results nor its efforts to mobilize program clients gave it access to government decision making.

The CCSD's first comprehensive social policy statement was *Social Security for Canada*, released almost simultaneously with the Orange Paper in 1973. It did not generate any enthusiasm among federal officials involved in the Review. As Reuben Baetz, the CCSD's executive director, later pointed out to Lalonde, the council's proposals "on income security [were] fairly consistent with those enunciated in your Orange Paper";[65] the initiatives recommended in the areas of social services and employment were also similar to the Orange Paper's. But the CCSD's statement adopted a negative tone that evoked dismay among federal officials. It maintained that the Orange Paper's proposed guarantee levels for support and supplementation were too low, that there was insufficient attention to social services, and that the employment objectives were excessively modest. As NHW officials pointed out privately, however, the Orange Paper did not specify definite guarantee levels, gave considerable attention to social services, and showed at least some flexibility with respect to the employment strategy.[66]

The council's other public comments on the Review during its first three years often had a negative tone. David Ross, the CCSD's leading analyst of income security issues from 1973 to 1976, on at least two occasions delivered highly publicized denunciations of the Orange Paper, arguing that it supported only a "bare subsistence income."[67] After one such outburst, Baetz was given to understand by Lalonde that the council's continued enjoyment of project grants from Health and Welfare would depend on its adopting a less adversarial approach. Baetz nevertheless was himself inclined to make occasional attacks on the Review – pointing out its slowness to reach agreement, the deficiencies of some of its premises, and the lack of sufficient consultation.[68] Some participants in the Review thought that Baetz's remarks reflected his partisan affiliation (he was elected under the Progressive Conservative banner to the Ontario legislature in 1975).

This hostility from the council evoked an equally sceptical response from Health and Welfare. The intimacy that had existed between the CWC and NHW during the 1960s was now a thing of the past. Federal welfare officials from both the old and the new guard criticized the council's policies and rejected some of its propositions as vague and ill-considered.[69] Lalonde's frustration with the council reached a peak at the organization's biennial meeting in June 1976, during a speech in which he denounced the CCSD, claiming that its hostility had undermined the Review.[70] The council's president responded by defending its record and registering her regret that "the process of the Review had been such that the opportunity to examine in detail official and authoritative proposals, and react to them, has not arisen in the past two years."[71] For his part, Baetz denounced the poverty organizations praised by Lalonde, referring to them as "dependents" of the federal government.[72]

This was a revealing remark. The CCSD never developed a rapport with poor program clients. Poor people were invited to each of its biennial conventions after 1970, but they fought with the largely middle-class council membership. At the 1970 conference, poor participants walked out of the meeting in protest.[73] At the 1974 conference, poor delegates organized by NAPO disrupted the meeting, denounced the Review and the council, and forced Baetz to leave the chair.[74] At the 1976 meeting, Baetz's criticism of poverty groups evoked an equally hostile response from the latter.

ORGANIZATIONAL BARRIERS TO NON-GOVERNMENTAL PARTICIPATION

The participation theme was influential within the federal government in the late 1960s and 1970s; but when the Social Security Review began, few mechanisms were in place to facilitate outside involvement. This reflected the impact of the institutionalized structures that had given rise to the Review and shaped its development.

The National Council of Welfare was supposed to represent the views of welfare clients in social policy making, but it failed in this mission. The Social Security Review created alternative avenues for non-governmental input, but these did not – indeed, they were never intended to – permit significant involvement by outside interests; the Review was very much a "governmental thing." Participants at both the federal and the provincial level had preconceived notions of the reforms they wished to implement, especially in the income security field, and they did not want to see them challenged. Also, both federal and provincial governments anticipated that the intra- and interjurisdictional tensions within the Review would create more than enough obstacles to reform; the involvement of non-governmental interests would only add to this burden.

NHW's Policy and Program Development and Coordination Branch (Welfare) included an "opinion analysis unit," which conducted liaison with non-governmental organizations during the Review.[75] That this responsibility was assigned to a branch that played a marginal role in the Review is evidence of its modest importance. At no time was the unit expected to bring outside interests into a meaningful dialogue with the leading federal reformers. In the words of a former senior official of the branch, the Review's objectives were "fixed in ministerial minds at the outset ... They wanted to bring people along but didn't expect them to have much impact." The unit conducted opinion polls to test the popularity of measures considered during the Review and contacted national interest groups for their views; it also arranged meetings between Lalonde and newspaper editors and other opinion leaders about the Review's objectives; in 1973 and 1974, it convened a number of "town hall meetings" across the country, enabling interested citizens to meet Lalonde and exchange views with him on social security issues. These consultations were designed to disseminate positive information about the Review, attract legitimacy to it, and sound out possible influential opposition. Representations that departed significantly from the Orange Paper's implied two-tier approach, particularly on income security issues, were quietly dismissed.[76] Only in the area of services did social agencies have some influence – on the provisions of the Social Services Act that dealt with day care. The opposition of non-governmental agencies to the block-funded Social Services Financing Act also played a role in convincing Bégin to abandon her department's support for that legislation.[77] But at no time did a senior participant in the Review wish to use public consultation to guide the basic direction of reform; consultation was conceived purely as an instrument to test the public's responsiveness to, and gain its acceptance of, the program outlined in the Orange Paper.

Federal reluctance to involve non-governmental interests therefore owed much to the institutionalized context of the Review and to the commitment of leading reformers to their preconceived systematic design. This reluctance, and that of provincial governments as well, also reflected another feature of this institutionalized setting – a desire to avoid multiplying the already substantial sources of conflict in the Review. Many federal and provincial participants believed that a more public process would have added considerably to the obstacles encountered on the road to reform.

At the *in camera* welfare ministers' conference in February 1974, Lalonde resisted significant involvement by welfare clients. He argued that "it is our responsibility as politicians to deal with [poor] people and to insure that their view is heard and if we don't hear it, we will hear about it. That would be my inclination rather than trying to have them as a special group bringing formal input at all kinds of levels of the Social Security Review. I would rather be concerned that we are going to end up with a much more complex operation than the one we have now which is already pretty complex, I'm afraid."[78] Consequently, it was left to each government to consult with interested groups within its jurisdiction; outside interests were given no standing in federal/provincial discussions.

Non-governmental consultation was greater in the social service strategy, but it remained limited. At a private meeting in September 1975, federal and provincial deputy ministers of welfare discussed "how confidential the Social Services Draft Legislation should be and whether provinces were free to discuss this with representatives of voluntary agencies." Ontario complained that some non-governmental groups were only interested in using the proposed legislation as a source of financing for themselves. The Manitoba deputy minister elaborated that "if you open this up for discussion with the voluntary agencies it is bound to get into the press and then the dialogue is over." His Quebec counterpart opined that "it was fundamental at this stage that the proposals remained confidential." He wanted to "wait for an official draft of the act before consulting any private agencies on its contents."[79] Thus, as with the other strategies, the development of the Social Services Act was largely an intergovernmental exercise. No province included non-governmental interests in its internal decision making about any of the Review's strategies or consulted them on a regular basis. Saskatchewan made the greatest effort to consult, but it had limited success because "the Review clearly had not been set up to accommodate input from the non-governmental sector."[80]

CONCLUSION

Chapters 5 to 7 traced the Social Security Review in an executive setting. It was found there that within the societal context of a liberal welfare state and a market-oriented accumulation strategy, the Social Security Review was largely shaped by the institutionalized structures of the federal and Quebec governments and of federal/provincial relations. In this chapter, we have assessed the impact on the Review of non-governmental interests acting outside executive settings. Chapter 1 anticipated that this impact would be limited; that expectation was largely corroborated by the evidence examined.

Organizations that reflected class influences played a marginal role. The political parties did take an interest in poverty and the concept of a guaranteed income, but the three national parties did not make it a major electoral or legislative priority. Reflecting its liberal origins, the GAI concept was expounded with the greatest enthusiasm by parties of the right. The modest role of parties reflected the absence of electoral incentives for them to pursue measures aimed at socially marginal voters; the NDP's ambiguous position also indicates the natural suspicion of parties of the left, which typically pursue social democratic objectives, about selective measures. Economic class organizations also played no significant role in the Review. Organized labour endorsed the GAI concept, but its support was qualified and muted by its social democratic agenda. Business federations were equally inactive; poverty reform was compatible with business's liberal agenda, but this same agenda suggested caution about the potential cost of new initiatives and about its implications for incentives.

Non-class actors were also of little importance. Lacking financial and analytical resources, the organizations of the poor were dependent on government financing – that is, on funds that could disappear if governments were antagonized. Middle-class organizations with an interest in poverty policy were equally ineffective. The CCSD had no significant impact on poverty policy along the paths provided by its new mandate: its policy research did not affect policy making within the federal and provincial governments, and it could not act as a conduit for the influence of program clients.

Finally, the leading federal reformers and most provincial participants did not want non-governmental involvement in the Review. This reflected institutionalized governmental structures. Many government actors approached the Review with their own preconceived systematic agenda for reform and did not want their objectives challenged. Outside interests were thought likely to add discord to a Review already torn by tensions among heterogeneous institutional actors.

CHAPTER NINE

Conclusion

This book has chronicled the development of an important but neglected element of Canada's postwar welfare state – its attempts to respond to persistent poverty. It has also tested the merits of synthesizing state- and society-centred approaches to the study of the modern state instead of simply championing one tradition at the expense of the other. I have attempted to demonstrate that the fate of poverty reform in Canada during the 1960s and 1970s reflected a combination of forces best explained on a societal level of analysis – the singular focus of the class perspective – and of factors reflecting organizations, the home domain of statism. This final chapter reviews the book's findings and takes a look at the poverty reform debate that began again in Canada after 1984.

THE SOCIETAL CONTEXT: A LIBERAL WELFARE STATE

Because of the relative weakness of its working class, Canada has never made a radical break with the selective, market-oriented, social policy model typical of all capitalist democracies in an earlier era. At the same time, the historic pursuit of a market-oriented accumulation strategy, represented above all by the department of Finance within the federal government, consistently acted as an impediment to poverty reform during the 1960s and 1970s. This societal context affected the Canada Assistance Plan and the Social Security Review differently, because different organizations and different economic circumstances prevailed when the two reforms were the focus of political debate.

Political Class Influences

The Canada Assistance Plan reflected liberal policy legacies, the most important of which was the continued influence of social assistance administrators. This was a trait emblematic of liberal welfare states, where assistance remains central, compared with non-liberal ones, where it has largely been eradicated. The Public Welfare Division of the Canadian Welfare Council, a vehicle for federal and provincial welfare bureaucrats, proposed most of the innovations eventually included in CAP, and welfare administrators remained the main inspiration of reform thereafter. Both the council's *Social Security for Canada* and numerous departmental memoranda prepared by Willard and Splane also gave evidence of the prevalence of pragmatic considerations in social policy making: by itself, extending the contributory and universal elements of Canada's welfare state would not provide for the most needy. An ideological preference for selective, market-oriented measures also appeared in the 1958 policy statement, but it did not become a central element of policy until later.

By contrast, explicitly ideological arguments did play a major role in motivating the Social Security Review. Most of the major government-sponsored recommendations for a new poverty reform agenda in the late 1960s and early 1970s explicitly cited liberal concerns – to create incentives and to direct resources to the least advantaged. The Orange Paper embodied a particularly eloquent and sophisticated statement of its market-oriented foundations. Documents of that period also gave evidence of pragmatic influences, but old-guard officials in federal and provincial welfare departments now had little impact.

Liberal policy legacies shaped CAP and the Review differently because of differences in organizations. CAP emerged during a period of organizational stability. The departmentalized structures that presided over its birth were those which had been in place during the preceding postwar assistance reforms. The administrators of earlier measures naturally were the source of the innovations that were implemented during the 1960s, and the changes embodied in CAP were elaborations and extensions of, rather than fundamental departures from, those programs. By contrast, the Social Security Review occurred after a period of institutional innovation. The administrators of existing measures were displaced from positions of influence, and the new reform agenda could therefore propose substantial departures from the status quo. The institutionalized structures also stimulated systematic policy analysis, and the reform documents produced during this period – above all, the Orange Paper – were a powerful reflection of this tendency. Liberal policy legacies – a societal phenomenon – shaped poverty reform during both periods, but in ways that differed because of the changing organization of government.

Neither political parties nor economic class organizations contributed directly to either of the two poverty reforms. For most analysts, this non-involvement signifies the irrelevance of class explanations. But the political variant of the class perspective alerts us to the need to relate the behaviour of class actors to fundamental class interests. Thus the preceding chapters showed that if the political parties did not champion poverty reform and if economic class organizations were similarly disengaged, it was because poverty reform affected no vital class-related interest.

In neither reform did political parties take a leading role. In the 1960s, comprehensive assistance reform was accepted by politicians after some resistance, but it had no independent base among the parties. Assistance was of little interest to politicians, whose primary concerns focused on Canada's modest universal and contributory social programs. The NDP led the way in championing a broader approach. In the 1970s, only the regional *Créditiste* Party made a significant issue of the guaranteed annual income as a solution to poverty.

The persistence of poverty-oriented measures reflects the liberalism of Canada's welfare state and the class relations underlying its development. But measures targeted at the socially and politically marginal held little appeal for the mass of middle-class and even working class voters. For that reason, they did not attract the attention of politicians who, sensitive to pressures from the left, had to attend to the electoral consequences of their programmatic commitments. Liberal ideological norms did motivate politicians – especially those of the political right – to support a GAI in the 1970s, but they did not make poverty reform a priority. Throughout the 1960s and 1970s, Canada's modest universal and contributory measures remained a greater object of concern among politicians. The preoccupation of the influential NDP with universality reflected a typically social democratic preference for market-curtailing social measures and a suspicion of solidarity-corroding, market-oriented selectivism.

The social policy agenda of organized labour paralleled that of the NDP. In the 1960s, labour's main concern with respect to social assistance was to prevent its being used to undermine working class interests; its main social goals were in the social democratic tradition. The GAI policy formulated during the 1970s by the Canadian Labour Congress did not depart from that tradition, and labour remained a minor influence in the poverty area. This muted approach to poverty reform reflected the problematical position of poverty issues, in a liberal context, for labour's social democratic interests. Because poverty-oriented measures tend intrinsically to erode working class solidarity, they attracted labour's suspicion; but the persistence of poverty in Canada's liberal welfare state created altruistic – and ulterior – reasons to support measures designed to alleviate it directly.

Business federations also had a limited role in both reforms. They consistently advanced a liberal perspective on social policy, preferring selective, incentive-creating measures. But because their market-oriented approach to capital accumulation implied an antithesis between government and market, they were prevented from actively supporting poverty reform. As the economic situation worsened during the 1970s, the major business groups opposed new social expenditures of any kind. At the same time, the interests of business were always best represented by organizations *within* the state – primarily, the department of Finance.

Functional Class Influences

A market-oriented accumulation strategy assumes that there is an opposition between government intervention (including government expenditures) and the needs of a prosperous private economy. Thus it is not surprising that in both of the periods examined here, the federal department of Finance opposed poverty reform. It was not the liberal underpinnings of reform that Finance objected to, but the assumption by reformers that market-oriented objectives should, or could, be achieved by increasing social expenditures of any kind. Only when improvements in poverty measures were seen as the only alternative to extending universal or contributory social security measures did Finance temporarily champion assistance reform.

During the creation of CAP, Finance opposed each provision of the new legislation that implied new expenditures. It relented only when bureaucratic reformers were able to obtain key political support for their cause from federal and provincial welfare ministers and from Tom Kent. Finance consistently premised its position on the putatively negative consequences of reform for the government's fiscal framework and for sound performance in the private economy.

The Social Security Review similarly met Finance's opposition from the very beginning; in 1975, that hostility administered a fatal blow to the initiative. Later, Finance was joined by other bureaux within the federal government – above all, the Prime Minister's Office – in championing a restrictive economic philosophy. Its opposition was again based on the market-oriented view that, despite the claims of its supporters, a GAI would undermine the incentive to work. The fact that Finance was much more successful in blocking reform during the 1970s reflected the failure of Lalonde and Johnson to achieve anything like the federal/provincial consensus in favour of change that had existed during the preceding decade; after 1974, the rapidly deteriorating state of the national economy also increased the influence of Finance.

Not all capitalist democracies responded similarly to the global economic crisis of the mid-1970s. Liberal welfare states such as Britain and the United States followed a dualist path, "cutting back the allocative and redistributive dimensions of the state's role, and encouraging the formation of a growing pool of unorganized and low paid workers."[1] Some European societies with social democratic or conservative traditions, by contrast, pursued a "corporatist" approach, involving cooperation between government, business, and labour rather than an attack on the interests of the latter. While Canada did not commit itself firmly to the dualist path in the 1970s, it took important steps in that direction. Economic arguments for restricting the welfare state were accepted by the major parties as a matter of common sense after 1975. In Esping-Andersen's terms, the modest solidarity characteristic of Canada's liberal welfare state created fewer barriers than elsewhere to the pursuit of a market-oriented, anti-labour response to economic crisis. The destruction of the Social Security Review reflected this new sensibility.

THE ORGANIZATIONAL CONTEXT: CANADA'S FRAGMENTED STATE

Changes in the structure of the Canadian state account for the most striking differences between CAP and the Review. The former emerged in an organizational setting suited to successful federal/provincial policy making; by contrast, the institutionalized context of the Review created enormous barriers to success. The two reforms differed in terms of each of the main features that distinguish departmentalized and institutionalized cabinet systems. In fact, they were, arguably, archetypal reflections of the quite different organizational structures that had given rise to them. Other policy developments during the 1960s were, in all likelihood, less unambiguous examples of a departmentalized cabinet system; and most policy making during the 1970s was probably less clearly driven by rationalist and comprehensive goals enunciated by staff bureaucrats.

The Canada Assistance Plan had its origins among line officials in a program department. By contrast, the Review was preceded by considerable preparatory work among planning officials in central agencies of the federal and Quebec governments; thereafter, it was led by staff officials.

The norms that permeated the two reforms reflected their distinctive origins. The CAP reformers were incrementalists, and strategic considerations about which jurisdiction would control, or benefit from, reform were usually not a central preoccupation. The federal reformers of the 1970s had a broader perspective. They developed a highly systematic, "ideal" conception of a social security system, proposing reforms that would adjust existing arrangements to conform to this model. The ideal model was often in conflict with competing "grand designs" from the provinces that also transcended the turf of any single department or program and often involved strategic bargaining. The need to resolve federal/provincial constitutional tensions was an important motivation for the Review, but as the latter progressed and the economic recession deepened, it gradually became more important to determine who would pay for, and control, any new program.

In scope, CAP was largely confined to measures within the responsibilities of the officials who promoted it. The discussion of work activity was the only exception to this pattern. The scope of the Review was broader: the Orange Paper gave considerable attention to programs typically administered by manpower or labour departments. It also linked the Review's objectives to goals in other policy areas, such as macroeconomics and the labour market. Its income security ambitions went beyond public assistance, encompassing demogrants and social insurance.

Thus CAP involved a much narrower range of participants than the Review. It was almost exclusively negotiated between welfare officials and their ministers. It was only intermittently subject to attacks on the fringe by officials at the department of Labour. By contrast, the range of organizations involved in the Review and the variety of divergent government-wide objectives that emerged, required a more formalized machinery – a continuing committee of responsible federal and provincial ministers, and a steering committee within the federal government. But these entities did not prevent the Review from becoming fragmented, at the very outset, among very different professional and departmental interests.

These organizational differences in poverty reform between the 1960s and 1970s resulted in the quite different patterns of conflict envisaged by Dupré. Reform was successful when it involved components that were entirely within the traditional jurisdiction of welfare departments and that reflected a consensus of federal and provincial officials – e.g., program integration; federal coverage of mothers' allowances, of administration and services, and of child welfare; and the preservation of cost-sharing for these measures. But when the reforms had a bearing on the concerns of other departments and were opposed by them – as in the case of work activity – or when no federal/provincial consensus emerged – as with the differential cost-sharing and national standards issues – reform was unsuccessful. Only where assistance reform in the 1960s departed from the pattern characteristic of a departmentalized cabinet model did it fail to benefit from the model's capacity to generate successes in federal/provincial policy making.

The array of interests involved at the federal level in the much broader Social Security Review contributed substantially to its destruction. Control of the employment strategy by a Manpower department that had no real interest in the Review's goals virtually assured the strategy's failure. At the same time, UIC officials opposed all meaningful efforts to involve their programs in the Review. The organizational hiatus between income-security and social service reform delayed the latter; service reform was also subject to friction from bureaucratic interests outside the Social Services Program Branch. As well, the Review was crippled by diverging government-wide objectives in an interjurisdictional setting. The liberal but reformist goals of the federal planners were challenged by a more purely market-oriented ideology from Ontario and Alberta, and by the social democratic alternative proffered by the provinces with NDP governments. These differences precluded any consensus on the design of support/supplementation or the community employment strategy. By 1975, strategic bargaining was another impediment to reform. The variety of players and agenda involved in the Review – a quintessential consequence of its institutionalized setting – crippled it from the outset.

THE RELEVANCE OF PLURALISM

For each reform, the activities of a number of interest groups were examples of pluralist power. Interest groups are, of course, a mainstay of pluralist analysis.[2] Even when their actions reflect their class and organizational contexts, they are also something more, in that they seek benefits for their individual members and their constituency. But none of these groups had a significant effect on either poverty reform.

During the CAP reform, groups representing the recipients of the categorical programs jealously protected their relatively privileged position among recipients of all social assistance. But they were unable to prevent the passage of CAP, and with the abolition of the categorical programs in 1966, these groups lost their influence as significant advocates in the poverty sector. During the 1970s, the major new interest groups were organizations of poor people. While these groups broadly advocated improvements in social security measures for their constituency, they failed to develop a coherent reform program. For this reason, and because they had limited financial and intellectual resources, and only a modest capacity to mobilize their constituency, poverty groups were negligible actors in the Social Security Review. Among middle-class organizations, the Canadian Council on Social Development abandoned the bureaucratic agenda championed by the old Canadian Welfare Council, but it did not cultivate a new constituency among the socially marginal or become an influential proponent of a new reform agenda. Finally, the institutionalized nature of the Review presented few opportunities for involvement by non-governmental interests.

CANADA'S CONTEMPORARY DEBATE ABOUT POVERTY

After the demise of the Social Security Review in 1978, there was little interest in poverty reform for a while. But in the mid-1980s, the GAI concept re-emerged as the subject of public debate. As with the previous reforms, these developments reflected their societal and organizational context.[3]

Widespread poverty persisted in Canada during the 1980s; as in the past, the proposed solutions reflected a liberal policy heritage. But there were also novel elements in this debate. Unlike in earlier times, poverty reform was now discussed as an alternative to retaining more inclusive elements of the Canadian welfare state. And also for the first time, poverty reform was championed by a governing national party – the federal Progressive Conservatives. The reintroduction of the GAI into policy debates reflected an aggressive reaffirmation of a market-oriented accumulation strategy during the 1980s. It was recommended in the report of the Macdonald Commission in 1985; the next year, it was advocated by Claude Forget's study committee on unemployment insurance.[4] In both cases, extensions of poverty-oriented measures were proposed at the expense of existing universal programs and the non-actuarial elements of contributory ones. Similar views were espoused by the major business federations.[5] Since its election in 1984, the Conservative government has broadly championed this agenda, which also permeated the Nielsen

Committee's report.[6] This approach represents an effort to "purify" the Canadian welfare state of at least some of its non-liberal elements. It has been justified with characteristically liberal arguments about the merits of targeting social security programs at those "who need them most" and with other arguments, grounded in a market-oriented strategy, about the need to rearrange the Canadian welfare state in order to ensure future economic prosperity.[7]

There has been resistance to this approach. Organized labour and the NDP continue to advocate universal social security and full employment.[8] Interest groups in the poverty field also oppose the extension of market principles in Canada's welfare state, generally advocating the retention and broadening of the existing mix of universal, contributory, and selective programs.[9]

Canada has not yet witnessed the wholesale redirection of social policies that occurred in Britain and the United States during the 1980s,[10] but important steps have been taken in that direction. The government's early effort to curtail universal Old Age Security payments was abortive, but limits were placed on family allowances. Both programs were subsequently subjected to a "claw back" provision that excludes upper-income earners from receiving benefits. Finally, in 1992 the family allowance was completely abandoned and replaced by a selective children's benefit. A series of program changes have also substantially curtailed the non-actuarial elements of the unemployment insurance program. In general, Canada's welfare state has been modified to increase selectivity, restrict access to benefits, and "increase the self-financing capacity of programs."[11]

This assault on non-selective elements in the postwar welfare state by the mainstream political right is unprecedented. While support for a gradually expanding welfare state in Canada eroded during the 1970s, it was only in the following decade that the universal and contributory measures achieved in an earlier era came under sustained attack. This development reflects a significant change in the societal context of policy making – the end of the postwar era of social Keynesianism (or "Fordism") and of the political consensus that ran throughout capitalist democracies in favour of government measures designed simultaneously to sustain levels of aggregate demand required by high-volume, standardized production and to improve social security.[12] The capitalist democracies have responded in quite different ways to the fundamental changes in the global capitalist economy that began in the 1970s. The market-oriented, anti-labour, dualist agenda is by no means universal: it has occurred mainly in those countries where postwar social reform took on a distinctly liberal flavour – the United Kingdom and the United States, for example – and where little solidarity had developed around the welfare state.[13] The emergence and increasing success of the Conservative agenda therefore reflects societal factors – the transition to a post-Keynesian world in a context of weak working class mobilization.

The new reform agenda also reflects its organizational context. In some respects, institutionalized structures persist in the contemporary federal government.[14] Poverty policies remain the concern of a number of departments, and the tensions in federal/provincial relations that typify institutionalized structures remain the norm. The major organizational change has been the substantial growth in stature of the department of Finance. Its new role was "designed to pursue the government's substantive policy priorities and in so doing to alter the configuration of power in the executive-bureaucratic arena."[15] It was intended to secure the predominance of a market-oriented strategy, now the preferred approach of the governing party, within the bureaucracy. Finance, through its Social Policy Division, has become the leading department in income security policy, though NHW and the department of Employment and Immigration continue to play important roles. The Social Policy Division has focused considerable attention on the possible use of the tax system to deliver social security measures selectively. If reductions in universal and social insurance measures are complemented by significant extensions of income-tested measures, the bureaucratic initiative for such an undertaking is likely to emanate from Finance. Future developments in poverty policy will reflect the combined impact of this societal and organizational setting.

Notes

ABBREVIATIONS

AO   Archives of Ontario
CCB   Canadian Council of the Blind
CCSD   Canadian Council on Social Development
CES   Community Employment Strategy
CLC   Canadian Labour Congress
CMA   Canadian Manufacturers' Association
CNIB   Canadian National Institute for the Blind
CWC   Canadian Welfare Council
ICPA   Interdepartmental Committee on Public Assis-
        tance
ICSS   Interdepartmental Committee on Social Security
MG   manuscript group
NA   National Archives of Canada
NAPO   National Anti-Poverty Organization
NCW   National Council of Welfare
NHW   National Health and Welfare
NUPE   National Union of Public Employees
PWD   Public Welfare Division
RG   record group

CHAPTER ONE

1 Korpi, "Social Policy," 299.
2 This is the conclusion of Rainwater et al. in *Income Packaging*, esp.
  chapter 11.
3 Korpi, "Social Policy," 310; Esping-Andersen, *Three Worlds*, 57, 73–5,
  127–8; Jones, *Social Policy*, 202–3.
4 Block, *State Theory*, 20–1.
5 Pal, "Relative Autonomy," 77.

6 Pal, *State, Class and Bureaucracy*, 91–3, 172.

7 Cuneo, "Restoring Class," 98.

8 Alford and Friedland, *Powers of Theory*, 3.

9 Alford, "Paradigms," 145–6.

10 *Powers of Theory*, 6, 421–2.

11 Ibid., 422.

12 On the American evidence about these phenomena, see Schlozman and Verba, *Injury to Insult*. In its 1971 *Report*, the Federal-Provincial Task Force on Alienation came to similar conclusions about the Canadian poor.

13 Alford and Friedland, *Powers of Theory*, 161; emphasis in original.

14 Badie and Birnbaum, *Sociology of the State*, chapter 3; Krasner, *Defending the National Interest*.

15 Tilly, "Reflections," 70.

16 Badie and Birnbaum, *Sociology of the State*, chapters 7 and 8; Heady, *Public Administration*, chapter 4.

17 Zysman, *Governments, Markets and Growth*, chapter 4; Zysman sees this state tradition as only one reason for France's industrial policy; see also Badie and Birnbaum, *Sociology of the State*, 111–12.

18 Atkinson and Coleman, *State, Business, and Industrial Change*, 60.

19 Ibid., 60, 63, 65.

20 Cited in Dupré, "Reflections," 2.

21 Ibid., 3.

22 Ibid., 3–5.

23 French, *How Ottawa Decides*, 22.

24 Stevenson, *Unfulfilled Union*, 224.

25 Alford and Friedland, *Powers of Theory*, 16–17.

26 Ibid., 307.

27 Korpi, "Social Policy," 298.

28 Wolfe, "Canadian State," 104.

29 Simeon and Robinson, *Development of Canadian Federalism*, 124.

30 Wolfe, "Canadian state," 105–6.

31 Ibid., 103, 112, 114, 119. Prime Minister Mackenzie King's sudden advocacy of family allowances in 1944, and his government's landmark Green Book proposals of 1945, occurred in the first of these two periods. The remaining postwar innovations in social security came during the second, as the Liberals made electoral commitments to contributory pensions and medicare in the wake of the disastrous 1958 election. In the context of a minority government and under the pressure exerted by the NDP, this resulted in legislation. See Granatstein, *Canada's War*, chapters 7 and 10; Bryden, *Old Age Pensions*, chapters 6, 8, and 9; Swartz, "Politics of Reform"; Newman, *Distemper of Our Times*, 412–16.

32 Esping-Andersen, *Three Worlds*, 22, 24.

33 Esping-Andersen, "Power and Distributional Regimes," 231–2.
34 Esping-Andersen, *Three Worlds*, 26, 33, 62–3.
35 Ibid., 70. On the persistence of selective measures in Canada's liberal welfare state, see also Manzer, *Public Policies*, 62–3.
36 NCW, *Welfare in Canada*, 8; Canada, Health and Welfare Canada, *Social Security Statistics*, 1987, 70, 78.
37 Wolfe, "Canadian State," 114.
38 Esping-Andersen and Korpi, "Institutional Welfare States," 41.
39 Esping-Andersen, *Three Worlds*, 73.
40 Apparently, social assistance is very decentralized in finance and administration, and there are few national standards for assistance in most continental European welfare states. This suggests a lack of significant bureaucratic resources that can be mobilized to perpetuate or expand poverty programs. See Walker, "Resources"; Furmaniak, "West Germany."
41 Wolfe, "Canadian State," 98.
42 Ibid., 112.
43 Wolfe, "Canadian State," 98, 101, 102–3, 108, 112.
44 Savoie, *Politics of Public Spending*, 73, 74–5; see also Phidd and Doern, *Politics and Management*, 199, 206.
45 Canada, Department of Reconstruction, *Employment and Income*.
46 Wolfe, "Canadian State," 112.
47 Wolfe, "Canadian State," 104, 112.
48 Hartle, *Budget Process*, 11.
49 French, *How Ottawa Decides*, 31.
50 Hartle, *Budget Process*, 12.
51 Savoie, *Politics of Public Spending*, 74–5, 148; Wolfe, "Canadian State," 109–10.
52 Alford, "Paradigms," 153.

CHAPTER TWO

1 Guest, *Emergence of Social Security*, chapters 5, 6, and 7.
2 Only Leonard Marsh's blueprint for a postwar welfare state appeared to envision a radical departure from the use of social assistance as an important element in the Canadian social security system; see Guest, *Emergence of Social Security*, chapter 8.
3 Canada, Dominion-Provincial Conference on Reconstruction, *Proposals*, passim.
4 Simeon and Robinson, *Development of Canadian Federalism*, 92–5; Granatstein, *Canada's War*, chapters 7 and 10.
5 Wolfe, "Canadian State," 106.
6 Guest, *Emergence of Social Security*, 137–8.

7 Canada, Statistics Canada, *National Income Expenditure Accounts*, table 50, 171.

8 Canada, Statistics Canada, *Social Security Statistics*, 1976, 511–12.

9 CWC, PWD, *Report, 1953–1954*, 18–19.

10 In 1959–60, the council's board of governors had 87 members, of whom 27 were listed in the *Canadian Who's Who*; of these, 17 were business persons; CWC, *Annual Report, 1959–1960*, 16.

11 The board of governor's composition allowed the claim, as was noted by participants at a PWD meeting in 1959, that the CWC "is representative of a broad cross-section of the Canadian public including representatives of the three levels of government, private welfare agencies, universities, labour, BUSINESS, the professions and other interested citizens, and is able to speak with authority on subjects in the field of social welfare. As a consequence, [its] briefs to government ... are usually given careful and sympathetic study." See NA, MG 28, I 10, box 150, PWD National Committee meeting, 4 March 1959; emphasis in original.

12 Ibid., *Report, 1959–1960*, 21–28.

13 Some of the confidential material handed over to the PWD is found in NA, MG 28, I 10, vol. 125, file E.

14 The PWD positions held by prominent provincial officials are listed in the division's annual reports for the years 1955 to 1963. The proximity of their views to those of the CWC was discussed in interviews with former NHW officials of that period.

15 Band informed the PWD of his disagreement with its policy in a letter dated 3 November 1958; see AO, RG 29, series 01, file 238. Band withdrew from the CWC on 1 April 1959.

16 CWC, PWD, *Report, 1957–1958*, 2.

17 NA, MG 28, I 10, vol. 101, Patrick to Davis, 25 June 1957; Cragg's response is conveyed by Davis in his reply to Patrick, dated 5 July 1957.

18 Ibid., Cragg to Farquhar, 11 July 1957.

19 Ibid., box 150, pt. 2, PWD, National Committee minutes, 3 October 1957.

20 CWC, PWD, *Report, 1957–1958*, 2–4.

21 Splane, "Social Welfare Development," 176.

22 NA, MG 28, I 10, box 150, vol. 2, PWD National Committee minutes, 4 March 1959, 1–2.

23 CWC, *Social Security for Canada*, 10–12.

24 Canada, Parliament, Senate, Special Committee on Manpower and Employment, *Proceedings*, "Submission to Special Committee on Manpower and Employment by the Canadian Welfare Council," 11 March 1961, 1251–3.

25 CWC, *Work for Relief*, 12.

26 CWC, *Social Security for Canada*, 3, 4–8, 13–17.

27 The view that the CWC was not an innovative force outside the welfare field was stressed in interviews conducted by the author. This was also the opinion of A. Andras, an official of the CLC during the 1950s; see NA, MG 28, I 103, reel H-44, Andras to Dodge, 22 May 1958; see also Bryden, *Old Age Pensions*, 198–200.

28 CWC, *Social Security for Canada*, 9–10.

29 The remaining issue was the inclusion of child welfare services, which was not raised until 1965.

30 Dyck, "Poverty and Policy-Making," 69–70.

31 Bella, "Right-Wing Welfare State," passim. Rogers' debt to the PWD was acknowledged in a speech given on 14 June 1965; see NA, MG 28, I 103, reel H-469.

32 NA, RG 29, vol. 921, "Manitoba" file; notes on a meeting dated 8–9 November 1959.

33 Dyck, "Poverty and Policy-Making," 72–4.

34 AO, RG 29, series 01, file 1663, Band to Cecile, 6 July 1962; Cecile to Monteith, 13 August 1962.

35 For documentation of provincial views on mothers' allowances, see Haddow, "State, Class and Public Policy," fn. 66, 135–6.

36 Newfoundland, Public Welfare Department, *Annual Report*, 1959, 28; Canada, Federal-Provincial Conference (July 1960), *Proceedings*, 39; Dyck, "Poverty and Policy-Making," 74.

37 NA, RG 29, vol. 2311, file 251–15–1, pt. 6, minutes of the August 1962 premiers' conference; *St. Catherines Standard*, 14 September 1962.

38 Haddow, "State, Class and Public Policy," fn. 71, 137.

39 NA, RG 29, vol. 2311, file 251–15–1, pt. 4, "Considerations in Amending the Unemployment Assistance Act: Draft", September 1959; ibid., Splane to Willard, 13 August 1960, 4 and 10 October 1960; ibid., vol. 921, "Alberta" file, Splane to Willard, 3 May 1960.

40 That is the title given to the document in an accompanying memo from Willard; see NA, RG 29, vol. 2311, file 251–15–1, pt. 4, Willard to Monteith, 4 November 1960. However, I have been unable to find a copy of the submission; there is no record of it in the Privy Council Office's lists of items for cabinet discussion, and that is what leads me to believe that the document never reached cabinet.

41 Ibid., Splane to Willard, 13 April 1961.

42 Ibid., vol. 1682, file 20-J-2A, "Memorandum to Cabinet – Re: Establishment of an Interdepartmental Committee to Consider Social Security Legislation," 19 June 1961.

43 Ibid., minutes of ICSS meeting, 24 July 1961, 2; ibid., 3 April 1961, 2.

44 Ibid., vol. 873, file 20-J-9, Willard to Taylor, 18 August 1961.

45 Ibid., vol. 1682, file 20-J-9A, ICSS minutes, 3 April 1961; ibid., vol. 873, file 20-J-9, Willard to Taylor, 11 August 1961; ibid., "Interim ICSS Report," August 1961.
46 Ibid., vol. 1682, file 20-J-9A, ICSS minutes, 24 July 1961, 2.
47 Ibid., vol. 863, file 20-J-9, Isbister to Bryce, 26 July 1961.
48 Ibid., vol. 1682, file 20-J-9A, ICSS minutes, 28 July 1961, 5.
49 NA, RG 19, vol. 3882, file 5514–04 (63/3)-2, pt. 1, Clark to Bryce, 22 November 1963.
50 NA, RG 29, vol. 1682, file 20-J-9A, Taylor to Willard, 17 August 1961.
51 Ibid., ICSS minutes, 28 July 1961, 5.
52 Cabinet document 311/61, "Report of the Interdepartmental Committee on Social Security," 29 August 1961, 14.
53 Ibid., 15–16.
54 Cabinet minutes, 12 October 1961, 48.
55 Cabinet minutes, 26 October 1961, 10.
56 Cabinet minutes, 23 October 1961, 6.
57 NA, RG 29, vol. 1526, file 201–16–2, Splane to Willard, 21 June 1962.
58 Ibid., vol. 1722, file 34–9–11, pt. 1, "Redrafting the Unemployment Assistance Act," 29. This document did not appear as an item for discussion in cabinet.
59 Ibid., vol. 1527, file 201–16–2A, Willard to White, 30 January 1963; NA, MG 28, I 103, reel H-477, speech given by Splane at a regional conference of the Canadian Association of Social Workers, 18 September 1962.
60 Kent, *Public Purpose*, 88; see also chapters 8 to 11 for the best available general discussion of the Liberal party's renewal during the early 1960s.
61 Kent's 1960 proposals did recommend "a concerted effort greatly to enhance social services and especially 'hard core' social work"; see ibid., 84.
62 *Canadian Party Platforms*, 266, 299.
63 NA, RG 29, vol. 1526, file 201–16–2, pt. 1, Willard to Splane, 30 April 1963. Rogers of Alberta expressed similar apprehension about the possible impact of Liberal and NDP preferences for categorical improvements; see ibid., vol. 921, "Alberta" file, 11 May 1962.
64 "The views of the Deputy Minister of Welfare in Alberta ... are indicative of a general feeling which will be encountered among the provinces when steps are taken to increase existing [i.e., categorical] benefit levels. That is, they would prefer to have the total area of public assistance systematically reviewed, with a view to rationalizing the existing programs and adopting new approaches which would allow greater flexibility in developing sound assistance measures suited to their particular needs within the framework of more positive federal standards";

see ibid., vol. 2311, file 251–15–1, pt. 7, Willard to LaMarsh, 29 April 1963.

65 Ibid., Willard to LaMarsh, 20 May 1963.

66 Ibid., Willard to LaMarsh, 23 May 1963.

67 Ibid., Willard to LaMarsh, 11 June 1963.

68 Ibid., vol. 2114, file 23–3–4, "Alternative Approaches Respecting Public Assistance for Presentation to the Federal-Provincial Conference on Problems Related to the Canada Pension Plan," 24 July 1963.

69 Cabinet minutes, 29 July 1963.

70 "Notes on the Federal-Provincial Conference, July 26–27, 1963," 32; cited in Dyck, "Poverty and Policy-Making," 102.

71 Quebec, Study Committee on Public Assistance, *Report*, 121–2, 125.

72 Splane reported Quebec's decision to Willard in a memo; see NA, RG 29, vol. 1526, file 201–16–2, 29 August 1963.

73 Dyck, "Poverty and Policy-Making," 101; NA, RG 29, vol. 1722, file 34–9–11, pt. 1, "Memorandum on Proposed Changes in Federal Public Assistance Programs," 11 October 1963.

74 NA, RG 29, vol. 1722, file 34–9–11, pt. 1, ibid.

75 This interpretation is strongly suggested by the passage cited above from NA, RG 19, vol. 3882, file 5514–04 (63/3)-2, pt. 1, Clark to Bryce, 22 November 1963.

76 Smiley, *Conditional Grants*, 41.

77 NA, RG 19, vol. 3882, file 5514–04 (63/3)-2, pt. 1, Isbister to Bryce, 23 August 1963; Abell to Isbister, 27 August 1963.

78 Ibid., file 5514–04 (63/3)-2, pt. 3, Bryce to Gordon, 22 October 1963.

79 Cabinet minutes, 30 October 1963; according to Splane, Finance expressed misgivings about the rising costs of UAA and other NHW programs in 1962; see NA, RG 29, vol. 2311, file 251–15–1, pt. 5, Splane to Willard, 8 March 1962.

80 The first extract is from Finance's November draft conference statement; see NA, RG 19, vol. 3906, file 5514–04 (63/3)-2, pt. 3. The second is from cabinet minutes, 30 October 1963.

81 NA, RG 19, vol. 3882, file 5515–04 (63/3)-2, pt. 1, Bryce to Clarke, 21 November 1963.

82 NA, RG 29, vol. 2114, file 23–3–5, Willard to Hardy, 11 September 1963.

83 Ibid., Splane to Willard, 23 September 1963.

84 Cabinet minutes, 21 November 1963.

85 Cabinet committee minutes, 22 November 1963.

86 NA, RG 19, vol. 3883, file 5514–04 (63/3)-3, pt. 1, "Notes on Federal-Provincial Plenary Conference, November 26–29, 1963," 30–2.

87 NA, RG 19, vol. 3906, file 5514–04 (63/2)-1, pt. 4, summary notes by Draper, 28 November 1963, 4.

CHAPTER THREE

1 This problem was discussed within the CWC on a number of occasions in the early 1960s; see NA, MG 28, I 10, box 150, pt. 3, CWC executive committee minutes, 27 November 1963; ibid., pt. 4, PWD National Committee minutes, 25 November 1964, 14 June 1965.

2 Ibid., vol. 1722, file 34–9–11, pt. 1, minutes of the ICPA, first meeting, 16 December 1963, 2–4; ibid., pt. 2, ICPA minutes, third meeting, 17 January 1964, 2–3.

3 The aspirations of federal welfare officials in the matter of national standards were spelled out privately in ibid., pt. 2, fourth ICPA meeting, 3 February 1964, 3.

4 Haddow, "State, Class and Poverty Policy," 153–4, fn. 13 to 17.

5 NA, RG 29, vol. 2113, file 23–1–5, "Federal-Provincial Working Group on Welfare Programs," verbatim minutes, 14–15 February 1964, 33–5, 43, 45, 216.

6 Ibid., 8–9.

7 Ibid., 85–6, 102–13, 131–3, 143–5.

8 Ibid., 27, 47–8, 51–5, 57–9, 61–5.

9 Cabinet document 191/64, "The Development of a New Public Assistance Plan," 4 May 1964.

10 Cabinet minutes, 21 May 1964, 3; 26 May 1964, 5.

11 NA, RG 29, vol. 2114, file 23–3–6, Willard to Splane, 9 March 1964.

12 Cabinet minutes, 21 May 1964, 13; 26 May 1964, 6.

13 Ibid.

14 Cabinet document 228/64, "Memorandum to Cabinet: Proposed New Public Assistance Plan," 22 May 1964, 2; cabinet minutes, 26 May 1964.

15 Cabinet minutes, 26 May 1964, 8.

16 For evidence of this, see cabinet document 48/65, "Memorandum to the Cabinet: The Canada Assistance Plan," 9 February 1965, appendix A, 1–2.

17 NA, RG 29, vol. 2115, file 23–4–5, Willard to LaMarsh, 8 and 16 July 1965; ibid., LaMarsh to provincial welfare ministers, 10 September 1965.

18 This paragraph is based on an interview with a former government official; see also Kent, Public Purpose, 353–60.

19 Simeon, Federal-Provincial Diplomacy, 293.

20 Morin, Quebec Versus Ottawa, 13–15.

21 NA, RG 19, vol. 3906, file 5660–08–1, pt. 4, Robertson to Bryce, 12 March 1964.

22 Ibid., vol. 3906, file 5660–08–1, pt. 4, "Notes on the Discussion by Federal and Provincial Officials of the Relations between Conditional Grant Programs and Fiscal Arrangements. Feb. 13, 1964"; ibid., vol. 4854, file

5508–02, pt. 1, "Report on the Federal-Provincial Officials Conference on Conditional Grants. Ottawa – 13 February, 1964."

23 Ibid., vol. 3906, file 5660–08–1, pt. 4, "Quebec's Proposals on the Matter of Joint Programs, Feb. 13, 1964."

24 Ibid., Bryce to cabinet committee, 19 March 1964.

25 Ibid., "Quebec's Proposals ... Feb. 13, 1964."

26 At the municipal level, statements on work-for-relief by the Canadian Federation of Mayors and Municipalities and by a number of its provincial affiliates clearly indicated that views were moderating; see NA, MG 28, I 10, vol. 125 (B), Saskatchewan Association of Municipalities to Baetz, 4 December 1963; ibid., Union of Alberta Municipalities to Baetz, 14 January 1964; ibid., Union of British Columbia Municipalities to Baetz, 5 December 1963; ibid., Baetz to Canadian Federation of Mayors and Municipalities, 26 November 1963.

27 NA, RG 29, vol. 1722, file 34–9–11, pt. 2, Haythorne to Campbell, 21 April 1964.

28 NA, MG 28, I 103, reel H-82, "Department of Labour News Release," 27 May 1964.

29 NA, RG 29, vol. 1722, file 34–9–11, pt. 2, Campbell to Haythorne, 10 September 1964.

30 An example of this can be found in cabinet document 48/65, "Memorandum to the Cabinet: The Canada Assistance Plan," 9 February 1965, appendix G, 1: "Several provinces ... indicated support for some form of program that would improve employment opportunities for assistance recipients who are not being absorbed in the labour market or trained for employment under existing measures."

31 NA, RG 29, vol. 2114, file 23–3–8, Willard to LaMarsh, 2 October 1964.

32 Ibid., vol. 2113, file 23–1–4, appendix B, LaMarsh to ministers, 10 November 1964.

33 Ibid., "Federal-Provincial Meeting on Welfare Measures for Increasing Work in Lieu of Assistance," minutes, 26 November 1964, 13–14.

34 Ibid., vol. 1722, file 34–9–11, pt. 2, "Memorandum to the Cabinet Committee on Social Security and Labour: The Development of a Public Assistance Act," 6 January 1965, 3; appendix G.

35 Ibid., Campbell to Haythorne, 27 July 1965.

36 Willard reviewed the results of the meeting in a memo to Haythorne on 8 February, saying that a "major revision" had been undertaken because of Labour's position; see ibid., accession 86–87/095, box 2, file 200–1–20A, pt. 2, Willard to Haythorne, 8 February 1965, and attachment.

37 Cabinet document 48/65, appendix G, 40–1.

38 NA, RG 29, vol. 1722, file 34–9–11, pt. 2, "Memorandum to the Cabinet Committee," 6 January 1965, 3; appendix G, 4.

39 Cabinet document 48/65, 3–5.

40 Ibid., 3, appendix A.

41 NA, RG 29, accession 86–87/095, file 200–20A, pt. 2, Bryce to Willard, 17 February 1965. CAP did, of course, come into effect in 1966, but this delay made it possible to extend the plan so as to include child welfare services; thus this postponement was a pyrrhic victory for Finance.

42 Ibid., Willard to Bryce, 19 February 1965.

43 Ibid., vol. 2113, file 23–2–3, Splane to Willard, 4 March 1965.

44 "Minutes of Cabinet Committee on Social Security and Labour," 12 March 1965, 1–3; "Memorandum to the Cabinet Committee on Social Security and Labour," 15 March 1965.

45 Cabinet minutes, 22 March 1965, 2.

46 Cabinet committee minutes, 12 March 1965, 3; Cabinet Committee on Labour and Social Security, minutes, 19 March 1965, 3–4.

47 Cabinet Committee on Labour and Social Security, minutes, 19 March 1965, 2–3.

48 Cabinet document 48/65, appendix B, 8; emphasis added.

49 Cabinet Committee on Labour and Social Security, minutes, 12 March 1965, 3.

50 Cabinet minutes, 22 March 1965, 3.

51 Cabinet document 152/65, "Memorandum to Cabinet: Canada Assistance Plan," 23 March 1965, 2.

52 Canada, Federal-Provincial Conference (July 1965), *Proceedings*, 53.

53 NA, RG 29, vol. 2115, file 23–4–4, "Federal-Provincial Conference of Deputy Ministers of Welfare, October 19–20," verbatim minutes, 2–10, 81, 83, 95.

54 NA, RG 29, vol. 1723, file 34–3–2, "Terms of Reference," May 1965.

55 NA, RG 29, vol. 2115, file 23–4–4, "Federal-Provincial Conference ... October 19–20," verbatim minutes, 137.

56 AO, RG 29, series 01, file 155, Band to Robarts, 14 May 1965; ibid., Borczak to MacDonald, 2 July 1965.

57 Canada, Federal-Provincial Conference (July 1965), *Proceedings*, 28–9.

58 Several NHW officials recall having had a very positive view of the inclusion of child welfare in CAP. One key official remembers "the delighted surprise in my mind that child welfare was going to become a possible inclusion."

59 So he told provincial officials at the October meeting; see NA, RG 29, vol. 2115, file 23–4–4, "Federal-Provincial Conference ... October 19–20, 1965," verbatim minutes, 116–18.

60 Ibid., 24, 108, 110, 112, 123; Dyck, "Poverty and Policy-Making," 169, 170.

61 NA, RG 29, ibid., 117–18.

62 Cabinet document 536/65, "The Canada Assistance Plan," 8 November 1965, 4.

63 NA, MG 28, I 103, reel H-137, NCW, minutes, 5–6 April 1965, 14.

64 NA, RG 29, vol. 2114, file 23–3–10, Willard to LaMarsh, 15 July 1965.

65 NA, MG 28, I 103, reel H-137, NCW minutes, 5–6 April 1965, 14. Finance officials were well aware of Ontario's traditional stand, and this may have encouraged them to oppose differential cost-sharing formulas in federal legislation; see NA, RG 19, vol. 4854, file 5508–02, pt. 3, "Provincial Statements Relating to Conditional Grants and Shared Cost Programs," 12 October 1966.

66 Cabinet document 536/65, 3–4, 7.

67 Cabinet minutes, 10 November 1965, 6–7.

68 Cabinet document 622/65, "Note to the Cabinet on the Canada Assistance Plan," 28 December 1966.

69 Cabinet minutes, 29 December 1965, 2–4.

70 Cabinet minutes, 5 January 1966, 4–7.

71 Cabinet minutes, 29 December 1965, 8.

72 NA, RG 29, vol. 2115, file 23–4–5, "Federal-Provincial Conference of Ministers of Welfare," 7–8 January 1966, 13, 22, 49–63, 106, 111.

73 Cabinet document 110/66, "Memorandum to Cabinet: The Canada Assistance Plan," 18 February 1966, 1, 4.

74 Cabinet document 179/66, "Memorandum to Cabinet: Canada Assistance Plan," 24 March 1966, 1; cabinet minutes, 31 March 1966.

75 NA, RG 29, vol. 2115, file 23–4–5, "Federal-Provincial Conference of Ministers of Welfare," verbatim minutes, 7–8 January 1966, 14, 40–1, 210; ibid., vol. 2115, file 23–4–5, communiqué, 8 January 1966.

76 Cabinet document 110/66, "Memorandum to Cabinet: The Canada Assistance Plan," 18 February 1966, 4.

77 Cabinet minutes, 31 March 1966, 7–9.

78 Cabinet minutes, 31 May 1966, 4–5.

CHAPTER FOUR

1 Canadian Party Platforms, 220–1, 233, 238–9, 248, 266, 277, 299. The Social Credit Party is not specifically discussed here, but its assistance policy did not significantly diverge from that of the other parties.

2 Canada, Parliament, House of Commons, Debates. For examples of Conservative MPs advocating categorical reform, see 16 January 1956, 153; 5 November 1957, 787; 3 June 1963, 594; 5 November 1963, 4399. For Liberal requests, see 12 January 1956, 64–5; 9 February 1961. For NDP requests, see 27 July 1956, 6592; 1 October 1963, 3067. There were many other examples of such requests by MPs of all three parties.

3 Ibid., 12 April 1962, 2885.

4 Ibid., 1 October 1963, 3067.

5 Ibid., 18 July 1963, 2346.

6 Referring to CAP in her memoirs, LaMarsh noted that "hand in hand with the work on the Pension Plan, there was being developed in the Department of National Welfare a plan to fill gaps within the public welfare sector"; see LaMarsh, *Bird in a Gilded Cage*, 119.

7 *Debates*, 15 June 1964, 4309, 4312; 28 July 1964, 6095; 11 September 1964, 7908–9.

8 Newman, *Distemper of Our Times*, 358.

9 *Debates*, 6 April 1965, 41.

10 Ibid., 27 May 1965, 1714.

11 Newman, *Distemper of Our Times*, 358.

12 *Canadian Party Platforms*, 314.

13 Bryden, *Old Age Pensions*, 152–3.

14 Canada, Parliament, Senate, Special Committee on Aging, *Final Report*.

15 Cabinet minutes, 4 April 1966, 4–5.

16 *Debates*, 14 June 1966, 6415–16.

17 Ibid., 14 June 1966, 6410–15; 21 June 1966, 6686, 6690–3.

18 *Globe and Mail*, 30 June 1966, 1 July 1966.

19 *Debates*, 28 June 1966, 6994.

20 Ibid., 30 June 1966, 7094.

21 *Globe and Mail*, 1 July 1966.

22 *Debates*, 8 July 1966, 7395–8, 7401, 7415–16.

23 Simeon and Robinson, *Development of Canadian Federalism*, 131–3; Kumar, "Union Growth," 127.

24 CLC, *Memorandum*, 1961, 16.

25 Ibid., December 1962, 13.

26 Ibid., 1961, 14–15.

27 CLC, *Submission*, 5.

28 CLC, *Memorandum*, 1965, 19.

29 Ibid., 1957, 11; ibid., 1957, 16; ibid., 1959, 21; NA, MG 28, I 103, reel H-558, CLC, "Policy Principles," 27 May 1964.

30 NA, MG 28, I 103, reel H-272, Andras to Armstrong, 6 January 1965.

31 Ibid., reel M-2039, CLC, subcommittee on Gill Report to MacEachen, October 1963, 15.

32 Ibid., accession 79/563, vol. 1, Andras to Morris, 27 July 1965.

33 CLC, *Memorandum*, 1966, 24; CLC, 6th constitutional convention, *Proceedings*, 68.

34 NA, MG 28, I 103, accession 79/563, vol. 5, Rintoul to Monteith, 18 April 1961.

35 Ibid., reel H-44, Andras to Dodge, 23 October 1961.

36 Ibid., reel H-279, CLC, National Committee on Employment, minutes, 22 November 1961.
37 Ibid., reel H-44, CLC, Internal Employment Committee, minutes, 17 August 1962.
38 Ibid., CLC, National Committee on Employment, minutes, 11 December 1962; CLC, *Memorandum*, December 1962. The passage of the memorandum on work-for-relief took up seventy lines, while assistance issues took up a total of forty-three lines of text in all CLC annual memos during the period from 1957 to 1963.
39 Ibid., 16.
40 NA, MG 29, vol, 1526, file 201–16–2, pt. 1, Splane to Willard, 11 December 1962. Splane even went so far as to call Andras to inform him of the views of one NDP Member of Parliament who favoured work-for-relief; see ibid. This led to a complaint by Andras to David Lewis about the views of Frank Howard, the MP in question; see NA, MG 28, I 103, reel H-477.
41 On 21 August and 2 October, respectively. Their statements are in ibid., reel H-44.
42 Ibid., reel H-477; NUPE *Highlights*, September 1962, 5.
43 Ibid., reel H-279, CLC, National Committee on Employment. minutes, 21 April 1965, 13–14.
44 Ibid., reel H-56, CLC, National Committee on Employment, minutes, 8 October 1964; ibid., reel H-469, CLC, Internal Employment Committee, minutes, 21 January 1965.
45 Ibid., reel H-139, NCW, minutes, 5–6 April 1965, 10.
46 See Burt's reference to the UAW policy at the executive committee meeting, 13 July 1964; ibid., reel M-2040.
47 Ibid., reel H-56, account in "Campaigns" document, 10 August 1964.
48 Ibid.
49 Ibid., reel M-2040, CLC executive committee, minutes, 13 July 1964.
50 CLC, *Memorandum*, 1966, 27–8.
51 CLC, 6th constitutional convention, *Proceedings*, 99–100.
52 Cabinet document 191/64, 4 May 1964, appendix I, 2; NA, MG 29, vol. 2115, file 23–4–5, "Federal-Provincial Conference of Ministers of Welfare," minutes, 7–8 January 1966, 151–2; minutes of the *in camera* meetings are in NA, MG 28, I 103, accession 79/563, vol. 8.
53 Canadian Chamber of Commerce, *Statement of Policy*, 1961, 47.
54 Canada, Committee of Inquiry into the Unemployment Insurance Act, *Exhibits and Briefs*, no. 5, 6–7.
55 Canadian Chamber of Commerce, *Report*, 1963–4, 9; ibid., 1964–5, 6–7; ibid., 1965–6, 6.
56 Canadian Chamber of Commerce, ibid., 1962–3, 5.

57 Canadian Chamber of Commerce, *Statement of Policy*, 1961, 20; ibid., 1964–5, 29; ibid., 1965–6, 31; ibid., 1966–7, 31.

58 Canadian Chamber of Commerce, *Submission* 42.

59 Canada, Committee of Inquiry into the Unemployment Insurance Act, *Exhibits and Briefs* no. 12, pp. 4, 6, 14–15.

60 CMA, *Report*, 1962, 22; ibid, 1965, 13; ibid., 1967, 16.

61 *The Canadian Banker* 71 (spring 1964), no. 1, 76–7; Canada, Committee of Inquiry into the Unemployment Insurance Act, *Exhibits and Briefs* no. 4, 4–6.

62 Canada, Royal Commission on Taxation, *Hearings* no. 94, 10 January 1964, 8674.

63 CNIB, *Annual Report*, 1935, 21.

64 Guest, *Emergence of Social Security*, 97–8.

65 CNIB, *Annual Report*, 1943, 13.

66 CCB *Outlook* 15 (January 1962), 3; 16 (April 1963), 8; ibid. (October 1963), 8.

67 AO, RG 29, series 01, file 1683, Magill (CNIB managing director) to Willard, 4 January 1965; CNIB, *Annual Report*, 1966, 4.

68 NA, MG 28, I 103, accession 79/563, vol. 1, Armstrong (national executive director, Canadian Rehabilitation Council for the Disabled) to Andras, CLC, 22 January 1965.

69 AO, RG 29, series 01, file 155, Borczak to Shaw (president, Ontario Federation for the Cerebral Palsied), 4 August 1965; NA, RG 29, vol. 2115, file 23–4–5, Shaw to Pearson, 23 September 1965.

70 NA, RG 29, vol. 1682, file 20-J-9A, ICPA meeting, 8 August 1961; cabinet document 311/61, 29 August 1961, appendix H, 1.

71 NA, MG 921, "Alberta" file, "Discussion by R. Draper with Deputy Minister of Public Welfare, Newfoundland," 7 January 1964; ibid., "Discussion with Alberta officials. R. Draper."

72 Cabinet document 191/64, "The Development of a New Public Assistance Plan," 4 May 1964, appendix B.

CHAPTER FIVE

1 Canada, Statistics Canada, *National Income and Expenditure Accounts*, 271; Canada, Health and Welfare Canada, *Social Security Statistics*, 1987, 318; Manzer, *Public Policies*, 63.

2 Esping-Andersen, *Three Worlds*, 70.

3 Harrington, *The Other America*; Townsend and Abel-Smith, *The Poor and the Poorest*.

4 Jones, *Social Policy*, 198–9, 104–6.

5 Lawson and Walker, "Lessons for the United Kingdom," 303–4.

6 Myles, "Decline or Impasse?"; Iacobacci and Seccareccia, "Full Employment."

7 Moynihan, *Politics of a Guaranteed Income*, 50.

8 Friedman, *Capitalism and Freedom*, 192.

9 Quebec, *Report of the Commission of Inquiry on Health and Social Welfare*, vol. 5, tome 1, title 2, 298–305.

10 Myles, "Decline or Impasse?", 94–5.

11 French, *How Ottawa Decides*, 19.

12 Doern and Aucoin, "Conclusions and Observations," 278; Phidd, "Central Advisory Councils," 205; Campbell, *Canadian Senate*, 87, 147–9.

13 Canada, Parliament, Senate, Special Committee on Aging, *Final Report*, vol. 1, v, xii, 9, 19.

14 Bryden, *Old Age Pensions*, 153.

15 Phidd, "Central Advisory Councils," 221.

16 Canada, Economic Council of Canada, *Fifth Annual Review*, 103, 105, 137.

17 Saywell and Stevens, "Parliament and Politics" (1968), 386.

18 Canada, Economic Council of Canada, *Fifth Annual Review*, 137.

19 Adams et al., "Renegade Report," 2.

20 Canada, Parliament, Senate, Special Committee on Poverty, *Report on Poverty*, xv-xx; Adams et al., *Real Poverty Report*, 190–200.

21 Canada, Royal Commission on the Status of Women in Canada, *Report*, 302, 324–5.

22 Canada, Economic Council of Canada, *Sixth Annual Review*, 118.

23 *Report on Poverty*, x, 180; *Real Poverty Report*, 181.

24 Canada, Economic Council of Canada, *Fifth Annual Review*, 130, 134.

25 *Report on Poverty*, 182, 184.

26 *Real Poverty Report*, 200.

27 Quebec, *Report of the Commission of Inquiry on Health and Social Welfare*, vol. 5, tome 1, title 2, 231; ibid., tome 3, title 4, 107–18.

28 Ibid., tome 1, title 2, 249, 252, 275.

29 Cutt, "National Economy," 365; Bellamy, "Welfare," 469.

30 *Canadian News Facts*, 13 August 1969, 22 November 1970, 10 November 1971; Canada, NHW, *Income Security for Canadians*, 25–7; Cutt, "Welfare and Unemployment Insurance," 348–9.

31 Cited in Dyck, "Poverty and Policy-Making," 376–7.

32 McInnis, "Federal-Provincial Negotiations," 125.

33 Ibid., 130.

34 Ibid., 123–8, 130, 132–5, 138.

35 Ibid., 130.

36 *Income Security for Canadians*, 25–7.

37 Johnson, *Social Policy*, 23.

38 McInnis, "Federal-Provincial Negotiations," 230, 251.
39 *Le Devoir*, 21 January 1971, 11 February 1971; Saywell and Stevens, "Parliament and Politics" (1971), 48.
40 Saywell and Stevens, ibid., 48.
41 NA, RG 29, vol. 1605, file 6, "Constitutional Conference, 3rd Working Session, Feb. 8–9, 1971, Statement of Conclusions," 8–9.
42 NA, RG 29, vol. 1545, file F1–1; Saywell and Stevens, "Parliament and Politics" (1971), 49; *Globe and Mail*, 9 June 1971.
43 Saywell and Stevens, "Parliament and Politics" (1971), 63.
44 *Le Devoir*, 10–11 September 1971.
45 Ibid., 23 September 1971; translation by the author.
46 Saywell and Stevens, "Parliament and Politics" (1972), 96, 98, 99; French in original translated by the author.
47 Ibid., 102–3; McInnis, "Federal-Provincial Negotiations," 297–300.
48 Canada, Rt. Hon. Pierre Elliot Trudeau, *Income Security and Social Services*, 66.
49 Ibid., 98.
50 French, *How Ottawa Decides*, 32–41.
51 A. W. Johnson, "Treasury Board of Canada," 347, 351, 353.
52 French, *How Ottawa Decides*, 37.
53 Based on McInnis, "Federal-Provincial Negotiations," 133.
54 Lalonde seemed to regard it as such, given his opening statement at the February 1973 welfare ministers' meeting; see NA, RG 29, vol. 2354, file 1, "Federal-Provincial Conference of Ministers of Welfare," 2 February 1973, verbatim minutes, 6.
55 Cutt, "Welfare and Unemployment Insurance," 349–50.
56 On the public demands, see *Canadian News Facts*, 5 and 15 November 1972. On private discussions, see Saltsman, "Party Politics and Social Policy," 269; Harder, "House of Minorities," 134.
57 *Canadian News Facts*, 4 January 1973; *Globe and Mail*, 5 January 1973.
58 Saltsman, "Party Politics and Social Policy," 269; Harder, "House of Minorities," 134.
59 *Canadian News Facts*, 11 January 1973.
60 Cutt, "Welfare and Unemployment Insurance," 350–1.
61 See Bellamy, "Welfare," 466.
62 Based on Gwyn, *Northern Magus*, 150; *Le Devoir*, 24 October 1972.
63 *Globe and Mail*, 5 January 1973.
64 Harder, "House of Minorities," 145–6.
65 NA, RG 29, vol. 2354, file 1, "Federal-Provincial Conference," 2 February 1973, verbatim minutes, 6, 23.
66 Saywell and Stevens, "Parliament and Politics" (1972), 102; *Le Devoir*, 26 October 1972.
67 Saywell and Stevens, "Parliament and Politics" (1972), 109.

68 NA, RG 29, vol. 1605, file 5, "Minutes of Provincial Welfare Ministers Conference," 27–28 November 1972, summary minutes, 18–19.

69 Ibid., communiqué, 28 November 1972.

70 Ibid., summary minutes, 20–1.

71 Saywell and Stevens, "Parliament and Politics" (1972), 104–5.

72 NA, RG 29, accession 85–86/343, file 3401–1/73–1, "April 1973 Meeting of Ministers of Welfare – Briefing Notes for Honourable Marc Lalonde," 1, 4–5; emphasis added.

73 Ibid., 2.

74 McInnis, "Federal-Provincial Negotiations," 343–4.

75 According to Leman, "as of October 1977 the Policy Research and Long Range Planning Branch (Welfare) had a staff of eighty-two, of whom forty had some education beyond college. Specialties were economics (twenty); mathematics, computing science, statistics (nineteen); sociology, demography (fifteen); and others"; see *Collapse of Welfare Reform*, 248. Interviews with participants confirmed that a similar pattern prevailed at the beginning of the Review.

76 Canada, NHW, *General Framework*, 20.

77 *Canadian News Facts*, 4 January 1973.

78 NA, RG 29, accession 85–86/343, file 3401–1/73–1, "April 1973 Meeting," 1.

79 Harder, "House of Minorities," 146.

80 *Globe and Mail*, 23 April 1973.

81 Cost calculations are based on cost increases for the two programs over the relevant years reported in Canada, Statistics Canada, *Social Security: National Programs, 1978*.

82 Canada, NHW, *Working Paper on Social Security*, 17, 29.

83 NA, RG 29, vol. 2354, file 2, "Federal-Provincial Conference of Ministers of Welfare, April 25–27, 1973," verbatim transcript, tape 3, 19; ibid., tape 4, 18, 21.

84 *Working Paper on Social Security*, 17, 28.

85 Ibid., 2.

86 Ibid., 3, 7–9.

87 Ibid., 8, 11, 12, 22–3; emphasis in original.

88 Ibid., 5.

89 Ibid., 6.

90 Therborn, *Why Some Peoples Are More Unemployed Than Others*.

91 *Working Paper on Social Security*, 7, 9; emphasis in original.

92 Ibid., 22, 23.

93 Ibid., 18, 19.

94 Ibid., 22–3.

95 Esping-Andersen, *Three Worlds*, 62.

96 Rachlis, "Ten Years After," 43–4.

97 *Working Paper on Social Security*, 26.
98 Ibid., 29.
99 This is strongly hinted at by A. W. Johnson in *Social Policy*, 21.
100 Andrew Johnson, "Political Leadership," 212–13.
101 A. W. Johnson, *Social Policy*, 24.
102 Leman, *Collapse of Welfare Reform*, 116.
103 A. W. Johnson, *Social Policy*, 27.
104 *Le Devoir*, 19 April 1973; *Globe and Mail*, 19 April 1973; *Canadian News Facts*, 18 April 1973.

CHAPTER SIX

1 Quebec's position was set forth at the *in camera* meetings of federal and provincial welfare ministers in February and April 1973; see NA, RG 29, vol. 2354, file 1, "Federal-Provincial Conference of Ministers of Welfare, February 2, 1973," verbatim transcript of minutes, tape 1, 14–22; ibid., file 2, "Federal-Provincial Conference of Ministers of Welfare, April 25–27, 1973," verbatim transcript of minutes, tape 1, 15–21. Other provinces also stated their initial positions at these meetings.
2 Ibid., file 1, tape 1, 10–13, 37–41, and tape 2, 1–2; ibid., file 2, tape 1, 5–14, 50–7.
3 Ibid., file 1, tape 1, 25–9, 34–6; file 2, tape 1, 27–36, 45–9; see also ibid., accession 85–86/343, file 3401–4/73–2, "British Columbia's Proposals on Income Security for Canada."
4 Ibid., vol. 2354, file 1, tape 1, 23–5, 29–33; ibid., file 2, "Federal-Provincial Conference ... April 25–27, 1973," tape 1, 22–5, 37–44.
5 At the April welfare ministers' meeting, Lalonde stated that these were the two major reasons for federal unwillingness to proceed with immediate reforms; see ibid., tape 6, 2–3. Both arguments also featured prominently in correspondence between Johnson and Lalonde; see ibid., accession 85–86/343, file 3401–4/73–3, Johnson to Lalonde, 9 October 1973.
6 The agreed-upon structure for the Review was elaborated in "Administrative Machinery for the Federal-Provincial Review of Social Security for Canada"; see ibid., vol. 1298, file 5619–3–731.
7 Ibid., vol. 1296, file 5619–3–731, "Deputy Ministers of Welfare Conference, May 29–30, 1973," verbatim transcript, tape 2–3, 29, 35–8.
8 The committee consisted of Johnson, Robinson (and, at times, one of his subordinates), and John Osborne. When social-service issues were being discussed, Brian Iverson from the corresponding branch of NHW would also be present. Reflecting the central role that he had played in shaping the Review, Claude Castonguay accepted Johnson's invitation to join the committee when he left his position as Quebec minister of Social Affairs in late 1973.

9 Ibid., accession 85–86/343, file 3401–4/73, Levi to Lalonde, 9 October 1973.

10 Ibid., vol. 2354, file 7, "Meeting of Federal and Provincial Ministers of Welfare, October 11–12, 1973," verbatim transcript, tape 3, 11–15, 21; tape 4, 12–17; file 8, tape 4, 20.

11 Johnson, "Canada's Social Security Review," 465–9.

12 NA, RG 29, vol. 1296, file 5619–2–741, "Ministers of Welfare Meeting, February 19–20, 1974," notes by G. Fortier dated 14 November 1974, 1–7; ibid., vol. 1613, file 10, Johnson to Cousineau (UIC commissioner), 14 May 1975; Leman, *Collapse of Welfare Reform*, 116.

13 An example of Lalonde's flexibility is found in NA, RG 29, vol. 1296, file 5619–2–742, "Federal-Provincial Conference of Ministers of Welfare of November 19–20, 1974," verbatim transcript, tape 2, 2.

14 Ibid., "Report on Income Support and Supplementation from the Continuing Committee on Social Security to the Federal and Provincial Ministers of Welfare, 19–20 November, 1974," 4–6.

15 Ibid., "Meeting of the Federal and Provincial Ministers of Welfare, November 19–20, 1974," notes by Blais-Grenier dated 10 December 1974, 3–11.

16 Ibid., vol. 1299, file 5619–3–751, "Federal-Provincial Conference of Welfare Deputy Ministers, 6–7 February, 1975," tape 1, 1–12, and tape 2, 1–9; ibid., vol. 1590, file 1024–1–2, pt. 3, "Memorandum to the Cabinet: The Social Security Review – Income Support and Supplementation," 20 January 1975; ibid., accession 85–86/343, file 3203–16–1, pt. 1, McLarty to Robinson, 5 September 1974; Clark to Osborne, 24 September 1974.

17 French, *How Ottawa Decides*, 28.

18 McCall-Newman, *Grits*, 223; Leman, *Collapse of Welfare Reform*, 122.

19 Wolfe, "Politics of the Deficit," 115–21.

20 In interviews, a number of major participants in the Review noted this fiscal shortfall as a major impediment to reform in 1975. Johnson discussed the problem with provincial deputy ministers at the time; see NA, RG 29, vol. 1299, file 5619–3–751, "Federal-Provincial Conference of Deputy Ministers of Welfare, February 6–7, 1975," verbatim transcript, tape 1, 5.

21 *Toronto Star*, 26 November 1974.

22 NA, RG 29, vol. 1297, file 5619–2–751, pt. 2, "Meeting of the Federal and Provincial Ministers of Welfare, February 18–20, 1975," summary minutes, appendix A, 9.

23 *Ottawa Citizen*, 19 February 1975; NA, RG 29, vol. 1297, file 5619–2–752, "Press Release: British Columbia Position on Supplementing the Working Poor," 20 February 1975.

24 Statement by Reisman, cited in *The Ottawa Journal*, 24 January 1976.

25 In interviews with the author, participants in the Review stressed that this was a major preoccupation for Reisman; see also Phidd and Doern, *Politics and Management*, 118.

26 Johnson referred to these competing ministerial objectives at his February meeting with the provincial deputy ministers; see NA, RG 29, vol. 1299, file 5619–3–751, "Federal-Provincial Conference of Deputy Ministers of Welfare, February 6–7, 1975," verbatim transcript, tape 1, 5.

27 See the article by John Grey in *The Ottawa Citizen*, 15 February 1975.

28 NA, RG 29, vol. 1297, file 5619–2–751, pt. 1, "Federal-Provincial Conference: Detailed Minutes," notes on the February 1975 welfare ministers' meeting by Pearson, 1–4, 9.

29 Ibid., 2–3, 6, 9–16.

30 Ibid., 24; ibid., "Meeting of the Federal and Provincial Ministers of Welfare, February 18–19, 1975," summary minutes by Fortier, 26–8.

31 Ibid., "Communiqué: Meeting of Federal and Provincial Ministers of Welfare, February 18 & 19, 1975," 1.

32 Ibid., vol. 1297, file 5619–2–752, Sadler (British Columbia deputy minister of welfare) to all other provincial deputy ministers, 20 February 1975; Johnson to Sadler, 25 February 1975; Sadler to Johnson, 27 February 1975; Desjardins (Manitoba welfare minister) to Lalonde, 26 February 1975; and Lalonde to Desjardins, 4 March 1975.

33 Ibid., "Meeting of the Federal and Provincial Minsters of Welfare, April 30–May 1, 1975," summary minutes by Fortier, 16–19.

34 Ibid., "Notes on Meeting of Continuing Committee on Social Security, April 16–17, 1975," summary conference minutes, 16–19; ibid., "Statement by the Honourable Marc Lalonde to the Conference of Federal and Provincial Ministers of Welfare," 30 April 1975, 3–6.

35 Ibid., "Statement by Mr Claude Forget, Minister of Social Affairs for the Province of Quebec," 30 April 1975; ibid., "Federal-Provincial Conference of Welfare Ministers, April 30–May 1, 1975," verbatim transcript, tape 2, 41–41D.

36 Ibid., "Meeting of the Federal and Provincial Ministers of Welfare, April 30–May 1, 1975," verbatim minutes by Fortier, 10–20; ibid., "Communiqué: Meeting of the Federal and Provincial Ministers of Welfare, April 30–May 1, 1975," 6; ibid., "Federal-Provincial Ministers Conference: Press Conference," verbatim transcript, 6–7.

37 Ibid., "Communiqué," 5.

38 Ibid., vol. 1299, file 5619–3–754, Rawson to provincial deputy ministers, 28 August 1975.

39 That this was already apparent is suggested by the minutes of a committee of federal and provincial welfare deputy ministers that met on 26 August; see ibid.

40 Therborn, *Why Some Peoples Are More Unemployed Than Others*, 10, 18.

41 Rachlis, "Ten Years After," 28–9.

42 Canada, NHW, *Working Paper on Social Security*, 18, 19.

43 Ibid., 7; NA, RG 29, vol. 1591, file 1024–6–3, pt. 1, 5, Johnson, "A Community Employment Plan," 21 January 1973.

44 NA, RG 29, vol. 1591, file 1024–6–3, pt. 1, "Interdepartmental Task Force on Direct Job Creation: Appendix B," 2; ibid., "A Direct Employment Planning Model: Appendix C," 1. Former Manpower officials interviewed by the author agreed with this assessment of the focus of their programs at the time.

45 Ibid., "Memorandum to Cabinet: A Planning and Action Framework for Direct Job Creation and Other Measures to Reduce Unemployment," by R. Andras, cabinet document 549/73, 31 May 1973, 1–2.

46 Ibid., vol. 1591, file 1024–6–3, pt. 2, Johnson to Lalonde, 4 June 1973, 3, 4.

47 NA, RG 118, file 3000–17–4–1, pt. 2, Manion to provincial members of the working party on employment, 28 August 1973.

48 NA, RG 29, vol. 1591, file 1024–6–3, pt. 2, Andras to Manpower officials, 12 June 1973, 2.

49 Johnson's views are recounted in ibid., accession 85–86/343, file 3203–16–1, pt. 1, Ferguson to Osborne, 14 December 1973, 3.

50 Ibid., vol. 1590, file 1024–2–2, pt. 1, Rawson to Lalonde, 12 November 1975. Their non-involvement was confirmed in interviews with former NHW officials.

51 NA, RG 118, accession 85–86/071, file 3000–17–4–1, pt. 1, Drew to Manion, 29 June 1973; ibid., file 3060–12–5–1, Boyd to Gotlieb, 6 March 1974.

52 Ibid., pt. 4, Johnson to Gotlieb, 25 January 1974.

53 Ibid., file 3060–12–5–1, Krupka to Manion, 29 January 1974.

54 NA, RG 29, vol. 1541, file 1003-W2–1, pt. 1, "Some Reflections Around the Concepts of Work and Working," by Cathy Stairs and Gail Stewart, 12 March 1972; ibid., "Community Employment: Some Basic Issues," by Stewart, August 1973; ibid., pt. 2, Stewart to Robinson, 15 February 1974.

55 Johnson responded to Stewart's views in marginal notes on the above documents – for example, on ibid., Stewart to Robinson, 7.

56 Ibid., Johnson to Robinson, 2 March 1974.

57 See NA, RG 118, accession 85–86/071, file 3000–17–4, "Delegates – Working Party on Employment Services," for evidence of the heterogeneous professional composition of officials working on the strategy. Many interviewees referred to the traditional hostility between welfare and labour officials. Johnson also alludes to these tensions in "Canada's Social Security Review," 471.

58 Ibid., pt. 2, Manion to working party on employment, 28 August 1973; ibid., Manion to Gotlieb, 18 September 1973.

59 NA, RG 29, vol. 2354, file 3, "Working Party on Employment, June 20–21, 1973," verbatim minutes, tape 1, side 2, 4, tape 2, 23–4.

60 Based on interviews with former Welfare and Manpower officials; see also A. W. Johnson, "Canada's Social Security Review," 464.

61 NA, RG 29, vol. 1541, file 1003-W2–1, pt. 1, Eberlee to Brunet, 24 September 1973; ibid., "Working Party on Employment Report to Continuing Committee on Social Security – Draft," 12 September 1973; NA, RG 118, accession 85–86/071, file 3000–17–4–1, pt. 2, Manion to Gotlieb, 18 September 1973; ibid., pt. 4, Manion to Gotlieb, 28 November 1973; ibid., Krupka to Manion, 5 December 1973.

62 Gotlieb acknowledged this in NA, RG 29, vol. 1298, file 5619–3–741, "Minutes of the Continuing Committee on Social Security, February 5–6, 1974," summary minutes by Osborne, 15.

63 Ibid., vol. 1296, file 5619–2–741, "Ministers of Welfare Meeting, February 19–20, 1974," summary notes by Fortier, 14 November 1974, 21–7.

64 Ibid., vol. 1541, file 1003–2–1, pt. 2, "Extract on Community Employment from Cabinet Document 78–74 of February 5," esp. 3.

65 So the conference communiqué indicated agreement on the experimental approach; see ibid., vol. 1296, file 5619–2–742.

66 Ibid., file 5619–2–741, "Federal-Provincial Conference of Ministers of Welfare, February 19–20, 1974," verbatim transcript, reel 2, 15.

67 Ibid., "Summary: Present Status of Community Employment."

68 Ibid., vol. 1591, file 1024–6–3, pt. 2, "Memorandum to Cabinet. Cab. doc. 412–74. Community Employment Strategy," by Andras, 26 July 1974, 2.

69 Ibid., 5; emphasis added.

70 Canada, Department of Manpower and Immigration, *Annual Report, 1974–75*, 14.

71 NA, RG 118, accession 85–86/071, file 3060–12–5–1, Van Loon to O'Neil and Rachlis, 1 August 1974. Krupka's negative response is summarized in a memo to Carter; see ibid., file 3060–18–1, pt. 3, n.d.

72 Recounted in NA, RG 29, vol. 1541, file 1003-W2–1, pt. 1, Johnson to Osborne, 19 July 1973.

73 AO, RG 29, accession 59–01, file 55–4–2–4, "Interim Report on Social Services in Canada"; on the report's significance, see NA, RG 29, vol. 1541, file 1003-W1–1, Osborne to Johnson, 31 October 1974.

74 Ibid., vol. 1298, file 5619–2–742, "Meeting of the Federal and Provincial Minsters of Welfare, November 19–20, 1974," summary minutes by Blais-Grenier, 14–15.

75 Ibid., vol. 1299, file 5619–3–751, "Special Meeting of the Continuing Committee on Social Security to Discuss Social Services … December 10, 1974," 5–6, 9.

76 Ibid., vol. 1298, file 5619–2–741, Fortier to Johnson, 24 October 1974.

CHAPTER SEVEN

1 Smiley, *Canada in Question*, 175.
2 NA, RG 29, vol. 1299, file 5619–3–754, minutes of the conference of federal and provincial deputy ministers of welfare, 23 September 1975.
3 Ibid., file 5619–3–753, "Support/Supplementation Design: Calgary WPIM Meeting, May 1975," summary minutes by Dickinson, 30 May 1975; ibid., accession 85–86/343, file 3401–4/75–4, Desjardins to Lalonde, 13 November 1975.
4 Ibid., vol. 1590, file 1024–1–2, pt. 2, "Outline for Cabinet Memorandum on a Proposed Income Support/Supplementation System," 8 December 1975, 2.
5 Ibid., pt. 1, Shoyama to Finance minister, 12 January 1975, 3–8.
6 Ibid., 5–6. In interviews conducted for this study, several participants stated that the position taken by the Finance minister in cabinet largely reflected the views expressed in Shoyama's memorandum.
7 Ibid., vol. 1297, file 5619–2–761, "Federal-Provincial Conference of Welfare Ministers, February 3–4, 1976," verbatim minutes, tape 4, 36; translation by the author.
8 Ibid., accession 85–86/343, file 3401–4/76–2, "Conversation with Heagle [an Ontario official]" by Osborne, 29 January 1976; ibid., "Briefing Note: Possible Positions by Ontario," February 1976.
9 Ibid., vol. 1297, file 5619–2–761, "Meeting of the Federal and Provincial Ministers of Welfare, February 3–4, 1976," summary minutes by Fortier, 40–1.
10 *Ottawa Citizen*, 5 February 1976, 37.
11 NA, RG 29, vol. 1297, file 5619–2–761, "Meeting of ... Ministers, February 3–4, 1976," summary minutes, 38–9; ibid., "Federal-Provincial Conference ... February 3–4, 1976," verbatim minutes, tape 4, 36–8.
12 Ibid., "Meeting of ... Ministers, February 3–4, 1976," summary minutes, 37–41; ibid., "Federal-Provincial Conference ... February 3–4, 1976," verbatim minutes, tape 4, 31–5.
13 Ibid., accession 85–86/343, file 3401–4/76–3, "Provincial Reactions to the Support/Supplementation Proposal," April 1976.
14 Ibid., file 3401–4/76–3, "Federal Income Support and Supplementation Proposal: Statement by the Honourable W. Darcy McKeough, Treasurer of Ontario."
15 Ibid., Fortier to Rawson, 5 April 1976.
16 Ibid., vol. 1296, file 5619–2–762, "Meeting of the Federal and Provincial Ministers of Welfare, June 1–2, 1976," summary minutes by Fortier, 1–4.
17 Ibid., accession 85–86/343, file 3401–4/76–3, "Possible Content for Final Communiqué from June Ministers' Meeting."
18 Ibid., 46–50.

19 Ibid., 62.

20 Ibid., 55–6, 65.

21 Ibid., vol. 1296, file 5619–2–762, "Communiqué – Meeting of Federal and Provincial Ministers of Welfare, June 1–2, 1976," 3–4.

22 Ibid., "Meeting of … Ministers of Welfare, June 1–2, 1976," summary minutes by Fortier, 47–65.

23 Ibid., accession 85–86/343, files 3203–16–2 and 3203–16–1, pt. 2.

24 Ibid., file 3203–16–1, pt. 4, "Income Supplementation: Considerations," 2.

25 Ibid., pts. 2 to 4, "Possible Options for Future Evolution of Income Support," 29 October 1976; ibid., Goodman to Transitional Committee on Income Support, 28 June 1977; ibid., "Report of the Transitional Committee on Income Support," 19 September 1977; ibid., W.A. MacDonald to Lyngseth, 7 November 1977; ibid., Clark to Osborne, 7 December 1977; ibid., "Income Support: Considerations."

26 Ibid., vol. 1296, file 5619–2–762, "Meeting of … Ministers of Welfare, June 1–2, 1976," summary minutes by Fortier, 52, 68–9.

27 Ibid., accession 85–86/343, file 3203–16–1, pt. 3, "The Tax-Transfer Integration Task Force: Situation Report," 1–4 March 1977; ibid., pt. 4, "Income Supplementation: Considerations," 18 January 1978, 1–2.

28 Ibid.

29 Ibid., 1.

30 Ibid., 6; emphasis in original.

31 Ibid., pt. 3, "The Tax-Transfer Integration Task Force," 6.

32 McCall-Newman, Grits, 236–7; Gwyn, Northern Magus, 312.

33 This interpretation of events is suggested by a number of informed federal actors from the period. Bégin herself has linked the restraint exercise to the origins of the Child Tax Credit; see L'assurance santé, 23–4.

34 Guest, Emergence of Social Security, 199; see also Leman, Collapse of Welfare Reform, 132–3.

35 NA, RG 29, vol. 1590, file 1024–1–2, pt. 1, Robinson to Johnson, 7 April 1975; ibid., Van Loon to Johnson, 12 March 1975.

36 Ibid., Record of Cabinet Decision, no. 213–75RD, 15 April 1975.

37 Ibid., Fortier to Johnson, 2 April 1975.

38 Ibid., vol. 1297, file 5619–2–752, "Federal-Provincial Conference of Ministers of Welfare, April 30–May 1: Communiqué," 2–3.

39 Ibid., Iverson to Lupien, 5 August 1975; ibid., "Draft Legislative Outline of Proposed Social Services Legislation," 10 September 1975.

40 Ibid,. vol. 1590, file 1024–1–2, pt. 1, Callbeck to Lalonde, 26 September 1975.

41 Ibid., vol. 1299, file 5619–3–753, "Press Statement: Provincial Ministers of Welfare, Sept. 25–26," 2.

42 Ibid., vol. 1590, file 1024–1–2, pt. 1, Callbeck to Lalonde, 26 September 1975.

43 Ibid., pt. 3, Iverson to Rawson, 12 December 1975; ibid., accession 85–86/343, file 3401-4/76-2, "Revised Outline no. II of Social Services Act," February 1976.

44 Ibid., vol. 1297, file 5619-2-761, "Communiqué: Meeting of Federal and Provincial Ministers of Welfare, February 3-4, 1976," 1.

45 Ibid., vol. 1299, file 5619-3-762, "Deputy Ministers Meeting, Montreal, 7-8 April, 76," handwritten notes by Fortier, 1.

46 Ibid., vol. 1298, file 5619-2-762, "Federal-Provincial Conference of Welfare Ministers, June 1-2, 1976," verbatim transcripts.

47 Ibid., vol. 1590, file 1024-1-2, pt. 1, 12 April 1975.

48 Ibid., Record of Cabinet Decision, 15 April 1975, 2.

49 Ibid., Gotlieb to Rawson, 11 September 1975; emphasis added.

50 Ibid., accession 85–86/343, file 3203-1-3-2, Gotlieb to Rawson, 5 September 1975.

51 Ibid., "Meeting with Gotlieb," handwritten notes, 11 September 1975.

52 Ibid., vol. 1590, file 1024-1-2, pt. 1, Iverson to Rawson, 10 September 1975.

53 Ibid., vol. 1625, file 7, "Social Services legislation meeting: Manion + Rawson," handwritten notes, 29 December 1975; ibid., vol. 1590, file 1024-1-2, pt. 3, Rawson to Manion, 30 December 1975.

54 Ibid., vol. 1299, file 5619-3-754, pt. 2, "Notes on the private meeting of deputy ministers of welfare ... September 23, 1975," summary minutes, 22–31; ibid., vol. 1297, file 5619-2-761, "Federal-Provincial Conference of Ministers of Welfare, February 3-4, 1976," summary minutes by Fortier, 4-9; ibid., vol. 1296, file 5619-2-762, "Meeting of ... Welfare Ministers, June 1-2, 1976," 23, 26.

55 Ibid., accession 85–86/343, file 3401-4/75-3, Cohen to Rawson, 23 September 1975.

56 Ibid., Rawson to Cohen, 2 October 1975.

57 Ibid., file 3401/75-4, Desjardins to Lalonde, 13 November 1975.

58 Ibid., accession 85–86/343, file 3401-4/76-2, "Section 3 (3) Residential Services for Adults," 1.

59 Ibid., file 3401/75-4, Desjardins to Lalonde, 13 November 1975; ibid., vol. 1296, file 5619-2-762, "Meeting of ... Welfare Ministers, June 1-2, 1976," summary minutes by Fortier, 29-33.

60 Ibid., accession 85–86/343, file 3203-1-1, pt. 2, "News Release: Social Services Act introduced to House of Commons," 20 June 1977.

61 Ibid., accession 85–86/343, file 3203-6-1, pt. 2, "Rationale."

62 Ibid.

63 Ibid., accession 85–86/343, file 3401-4/78-1, "A Federal Government Proposal for an Alternate Funding Arrangement for Social Services," 15 August 1977, 1.

64 Ibid., file 3401-2-2/78-1, "Communiqué: Federal and Provincial Ministers of Social Services," 7-8 March 1978, 1-2.

65 Ibid., file 3203–6–1, pt. 1, Hunley to Lalonde, 26 September 1977.
66 Ibid., pt. 3, "Reactions of Provinces," 30 November 1977.
67 Ibid., Bégin to provincial ministers, 14 December 1977.
68 Ibid., "Summary of Decisions: Conference of Deputy Ministers of Welfare," 26 January 1978.
69 Ibid., pt. 5, Rawson to provincial deputy ministers, 28 July 197?.
70 Smiley, *Federalism in the Eighties*, 170, 177.
71 A number of interviewees confirmed that this was Chrétien's strategy; see also Guest, *Emergence of Social Security*, 199.
72 NA, RG 29, vol. 1590, file 1024–1–2, pt. 3, Rawson to Lalonde, 12 November 1975; emphasis added.
73 Ibid., pt. 1, "Deputy Ministers Conference: Discussion of CES," 23–24 September 1975, 22–31.
74 Canada, Employment and Immigration Canada, *Community Employment Strategy*.

CHAPTER EIGHT

1 *Canadian News Facts*, 4 May, 15 May, 7 and 11 June 1968.
2 Saywell and Stevens, "Parliament and Politics" (1968), 41, 58–9.
3 *Canadian News Facts*, 13 August 1969; 20 and 22 November 1970.
4 Ibid., 22 August, 8 September, and 9–13 October 1969.
5 Examples include Canada, Parliament, House of Commons, *Debates*, 28th Parliament, 2nd session, statement by Laprise, 28 April 1970, 6364; 3rd session, statement by Lambert, 22 October 1970, 483; statement by Caouette, 25 November 1971, 9879.
6 *Globe and Mail*, 29 and 31 October 1969.
7 *Debates*, 25 January 1971, 2718.
8 *Canadian News Facts*, 1, 14, 20, and 24 September 1972; 9 October 1972.
9 Ibid., 15 September 1972; 8 October 1972.
10 *Debates*, 29th Parliament, 1st session, 9 January 1973, 131; emphasis added. See also his remarks on 18 April 1973, 3405–8.
11 An example was Lalonde's response to another statement about the GAI by Caouette; see ibid., 17 September 1973, 6624.
12 *Canadian News Facts*, 22 July 1973; 21 August 1973.
13 Saywell and Stevens, "Parliament and Politics" (1974), 38–9.
14 *Canadian News Facts*, 26 and 27 May 1974; 4, 5, and 10 June 1974; 3 July 1974.
15 *Debates*, 30th Parliament, 1st session, 20 February 1975, 3389–90; 17 March 1975, 4154; 18 June 1975, 6894; passim.
16 Simeon and Robinson, *Development of Canadian Federalism*, 218–9.
17 NA, MG 28, I 103, reel H-517, Andras to Lewis, 18 March 1966; ibid., reel H-478, Andras to Godfrey, 16 September 1968; ibid., reel H-698, Andras to McCaffrey, 3 February 1970.

18 *Canadian Labour* 14 (1969), no. 3, 9.

19 Ibid., 15 (1970), nos. 7–8, 29, 34; see also Canada, Parliament, Senate, Special Committee on Poverty, *Proceedings*, "Canadian Labour Congress," 3 November 1970, 8:8, 8:42.

20 Ibid., 8:18–19.

21 NA, MG 28, I 103, reel H-824, McCaffrey to Beaudry, 3 August 1973, 2.

22 Ibid., Kerwin to directors of departments, 20 December 1973.

23 Ibid., "Working Paper on Social Security in Canada," by P. Kerwin, n.d., 1–4; ibid., Kerwin to directors, 3 May 1973, 1, 4; ibid., "CLC's Reaction to the Working Paper on Social Security," n.d., 2–3.

24 Canada, Parliament, Senate, Special Committee on Poverty, *Proceedings*, "Canadian Chamber of Commerce," 51:39, 51:41–5.

25 Shifrin, "Politics of Income Security," 62.

26 NA, RG 29, accession 84–85/085, file 3402–1–4, pt. 2, Canadian Chamber of Commerce, "Submission on the Working Paper on Social Security in Canada ... by the Executive Council," April 1974, 1, 4, 5, 7.

27 Ibid., Johnson to Lalonde, 13 November 1974; ibid., "Presentation to the Prime Minister and Cabinet by President, Canadian Chamber of Commerce," 20 January 1975, 18; ibid., Johnson to Lalonde, 11 April 1975; ibid., "Chamber of Commerce, Feb. 23, 1976."

28 Ibid., Lalonde to vice president, Canadian Chamber of Commerce, 2 January 1975; ibid., Lalonde to vice president, Canadian Chamber of Commerce, 5 August 1975; ibid., "Notes Responding to Social Security Issues Raised by the Chamber of Commerce," by Osborne, n.d; ibid., chairman, Canadian Chamber of Commerce, to Lalonde, 9 December 1975.

29 Ibid., "Canadian Chamber of Commerce, Feb. 23, 1976," 1.

30 Ibid., file 3402–1–12, Osborne to departmental correspondence file, 19 November 1973; ibid., executive director, CMA, to Lalonde, 14 May 1976, 1–2, 4.

31 Ibid., Lalonde to president, CMA, 30 June 1976, and attachment entitled "CMA Questions/Comments Relating to Social Security Policy."

32 "Is There Really Poverty in Canada?" *The Canadian Banker* 79 (1972), no. 3, 2–3; "The High Cost of Health," ibid., 80 (1973), no. 6, 2–3; ibid. 82 (1975), no. 2, 4, 7.

33 Felt, "Militant Poor People," 418.

34 Canada, NHW, *Low Income Interest Groups in Canada*.

35 Felt, "Militant Poor People," 418; see also Loney, "Political Economy," 467–8.

36 Besides NHW, federal departments and agencies with an interest in the field included the Secretariat of State, Indian and Northern Affairs, and the Canada Mortgage and Housing Corporation; see D. Walker, "Poor People's Conference," 27–8.

37 Canada, Health and Welfare Canada, *Chronology*, section 7.

38 Splane, "Social Policy-Making," 215–16; Walker, "Poor People's Conference," 44–5; Canada, Federal-Provincial Study Group on Alienation, *Final Report*.

39 Walker, "Poor People's Conference," 9–10.

40 Loney, "Political Economy," 456.

41 NA, RG 29, vol. 1605, file 7, press release by Munro, December 1971.

42 Walker, "Poor People's Conference," 39.

43 Chapin and Deneau, *Policy-Making Process*.

44 Chapin, "Citizen Involvement," 141.

45 Ibid., 112, 140–1; Chapin's interpretation of the role of subnational poverty organizations in the Review was largely corroborated in interviews.

46 NA, MG 28, I 103, reel H-704, NHW, news release, January 1970.

47 Wharf and Halliday, *Advisory Councils*, 35–8.

48 NA, RG 118, accession 85–86/71, file 3060–18–1, pt. 2, "Summary Report on the National Council of Welfare on the 'Orange Paper'," 29 November 1973.

49 NCW, *Incomes and Opportunities*, esp. 41–2.

50 NA, RG 29, vol. 1298, file 5619–2–762, pt. 2, "Final Plenary of CCSD: Report of Georgio Gaudet," Becker to Lalonde, June 1976.

51 See also Wharf and Halliday, *Advisory Councils*, 56–8.

52 Walker, "Poor People's Conference," 2.

53 *Canadian News Facts*, 25 January 1971; Kinnon, "Pressure Group Politics." 4.

54 Leman, *Collapse of Welfare Reform*, 51.

55 NAPO, "More About NAPO," n.d.

56 NAPO, *Towards a Guaranteed Income*.

57 Leman, *Collapse of Welfare Reform*, 122.

58 *Globe and Mail*, 18 February 1975; *Ottawa Citizen*, 17 February 1975.

59 NA, RG 29, vol. 1298, file 5619–2–762, pt. 2, "Final Plenary of CCSD"; *Toronto Star*, 17 June 1976.

60 Canadian Rehabilitative Council for the Disabled, "Brief Presented to the Federal-Provincial Working Parties."

61 Among PWD meetings where these discussions occurred were those of 20 January 1967 and 22 April 1968; see NA, MG 28, I 103, reels H-278 and H-478.

62 NA, MG 28, I 10, box 150, pt. 4, "Next Steps in Welfare," by White, 20 September 1965; ibid., I 103, reel H-478, minutes of CWC consultative meeting, 20–22 October 1967.

63 Ibid., reel H-500, "The Commission on Functions and Organization has Pleasure in Submitting its Report to the Board of Governors of the Canadian Welfare Council," by H. Carver, February 1969, sections 2–3.

64 Ibid., I 10, reel H-500, PWD National Committee and general meeting, 25–27 June 1969; ibid., "Report of the Committee on the Implications of the Carver Report," 15 November 1969.

65 NA, RG 29, accession 84–85/085, file 3402–1–5, pt. 3, Baetz to Lalonde, 3 September 1974.

66 Ibid., pt. 2, "Report on Social Security in Canada by the Canadian Council on Social Development," 13 September 1973.

67 Ibid., "An Examination of 'The Critique of the Working Paper on Social Security'," 8 March 1974; *Ottawa Journal* and *Ottawa Citizen*, 14 May 1974.

68 NA, RG 29, accession 84–85/085, file 3402–1–5, pt. 2, "Briefing Notes on CCSD," 8 March 1974; Leman, *Collapse of Welfare Reform*, 124–5. Baetz's antagonistic disposition was also frequently mentioned in interviews.

69 NA, RG 29, accession 84–85/085, file 3402–1–5, pt. 2, "Briefing Notes on the CCSD," 8 March 1974.

70 *Canadian News Facts*, 18 June 1976; Lalonde's arguments were treated in some detail in the counter-speech by the CCSD president; see NA, RG 29, accession 84–85/085, file 3402–1–5, pt. 3, speech by J. Séguin, 17 June 1976.

71 Ibid., 3.

72 *Toronto Star*, 17 June 1976.

73 Walker, "Poor People's Conference," 24.

74 Leman, *Collapse of Welfare Reform*, 122.

75 Ibid., 159–60.

76 For example, see NA, RG 29, accession 85–86/343, file 3302–3–2–1, pt. 1, "Submission to the Government of Nova Scotia and the Government of Canada Regarding Federal Proposal for Income Support and Supplementation," 28 May 1976; ibid., "Comments on Halifax Coalition Criticisms," by Osborne, 21 June 1976.

77 For evidence of the unpopularity of the block-funding proposal, see ibid., file 3203–6–1, pt. 3, Osborne to Rawson, 20 September 1977.

78 Ibid., vol. 1296, file 5619–2–741, "Federal-Provincial Conference of Ministers of Welfare," verbatim minutes, tape 1, 25.

79 Ibid., vol. 1299, file 5619–3–754, pt. 2, "Notes on the Private Meeting of Deputy Ministers of Welfare at St. Andrews, New Brunswick, on Tuesday, September 23, 1975," 1–3.

80 Chapin, "Citizen Involvement," 125.

CHAPTER NINE

1 Simeon and Robinson, *Development of Canadian Federalism*, 218.

2 Alford and Friedland, *Powers of Theory*, 35–40.

3 Contemporary developments are treated in greater detail in Haddow, "Poverty Policy Community," 225–34.

4 Canada, Royal Commission on the Economic Union and Development Prospects for Canada, *Report*, volume 2, part 5, esp. 824–7; Canada, Commission of Inquiry on Unemployment Insurance, *Report*, chapter 7.

5 The Business Council on National Issues, the Canadian Chamber of Commerce, and the Canadian Manufacturers' Association all recommended the restriction of social expenditures and greater selectivity in remaining benefits; see *Canadian News Facts*, 19 April 1985; 10 September 1986; 19 and 26 November 1986.

6 Canada, Task Force on Program Review, *Introduction*, 19–20, 30–1.

7 Houle, "Economic Renewal," 430–1.

8 CLC, "Adequate Incomes."

9 NCW, "The June 1982 Budget"; ibid., *Welfare in Canada*; CCSD, *Annual Report*, 1987–8, S-3 to S-8; NAPO, "Mission Statement"; ibid., "Election '88."

10 Houle, "Economic Renewal," 432.

11 Houle, "Economic Renewal," 432.

12 Lipietz, *Mirages and Miracles*, esp. chapter 2; Wolfe, "Canadian State," 115–16.

13 Mishra, *Welfare State in Crisis*, 25.

14 Aucoin, "Mulroney Government," 345–7.

15 Ibid., 335, 338.

Bibliography

ARCHIVAL COLLECTIONS AND
CABINET DOCUMENTS

(i) National Archives of Canada
     RG 19, department of Finance;
     RG 29, department of National Health and Welfare;
     RG 118, department of Manpower and Immigration;
     MG 28, I 10, Canadian Council on Social Development;
     MG 28, I 103, Canadian Labour Congress.
(ii) Archives of Ontario
     RG 29, ministry of Community and Social Services.
(iii) Minutes and documents of the federal cabinet, 1961–6.

INTERVIEWS

Confidential interviews were conducted with 42 individuals – former officials
of the departments of National Health and Welfare, Finance, and Manpower
and Immigration, as well as officials of the Canadian Welfare Council, the
Canadian Council on Social Development, the National Council of Welfare,
the Canadian Labour Congress, and the provincial governments of Nova
Scotia, Ontario, and Quebec. Each of the interviewees was familiar with
events that transpired during the creation of the Canada Assistance Plan
and during the Social Security Review.

PRINTED MATERIAL

Adams, Ian, et al. *The Real Poverty Report*. Edmonton: Hurtig, 1971.
– "The Renegade Report on Poverty." *The Last Post* 1 (1971), no. 8.

Alford, Robert. "Paradigms of Relations between State and Society." In *Stress and Contradiction in Modern Capitalism*, edited by L. Lindberg et al. Lexington, Mass: Lexington Books, 1979.

Alford, Robert, and Roger Friedland. *Powers of Theory*. Cambridge: Cambridge University Press, 1985.

Atkinson, Michael, and William Coleman. *The State, Business, and Industrial Change in Canada*. Toronto: University of Toronto Press, 1990.

Aucoin, Peter. "The Mulroney Government, 1984–1988: Priorities, Positional Policy and Power." In *Canada Under Mulroney*, edited by A. Gollner and D. Salée. Montreal: Véhicule Press, 1989.

Badie, Bertrand, and Pierre Birnbaum. *The Sociology of the State*. Chicago: University of Chicago Press, 1983.

Bégin, Monique. *L'Assurance santé: Plaidoyer pour le modèle canadien*. Montreal: Boréal, 1987.

Bella, Leslie. "The Politics of the Right-Wing Welfare State." Ph.D. thesis, University of Alberta, 1981.

Bellamy, David. "Welfare." In *Canadian Annual Review of Politics and Public Affairs, 1970*, edited by J. Saywell. Toronto: University of Toronto Press, 1971.

Block, Fred. *Revising State Theory*. Philadelphia: Temple University Press, 1987.

Bryden, Kenneth. *Old Age Pensions and Policy-Making in Canada*. Montreal: McGill-Queen's University Press, 1974.

Campbell, Colin. *The Canadian Senate*. Toronto: MacMillan, 1978.

Canada. Committee of Inquiry into the Unemployment Insurance Act. *Exhibits and Briefs* no. 4, Canadian Bankers' Association; no. 5, Canadian Chamber of Commerce; no. 12, Canadian Manufacturers' Association. Ottawa: Queen's Printer, 1962.

– *Report*. Ottawa: Queen's Printer, 1962.

Canada. Commission of Inquiry on Unemployment Insurance. *Report*. Ottawa: Supply and Services Canada, 1986.

Canada. Department of Manpower and Immigration. *Annual Report, 1974–1975*.

Canada. Department of Reconstruction. *Employment and Incomes with Special Reference to the Initial Period of Reconstruction*. Ottawa: King's Printer: 1945.

Canada. Dominion-Provincial Conference on Reconstruction. *Proposals of the Government of Canada*. Ottawa: King's Printer, 1945.

Canada. Economic Council of Canada. *Annual Review*. 5th, 1968; 6th, 1969. Ottawa: Queen's Printer: 1968, 1969.

Canada. Employment and Immigration Canada. *Community Employment Strategy, 1976–77*, Ottawa: 1977.

Canada. Federal-Provincial Conference, July 1960. *Proceedings*. Ottawa: Queen's Printer, 1965.

Canada. Federal-Provincial Conference, 19–22 July 1965. *Proceedings*. Ottawa: Queen's Printer, 1965.

Canada. Federal-Provincial Study Group on Alienation. *Report*. Ottawa: 1971.

Canada. Health and Welfare Canada. *Chronology of Selected Federal Social Welfare Legislation by Program, 1876–1980*. Ottawa: Supply and Services, n.d.

Canada. National Health and Welfare. *A General Framework for the Evaluation of Social Security Policies*, by T. Russell Robinson. Ottawa: 1975.

– *Income Security for Canadians*, by John Munro. Ottawa: Queen's Printer, 1970.

– *Low Income Interest Groups in Canada*, by Mario Caroto. Ottawa: 1970.

– *Social Security Statistics, Canada and the Provinces*. Ottawa: Supply and Services Canada, 1976.

– *Social Security Statistics, Canada and the Provinces, 1960–61 to 1984–85*. Ottawa: Supply and Services Canada, 1987.

– *Working Paper on Social Security in Canada*, by Marc Lalonde. Ottawa: 1973.

Canada. Parliament. House of Commons. *Debates*. Various years and dates, 1956 to 1978.

Canada. Parliament. Senate. Special Committee on Aging, *Final Report 1966* [first Croll Report]. Ottawa: Queen's Printer, 1966.

– Special Committee on Manpower and Employment. *Proceedings*. Ottawa: Queen's Printer, 1961.

– Special Committee on Poverty. *Report on Poverty* [second Croll Report]. Ottawa: Queen's Printer, 1971.

– Special Committee on Poverty. *Proceedings* no. 8, Canadian Labour Congress; no. 12, Canadian Welfare Council; no. 51, Canadian Chamber of Commerce. Ottawa: 1971.

Canada. Right Honourable Pierre Elliot Trudeau. *Income Security and Social Services*. Ottawa: Queen's Printer, 1969.

Canada. Royal Commission on Taxation. *Hearings* no. 94, Canadian Bankers Association. Ottawa: Queen's Printer, 1964.

Canada. Royal Commission on the Economic Union and Development Prospects for Canada. *Report*. Ottawa: Supply and Services Canada, 1985.

Canada. Royal Commission on the Status of Women in Canada. *Report*. Ottawa: Queen's Printer, 1970.

Canada. Statistics Canada. *National Income and Expenditure Accounts: Annual Estimates, 1926–1974*. Ottawa: 1976.

– *Social Security: National Programs, 1978*. Ottawa: 1978.

Canada. Task Force on Program Review. *An Introduction to the Process of Program Review*. Ottawa: Supply and Services Canada, 1986.

Canadian Bankers' Association. *The Canadian Banker* 71 (1964), no. 1; 79 (1972), no. 3; 80 (1973), no. 6; 82 (1975), no. 2.

Canadian Chamber of Commerce. *Report of Annual Meeting*. 1962–63; 1963–64; 1964–65; 1965–66.

- *Submission to the Minister of Finance and the Minister of National Revenue.* 1961–64, 1966.
- *Statement of Policy.* 1961, 1964–67.
Canadian Council for the Blind. *CCB Outlook* 15 (1962), no. 1.
Canadian Council on Social Development. *Social Security For Canada, 1973.* Ottawa: 1973.
- *Annual Report, 1987–1988.*
Canadian Labour Congress. *Canadian Labour* 9 (1964), no. 2; 10 (1965), no. 1 and 7–8; 13 (1968), no. 12; 14 (1969), nos. 3, 7–8, 9, and 10; 15 (1970), nos. 4 and 7–8; 20 (1975), no. 2.
- Constitutional Convention. *Proceedings.* 1st convention, 1956; 4th convention, 9–13 April 1962; 6th convention, 25–29 April 1966.
- *Memorandum to the Government of Canada.* February 1957; November 1957; January 1959; February 1961; December 1962; March 1965; February 1966; March 1970.
- *Submission to the Special Joint Committee of the Senate and of the House of Commons on the Canada Pension Plan (Bill C-136), January 22, 1965,* Ottawa, 1965.
- "Adequate Income for All Canadians: A Working Future (Policy Statement on A Guaranteed Annual Income)." 17th constitutional convention, 9–13 May 1988.
Canadian Manufacturers' Association. *Report of Annual Meeting.* Toronto: 1962, 1965, 1967.
Canadian National Institute for the Blind. *Annual Report.* 1935, 1943, 1966.
Canadian News Facts. 1968–78; 1985–86.
Canadian Party Platforms, 1867–1968, edited by Owen D. Carrigan. Toronto: Copp Clark, 1968.
Canadian Rehabilitative Council for the Disabled. "A Brief Presented to the Federal-Provincial Working Parties on Social Security by the National Steering Committee of the Physically Disabled." Ottawa: 1974.
Canadian Welfare Council. *Annual Report.* 1946–47, 1959–60.
- *Public Assistance in Canada.* Ottawa: 1951.
- *Social Security for Canada.* Ottawa: 1958.
- *Work for Relief.* Ottawa: 1963.
- *A Policy Statement on the Canada Assistance Plan.* Ottawa: July 1966.
- *Social Policies for Canada, Part 1.* Ottawa: 1969.
- Public Welfare Division. *Report.* 1952–63.
Chapin, Henry. "Citizen Involvement in Policy-Making." In *Issues in Canadian Social Policy: A Reader.* Vol. 1. Ottawa: Canadian Council on Social Development, 1982.
Chapin, Henry, and Denis Deneau. *Access and the Policy-Making Process.* Ottawa: Canadian Council on Social Development, 1978.

Cuneo, Carl. "Comment: Restoring Class to State Unemployment Insurance." *Canadian Journal of Political Science* 19 (1986).

Cutt, James. "The National Economy." In *The Canadian Annual Review of Politics and Public Affairs, 1971*, edited by J. Saywell. Toronto: University of Toronto Press, 1972.

– "Welfare and Unemployment Insurance." In *The Canadian Annual Review of Politics and Public Affairs, 1972*. Toronto: University of Toronto Press, 1972.

Devoir, Le. Various dates, 1971–3.

Doern, G. Bruce, and Peter Aucoin. "Conclusions and Observations." In *The Structures of Policy-Making in Canada*, edited by G. B. Doern and P. Aucoin. Toronto: MacMillan, 1971.

Dupré, Stefan. "Reflections on the Workability of Executive Federalism." In *Intergovernmental Relations*, edited by R. Simeon. Toronto: University of Toronto Press, 1985.

Dyck, Rand. "Poverty and Policy-Making in the 1960s: The Canada Assistance Plan." Ph.D. thesis, Queen's University, 1973.

– "The Canada Assistance Plan: The Ultimate in Cooperative Federalism." *Canadian Public Administration* 10 (1976).

Esping-Andersen, Gösta. "Power and Distributional Regimes." *Politics and Society* 14 (1985).

– *The Three Worlds of Welfare Capitalism*. Princeton: Princeton University Press, 1990.

Esping-Andersen, Gösta, and Walter Korpi. "From Poor Relief to Institutional Welfare States: The Development of Scandinavian Social Policy." In *The Scandinavian Model*, edited by R. Erikson. London, U.K.: Sharpe, 1987.

Felt, Lawrence. "Militant Poor People and the Canadian State." In *Modernization and the Canadian State*, edited by D. Glenday et al. Toronto: MacMillan, 1978.

French, Richard. *How Ottawa Decides*. Toronto: Lorimer, 1980.

Friedman, Milton. *Capitalism and Freedom*. Chicago: University of Chicago Press, 1962.

Furmaniak, Karl. "West Germany: Poverty, Unemployment and Social Insurance." In *Responses to Poverty*, edited by Robert Walker et al. London, U.K.: Heinemann, 1984.

Globe and Mail, The. Various dates, 1966–78.

Granatstein, J. L. *Canada's War*. Toronto: Oxford University Press, 1975.

Guest, Denis. *The Emergence of Social Security in Canada*. Vancouver: University of British Columbia Press, 1980.

Gwyn, Richard. *The Northern Magus*. Toronto: McClelland and Stewart, 1980.

Haddow, Rodney. "The Poverty Policy Community in Canada's Liberal Welfare State." In *Policy Communities and Public Policy in Canada*, edited by W. Coleman and G. Skogstad. Toronto: Copp Clark Pitman, 1990.

– "State, Class and Public Policy: Canadian Poverty Policy, 1963–1978," Ph.D. thesis, University of Toronto, 1991.

Harder, Vernon. "A House of Minorities," M.A. thesis, Queen's University, 1977.

Harrington, Michael. *The Other America*. New York: MacMillan, 1962.

Hartle, Douglas. *The Expenditure Budget Process in the Government of Canada*. Toronto: Canadian Tax Foundation, 1978.

Heady, Ferrel. *Public Administration: A Comparative Perspective*. Englewood Cliffs, N.J.: Prentice-Hall, 1966.

Houle, François. "Economic Renewal and Social Policy." In *Canadian Politics: An Introduction to the Discipline*, edited by A. Gagnon and J. Bickerton. Peterborough, Ont.: Broadview Press, 1990.

Iacobacci, Mario, and Mario Seccareccia. "Full Employment versus Income Maintenance." *Studies in Political Economy* 28 (1989).

Jessop, Bob. *The Capitalist State*. Oxford: Martin Robertson, 1983.

Johnson, A. W. "The Treasury Board of Canada and the Machinery of Government of the 1970s." *Canadian Journal of Political Science* 4 (1971).

– "Canada's Social Security Review 1973–1975: The Central Issues." *Canadian Public Policy* 1 (1975).

– *Social Policy in Canada: the Past as it Conditions the Present*. Ottawa: Institute for Research in Public Policy, 1987.

Johnson, Andrew. "Political Leadership and the Process of Policy-Making: the Case of Unemployment Insurance in the 1970s." Ph.D. thesis, McGill University, 1983.

Jones, Catherine. *Patterns of Social Policy*. London, U.K.: Tavistock, 1985.

Kent, Tom. *A Public Purpose*. Kingston: McGill-Queen's University Press, 1988.

Kinnon, Dianne. "Pressure Group Politics in Canada: A History of the National Anti-Poverty Organization." Mimeograph, 1986.

Korpi, Walter. "Social Policy and Distributional Conflict in the Capitalist Democracies." *West European Politics* 3 (1980).

Krasner, Stephen. *Defending the National Interest*. Princeton: Princeton University Press, 1978.

Kumar, P. "Union Growth in Canada: Retrospect and Prospect." In *Canadian Labour Relations*, edited by C. Riddell. Toronto: University of Toronto Press, 1986.

LaMarsh, Judy. *Bird in a Gilded Cage*. Toronto: McClelland and Stewart, 1968.

Lawson, Roger, and Robert Walker. "Lessons from Europe." In *Responses to Poverty*, edited by R. Walker et al. London, U.K.: Heinemann, 1984.

Leman, Christopher. *The Collapse of Welfare Reform: Political Institutions, Policy, and the Poor in the United States*. Cambridge, Mass.: MIT Press, 1980.

Lipietz, Alain. *Mirages and Miracles*. London, U.K.: Verso, 1987.

Loney, Martin. "A Political Economy of Citizen Participation." In *The Canadian State*, edited by L. Panitch. Toronto: University of Toronto Press, 1977.

Manzer, Ronald. *Public Policies and Political Development in Canada*. Toronto: University of Toronto Press, 1985.

McCall-Newman, Christina. *Grits*. Toronto: MacMillan, 1982.

McInnis, Simon. "Federal-Provincial Negotiations: Family Allowances, 1970–1976." Ph.D. thesis, Carleton University, 1978.

Mishra, Ramesh. *The Welfare State in Crisis*. Brighton, u.k.: Wheatsheaf, 1984.

Morin, Claude. *Quebec Versus Ottawa*. Toronto: University of Toronto Press, 1976.

Moynihan, Daniel P. *The Politics of a Guaranteed Income*. New York: Vintage, 1973.

Myles, John. "Decline or Impasse? The Current State of the Welfare State." *Studies in Political Economy* 26 (1988).

National Anti-Poverty Organization. *Towards a Guaranteed Income for Canadians: An Analysis of the Three Choices Now Being Considered by the Federal-Provincial Review*, by Marjorie Hartling. Ottawa: n.d.

– "napo's Mission Statement," n.d.

– "Election '88: What About Poverty?" n.d.

– "More About napo," n.d.

National Council of Welfare. *Incomes and Opportunities*. Ottawa: 1973.

– "The June 1982 Budget and Social Policy." Mimeograph, July 1982.

– *Welfare in Canada*. Ottawa: 1987.

National Union of Public Employees. nupe *Highlights*, September 1962.

Newfoundland. Public Welfare Department. *Annual Report*, 1959.

Newman, Peter C. *The Distemper of Our Times*. Toronto: McClelland and Stewart, 1978.

Ottawa Citizen, The. 14 May 1974; 15, 17, and 19 February 1975; 5 February 1976.

Ottawa Journal, The. 14 May 1974; 15 February 1975.

Pal, Leslie. "Relative Autonomy Revisited: The Origins of Canadian Unemployment Insurance." *Canadian Journal of Political Science* 19 (1986).

– *State, Class, and Bureaucracy*. Montreal: McGill-Queen's University Press, 1988.

Phidd, Richard. "The Role of Central Advisory Councils: The Economic Council of Canada." In *The Structures of Policy-Making in Canada*, edited by Bruce Doern and P. Aucoin. Toronto: MacMillan, 1971.

Phidd, Richard, and G. Bruce Doern. *The Politics and Management of Canadian Economic Policy*. Toronto: MacMillan, 1978.

Quebec. Study Committee on Public Assistance. *Report*. Québec: 1963.

– *Report of the Commission of Inquiry on Health and Social Welfare*, Vol. 5, *Income Security*. Three tomes. Quebec: 1971.

Rachlis, Charles. "Ten Years After: The Social Security Review." Mimeograph, n.d.

Rainwater, Lee, et. al. *Income Packaging in the Welfare State*. Oxford: Clarendon Press, 1986.

Rice, James. "Restitching the Safety Net: Altering the National Social Security System." In *How Ottawa Spends, 1987–88*, edited by M. Prince. Toronto: Methuen, 1987.

Saltsman, Max. "Party Politics and Social Policy: the Party in Opposition." In *Canadian Social Policy*, edited by S. Yeleja. Waterloo: Waterloo University Press, 1978.

St. Catherines Standard, The. 14 September 1962.

Savoie, Donald. *The Politics of Public Spending in Canada*. Toronto: University of Toronto Press, 1990.

Saywell, John, and John Stevens. "Parliament and Politics." In *Canadian Annual Review, 1968*, edited by J. Saywell. Toronto: University of Toronto Press, 1969.

– "Parliament and Politics." In *Canadian Annual Review of Politics and Public Affairs, 1971*, edited by J. Saywell. Toronto: University of Toronto Press, 1972.

– "Parliament and Politics." In *Canadian Annual Review of Politics and Public Affairs, 1972*, edited by J. Saywell. Toronto: University of Toronto Press, 1974.

– "Parliament and Politics." In *Canadian Annual Review of Politics and Public Affairs, 1974*, edited by J. Saywell. Toronto: University of Toronto Press, 1975.

Schlozman, Kay and Sidney Verba. *Injury to Insult*. Cambridge, Mass.: Harvard University Press, 1979.

Shifrin, Leonard. "The Politics of Income Security." In *Family Income Security Issues*. Toronto: Social Planning Council of Metropolitan Toronto, 1975.

Simeon, Richard. *Federal-Provincial Diplomacy*. Toronto: University of Toronto Press, 1972.

Simeon, Richard, and Ian Robinson. *State, Society, and the Development of Canadian Federalism*. Toronto: University of Toronto Press, 1990.

Smiley, Donald. *Conditional Grants and Canadian Federalism*. Toronto: Canadian Tax Foundation, 1963.

– *Canada in Question: Federalism in the Eighties*. Toronto: McGraw-Hill Ryerson, 1980.

Splane, Richard. "Social Policy-Making in the Government of Canada: Reflections of a Reformist Bureaucrat." In *Canadian Social Policy*, edited by S. Yeleja. Waterloo, Ont: Wilfred Laurier University Press, 1978.

– "Social Welfare Development in Alberta: The Federal-Provincial Interplay." In *Canadian Social Welfare Policy: Federal and Provincial Dimensions*, edited by J. Ismael. Kingston: McGill-Queen's University Press, 1985.

Stevenson, Garth. *Unfulfilled Union*. Toronto: Gage, 1979.

Swartz, Donald. "The Politics of Reform: Conflict and Accommodation in Canadian Health Care." In *The Canadian State*, edited by L. Panitch. Toronto: University of Toronto Press, 1977.

Therborn, Goran. *Why Some Peoples Are More Unemployed Than Others*. London, U.K.: Verso, 1986.

Tilly, Charles. "Reflections on the History of European State-Making." In *The Formation of National States in Western Europe*, edited by C. Tilly. Princeton: Princeton University Press, 1975.

Toronto Star, The. Various dates, 1971–6.

Townsend, Peter, and Brian Abel-Smith. *The Poor and the Poorest*. London, U.K.: Bell, 1966.

Van Loon, Richard. "Reforming Welfare in Canada." *Public Policy* 27 (1979).

Walker, David. "The Poor People's Conference." M.A. thesis, Queen's University, 1971.

Walker, Robert. "Resources, Welfare Expenditures and Poverty in European Countries." In *Responses to Poverty*, edited by R. Walker et al. London, U.K.: Heinemann, 1984.

Wharf, Brian, and Allan Halliday. *The Rise of Advisory Councils in Forming Social Policies: A Case Study of the National Council of Welfare*. Hamilton: McMaster University Press, 1974.

Wolfe, David. "The Politics of the Deficit." In *The Politics of Economic Policy*, edited by G. B. Doern. Toronto: University of Toronto Press, 1983.

– "The Canadian State in Comparative Perspective." *Canadian Review of Sociology and Anthropology* 26 (1989).

Zysman, John. *Governments, Markets and Growth*. Ithaca: Cornell University Press, 1983.

Index